NEVER
SHUT UP

NEVER SHUT UP

THE LIFE, OPINIONS, AND UNEXPECTED ADVENTURES OF AN NFL OUTLIER

MARCELLUS WILEY

DUTTON

DUTTON
An imprint of Penguin Random House LLC
375 Hudson Street
New York, New York 10014

Copyright © 2018 by Dat Dude Entertainment, Inc.
Penguin supports copyright. Copyright fuels creativity, encourages diverse voices,
promotes free speech, and creates a vibrant culture. Thank you for buying an authorized
edition of this book and for complying with copyright laws by not reproducing, scanning,
or distributing any part of it in any form without permission. You are supporting writers
and allowing Penguin to continue to publish books for every reader.

DUTTON and the D colophon are registered trademarks of Penguin Random House LLC.

A request for cataloging has been submitted to the Library of Congress.

ISBN 9781524743222

Printed in the United States of America
1   3   5   7   9   10   8   6   4   2

Book design by George Towne

Penguin is committed to publishing works of quality and integrity. In that spirit,
we are proud to offer this book to our readers; however, the story,
the experiences, and the words are the author's alone.

For Mama and Grandma, who are always looking out for me
up in the Bank in the Sky

CONTENTS

INTRODUCTION

THE CAMERA CREW got to our apartment at six in the morning that Saturday. A whole team from CNN—sound, makeup, producers, the whole deal—squeezed into my tiny childhood home in South Central, there to broadcast live during the 1997 draft.

This was the same place I had grown up. Sharing a room with my sister that wasn't even a room, just a nook with a sheet hung up for privacy. Listening to NWA songs about shootings and drugs and gangs, about things I saw every day on the streets. Sitting on the floor my freshman year of high school, staring into space as I iced my aching, inflamed knees, wondering if I'd ever achieve my NFL dreams and get my family out of the hood.

Now, after all those years, all those struggles, here was a CNN camera crew right in our living room to watch as I finally got chosen by some team, any team, to play in the League.

Of course, first they had to figure out how to fit all their shit into the damn place.

By the time they unloaded all their gear, all their equipment, all their mics and cameras, we looked around and realized there was nowhere left for any actual people to sit! The CNN guys took a look around, scratched their heads, and promptly got rid of half their stuff, making barely enough room for me and my family to watch my fate unfold on TV.

A lot of the potential first-round picks were actually attending the draft, which was in New York City, but I didn't get a formal invite. I'd flown myself home for the weekend, using some of the money from my agent's advance. Besides, I wanted the world to see my roots, see where I was from, a background I was both proud of and fought every day to improve on.

I also wanted to be around plenty of my friends and family—to help me through both potential "oh shit" moments. That's "Oh shit, I just got picked in the first round and let's party" *or* "Oh shit, it's the seventh round and are these people ever gonna call my damn name?" I was projected to go somewhere in the first couple rounds, but that's the thing about draft projections. No matter what Mel Kiper might say, he wasn't the one signing the contracts. It all came down to the teams, and no one—no one—could predict exactly what they'd do.

I settled in with Mama, my dad, Grandma, my sister, Tiki, and my best friend, Jabari, and every other uncle, second cousin, and halfway former acquaintance from down the block who could cram into our place. When a kid from the block was about to make it big, *everyone* wanted a piece.

Because we were on the West Coast, three hours behind the New York broadcast, it was early as hell, but I was so pumped my eyes were peeled wide open. I knew there was no way I'd get chosen in the first few picks—those spots were reserved for college superstars, not standouts like me from Columbia University, an Ivy League school with a notorious history of awful football teams.

But I didn't care, I was still listening to those announcements with every cell of my ear canal. I wasn't even waiting for my name, a syllable or two would've been enough to set me off.

Mmmaaaa—

Mmmmmaaaaarrrrr—

Mmmmmmmaaaaarrrrcelllll—

Give me a sound, baby! That's all I need! I'm begging you!

But no. Pick one came, and the name I heard didn't start with an "M."

"Orlando Pace, of Ohio State!"

Oh yeah, I forgot that *everyone in the world* knew number one was gonna be Pace. Shit, I needed to chill! Okay, fuck that, time to focus on number two.

"Darrell Russell, of USC!"

Okay, alright. I knew Russell would be up there too, that made sense. Just had to look at three.

"Shawn Springs, of Ohio State!"

Fine, fine! So I wasn't gonna be three. No one even thought I would be three, whatever. On to the next one. And the next, and the next.

What really killed me, though, wasn't even the names that were popping out. It was the wait between each announcement. That wait had always seemed easy in past years, when I had been watching for fun—minutes upon minutes spent interviewing the most recent pick, talking to the usual sports prognosticators, and, of course, giving the teams time for all their backroom deals and machinations—but now? When I was an actual prospect? When it was *my* life on the line? That wait felt interminable.

Finally, right around pick fifteen, I started hearing those magic "Marcellus" syllables. Hold up, hold up—not because I was actually *chosen*, nothing that good. But because Mel and all the other talking heads thought I was finally in range. One of the top five or six best available prospects, who could get picked literally any minute.

Alright, cool, I thought. *So I can be top twenty. I'm good with that, totally chill.*

All while sitting on the edge of my seat and gritting my teeth down to the damn roots.

Shit! There went number twenty. And before I knew it, twenty-four. And then twenty-eight.

By now, my name was at the very top of Mel's list of dudes who hadn't been selected yet.

Fine, I thought. *Second round it is.*

Every now and then CNN would check in on me, ask me how I was doing. I'd give them my usual big smile, admit that I was feeling nervous—both because I was and because I knew that's what they wanted to hear, what made for a good story. But deep down, at the bottom of my soul, I still felt good, still felt confident about everything.

See, I was playing with house money. No one—*no one*—had expected me to get this far. I had grown up with so many guys who played college ball at the big, flashy schools, the USCs, the Notre Dames, the Florida States. But where were they now? None of them were projected to go as high as I was in the draft. Hell, none of them even got invited to the combine!

They had faced huge expectations and hadn't lived up to any of them, despite all the advantages, despite doing exactly what they were supposed to do. I, on the other hand, had made my own path. I had always strived to be true to myself. To embrace my individuality and never follow the herd. To do everything I could to help my family in my own unique way.

I could've gone to a major football program in a premier conference if I had wanted to. But I chose to put my education first instead, to get an Ivy League degree as my safety net in case football didn't work out. So I went to a school no one in my neighborhood had ever even heard of, and now, here I was, on the cusp of making it to the NFL.

Did I want to go high up? Of course. The higher you went, the more guaranteed money you were likely to get in your contract. But as long as I got in, as long as I made it into the League, I'd be happy no matter what the round. I had made my own path in the past, and I could do it again.

As the names and the minutes passed by, I started to zone out. All the emotional swings, all the anticipation and waiting, not to mention that early-ass morning, were taking a toll. For hours I had been watching the TV, then suddenly it felt like the TV was watching me.

I closed my eyes, just for a little, I told myself. Not to fall asleep, just to take a rest. Just to relax for a couple quick minutes.

"Alright!"

My peace was shattered by that single word from my dad, a man of very few words who generally only expressed happiness when Emmitt Smith and his beloved Cowboys did something amazing on the field.

But this time, this word was for me.

"ALRIGHT!"

I opened my eyes, shook my head until the fog cleared from my mind, and it hit me—I just got drafted.

The next thing I was aware of was simply screaming. My daddy was screaming, my mama was screaming, everyone was screaming. I looked at the TV and saw my name next to a big blue-and-red logo. I was the fifty-second pick of the draft, selected in the second round by the Buffalo Bills.

"Bruce Smith!" was the very first sound that came out of my mouth.

Followed very closely by "Marv Levy!"

At this point, the Bills of that era are remembered more for losing four Super Bowls in a row than anything else. But remember—to lose those Super Bowls, they had to get there first. They were a good fucking team, starring Bruce Smith, the greatest defensive end to ever put on a helmet.

To me, it felt like the universe had put me in the ideal situation. D-end was my position too. I was physically gifted, yes—that's why the Bills were taking a gamble on me—but I was also incredibly raw. I only had two years' experience playing my position, something almost unheard of for a second-round NFL draftee. And here I was about to play alongside the best D-end in the business. That wasn't intimidating—that was a chance to learn, to grow, to hone my technique.

"ALRIGHT THEN!"

My dad was officially setting a record for word count.

The phone rang, and if shit wasn't already real, it got even realer.

"Hi, Marcellus," the voice on the other end said. "Congratulations!"

It was John Butler, the Bills general manager—a man I had never met who was now officially my favorite person in the world.

"Are you ready to be a Buffalo Bill?"

"Yessir," I said.

"Hold on, I want to let you talk to your coach."

He put Coach Levy on, and I barely remember a word he said.

All I could think was, *I'm sitting in my tiny apartment off Slauson Avenue in South Central LA, surrounded by my family, my friends, and a CNN camera crew, and I'm on the phone with Marv Levy of the Buffalo Bills.*

My crazy-ass life had gotten even crazier. And it was just getting started.

CHAPTER ONE

FINDING MY OWN PATH, AND GETTING MY ASS BEAT ALONG THE WAY

FIRST FOUND OUT who I was when I was seven years old.

I was playing tetherball during recess with some other kids when a girl who was bigger and older than me pushed me out of the way, knocked me to the ground.

Now what do you think I'm gonna say? That I learned how to fight back? That I stood up for myself and finally became a man when I was in the third grade?

Hell naw!

I grew up in the toughest, meanest neighborhood in America—South Central LA. This was 1982, years before movies like *Boyz n the Hood* and rap groups like NWA made us famous—but the stuff they made us famous for? The gangs and the drugs and the violence? That was already everywhere. I got a Boston Red Sox cap as a gift once, and that thing almost never left our apartment. Not because I had anything against the Sox, but because it was red, and that was the Bloods' color. You had to be smart about anything blue too. Blue jeans were fine, yeah, but you couldn't wear any blue hats, no blue flannel shirts, nothing *explicitly* blue, because that would've marked you as one of the Crips. Every few blocks were carved into a different territory, belonged to a different set. And if anyone ever asked, "Where you from?" that wasn't polite conversation, that meant "What gang you in?" and it almost always ended in assault or death.

Me? I had my own unique coping mechanism. Someone wanted to start something, I'd mock them with the best vocabulary they'd ever heard, and if that didn't work? Well then, I'd turn on my heel and run like hell. Lucky for me, I was fast as shit, even at a really young age, so it almost always worked. Thank God for that, because I was *not* a fighter.

My sister, Tiki, though? Now she would fuck your shit up.

"Tiki" was short for "L'Tashika." That's right, her name got an apostrophe in it and everything, most ghetto name you could imagine, and I still tease her about it to this day. But man, did she own it. She was undefeated in all her fights—and there were a *lot*—quick as lightning, with an amazing connect rate for a fourth grader.

She was two years older than me, and she was always trying to protect me, always had my back, even when I didn't exactly want her to. Tiki found me crying after the tetherball game, asked me what happened, then she found that girl—and there was no asking required.

One punch, two punches, then *yayaya*!

Over!

There was one small problem. The girl whose ass Tiki beat also happened to have a brother. He was older, in high school, and he was a member of the Rollin 60s Crips. So yeah. It wasn't over at all.

It was just getting started.

The next day, on our way home from school, guess who's right there at the corner waiting for us? The girl, her brother, and one of his high school friends. Both the brother and his friend, by the way, ended up going to prison a few years later, and one of them was killed after that.

That day, I wanted to run, of course, but my sister wasn't going anywhere. They took us on, and even Tiki couldn't stop them. They hit us with body blows like thunder to the chest, left me crying, and left my sister mad as hell because there was nothing she could do about it. There were three of them and two of us—one of us considering that I wasn't much help—and two of them were in high school. We weren't even in junior high yet!

I bawled as Tiki and I walked home.

"Would you shut up?" she said. "They just want to punk us, Teddy Bear."

That was her nickname for me—Teddy Bear. Did I mention I wasn't much of a fighter?

"I'm gonna tell Mama!" I sobbed.

"You ain't telling *nobody*," she said. "And you know why."

She was right, I did.

In our world, even something as minor as a few kids getting into a fight over tetherball could escalate fast. If I told Mama, she'd tell Grandma. If she told Grandma, next thing you know my uncles would get involved. My uncles weren't your stereotypical "crazy uncles you see at Thanksgiving and Christmas." They were gang members themselves, Palmer Blocc Crips out of Compton. Two of them ended up getting murdered, while a third went to prison and later committed suicide so he wouldn't have to go back.

So if my uncles got involved, they wouldn't just *talk* to those kids who were punkin' us. At the very least, they'd beat their ass—if the kids were lucky. If they weren't so lucky? They could get smoked. And the next thing you'd know, people would be dead. All over tetherball.

For better or worse, living in the hood forced us to be independent at a young age, to try to figure shit out on our own before we went to anyone else. I felt like the world was resting on my shoulders— and it wouldn't be the last time.

MY MAMA'S NAME was Valerie Howard. She'd given birth to me when she was nineteen, to my sister at the age of seventeen. Mama was big and imposing, six foot one and slim, but still well over two hundred pounds at the time. She had a small dent in the palm of her left hand, a scar from falling on a nail as a little girl.

Mama was smart—she had gotten all As in high school and was college-bound before she had us kids and decided to stay home to raise us—but she was young. She raised us on welfare and food stamps, which I knew was an act of love on her part, of devotion, because not having a job meant she could be at home for us at all times. But that lifestyle also included a lot of talking, which felt like a bunch of gossiping and complaining to me, with not much else to improve our situation.

My dad was eight years older than my mom. His name was Charles. A tall, skinny guy, a couple inches taller than Mama. They weren't married, but it felt like they were. He lived with us, was always there for us. That—the simple fact that he was *present*—gave me a huge advantage over most of my friends, who didn't have any father around. He was steady, Steady Eddie, I like to call him, and he had a good job with the Post Office. He talked to me about important things in life, like values and principles, but he wasn't expressive with his emotions. He mostly communicated through sports, almost like a code for how he was feeling.

"How are you, Daddy?"

"Aw, man," he'd say. "Those Cowboys!"

So when Tiki and I were outside the walls of our small one-bedroom apartment, it felt like me and her against everyone else. Everyone.

After those two high school gangbangers beat us up that afternoon, they *kept* beating us up—every single day after school, in the exact same place every single time. Five days, ten days, fifteen days, twenty. Always being sure to hit us in the body, in the arms and the chest, so no one would see any marks.

I begged Tiki to take a different way home after school, a different path.

"Please!" I'd say. "Let's take another street! Just this once!"

"Come on, fool!" she'd shout, leading the way down the same path. "We ain't running!"

"Fuck!" I'd shout, and go right after her.

Tiki was proud. She wasn't going to let these fuckers push her and her brother around. She never ran, she never gave ground, and she always talked shit.

But I wasn't my sister. Even with her at my side, I was terrified. Not only terrified, but confused.

What was the point of what we were going through? My sister felt like we were proving something. Like we were protecting our turf, guarding our honor, our dignity. But I didn't feel that way. I felt like the whole thing proved how futile, how pointless, fighting in our world really was. So what if we kept going home the same way? We still got our ass beat every time!

I loved my sister. I respected her. And I didn't know what to do.

One weekend, I was sitting by myself at my grandma's house. My mama's mom wasn't just my flesh and blood—she was the foundation of my life, of *all* our lives. She was five foot six, two hundred pounds plus, small, round, and hard, like a little human bowling ball. She had her very own house in Compton with a front yard *and* a backyard, so naturally I thought she was rich. We lived with her until I was five years old, and even after we got our own place we spent most Saturdays and Sundays there, chilling, barbecuing out back, just being family.

Grandma also had a way with words. She was always ready with a saying or phrase that fit about any situation. Her wisdom always cut right to the core of life—and if she needed to cuss to get her point across, then so be it.

Let's say you did something stupid and got in trouble for it. She wouldn't come back with some lame-ass stuff like "I told you so" or "You get what you deserve." Nope. For her it was "Play pussy, get fucked." Or to translate: if you choose to play around with pussy, you're bound to get fucked—both literally and figuratively.

You choosing to gangbang? Go ahead, you'll wind up dead like your uncles. *Play pussy, get fucked.* You choosing to mess around with drugs? Fine, you'll get your ass thrown in jail. *Play pussy, get fucked.* You wanna skip school and not do your homework? Welcome to life on welfare. *Play pussy, get fucked.*

Grandma was a lot of things, but she was *not* a shrinking violet.

So when she saw me at her house that day, about a month after the daily beatings had started, she wasn't about to ignore me and mind her own business. No way. She saw me sitting by myself, worried, nervous, alone, and she stopped what she was doing immediately.

"What's wrong with you, boy?" she asked.

I took a deep breath. I knew I wasn't supposed to snitch, but I couldn't hold it in any longer.

I told her bullies had been messing with me. I told her I didn't want anyone else to know, but that I wasn't sure if I was doing the right thing.

"Is it bad that I don't want to fight people, Grandma?"

She looked at me and smiled.

"Alright," she said. "Go get a piece of paper, bring it back here, and write down who you are."

"Huh?" I said.

"You heard me. Go get a piece of paper and write down who you are."

I got a piece of paper, sat down at the table, and wrote my name. Marcellus Vernon Wiley.

"Okay, good," she said. "Now write down three things about you that make you who you are."

I thought for a second, and wrote my first thing.

"Well," I said, "I'm smart."

"Why?" she said.

"Because I work hard at school and I always get As. Sometimes Bs, but mostly As."

I was a huge nerd. I was on the academic decathlon team and came in second in my school spelling bee. I lost to Kenya Petteway because I didn't say "capital 'Q'" when they asked me to spell "Queen," as in "Queen Elizabeth." I spelled "queen" right, I just didn't say the "Q" should be capitalized. So I lost! Now I ask you, is that fair?

"That's my baby," she said. "What next?"

I wrote down my second thing.

"I'm an athlete," I said.

"Why?"

"Because I beat everyone at my school in running every single morning."

And it's true, I did. Every single morning before class I would challenge everyone in my school to racing, and I'd beat them all, even the older kids. Well, all except one other boy named Hanky, who I knew was faster than me. I made sure he was using the bathroom whenever I told people I wanted to race.

"Very good," she said. "And what last?"

I wrote down my third and final thing.

"I'm nice," I said. "I like everybody. Even if they don't like me, I still like them."

Grandma didn't even have to ask me why. We both knew that was who I was—and that it was why I hated to fight. Not because I wasn't strong enough to, not even because I was scared. But because I was a genuinely warm, caring person. Fighting wasn't in my nature.

"Perfect," she said. "Now take that piece of paper, fold it up, and put it under your bed. For the rest of your life, if someone calls you by one of those three things, listen to them. If they call you anything else, I don't care what it is—buster, geek, sissy, *anything*—you don't listen to a damn word they say. You understand me?"

"Yes, Grandma."

"Good. And don't you forget—it's not only what you are that matters, but what you are not. And you ain't no gangbanger."

A couple days later, the beatings finally stopped. It had been four long, painful weeks.

Now, I wish I could say my grandma's advice somehow magically made the gang members go away, but this was life in the hood, not a fairy tale. What actually happened was my grandma told my mama, who told my uncles, who had a good long private "talk" with the teenagers who were screwing with us. Lucky for them, it stopped there and no one wound up dead. When it was all said and done, my uncles were grown-ass men and these were some teen punks—beating their butts was enough to get the message across.

But that wasn't the most important thing that happened. Not even close.

That was the piece of paper. I kept it hidden away, exactly like my grandma said. When I was feeling bad, or confused, I'd get it out and I'd look at it, and I'd remember who I was. I'd remember that who I was came from inside me, not from the world I lived in. I'd remember that I was different, and that that was a good thing.

With that piece of paper, I had taken my first right turn onto my very own path.

Soon after that, I discovered something else that would be a big part of my new path: football.

Like I told my grandma, I was fast—maybe not Hanky fast, but still pretty damn fast—and I knew it. Besides racing older boys every day before school, I also played a lot of football on the streets in my neighborhood. Nothing organized, nothing serious, just a few kids getting together and playing ball, light pole to light pole.

Until one summer day when I was about eight years old, I was playing with a few of my boys, including a cat by the name of Dominique Walker at quarterback.

Dominique called a streak play—I say, "called a play," but he probably just said, "Run over there!" So that's what I did. I ran. Sprinted down the side, past everyone.

Dominique chucked the ball in the air, and I dove for it, slamming my body into a parked car and hitting the pavement hard. Popped up like it was nothing with the football in my hands.

"Caught it!" I shouted.

Dominique jogged over to me shaking his head.

"Dog, you crazy!" he said.

"That's right," I said.

"*And* you fast. You gotta play football!"

This made no sense to me. I thought we *were* playing football.

"What do you mean?" I said. "Where?"

"For a team, man!" he said, laughing.

"For real?" I said. "You can do that?"

To me, organized football was something that happened on TV. Something that grown men did, the best of the best, and got paid money for it. We lived in LA, where almost everyone loved the Raiders, but the Dallas Cowboys were my dad's favorite team. The Cowboys liked to call themselves "America's Team," but my daddy wasn't another bandwagon guy. He was from Tyler, Texas, born and bred a Dallas fan, and he watched their games every Sunday. That was what adults did.

But kids playing *real* football? No way.

"Yeah, man," Dominique said. "I play for Inglewood. You go sign up, pay 'em some money, and you there."

Aw, shit. Everything was going great until he mentioned the money. That meant I had to run it by the toughest, tightest, completely not-certified accountant this side of Crenshaw.

"Sixty-five dollars!" my mama said. "You crazy?"

"Pleeeeeease!" I begged. "You get a whole lotta stuff with it, like a jersey with your own number on it and shoulder pads and a helmet and everything. And they let you sell candy and stuff to help pay for it!"

She finally relented, as long as I kept my grades up. I already got good grades, but if I needed any extra motivation, this was it.

Just like Dominique, I played for the Inglewood Mohawks peewee football team. I'd love to be able to tell you I came out and dominated straight away, but I was a flickering lightbulb compared with the true star on our team, Stais Boseman. He was so fast, he put Hanky to shame. As a running back, my dog averaged four touchdowns a game. *Averaged.*

Sounds nuts, I know—if a running back averaged four touchdowns a game in the NFL, he'd automatically be the greatest player in the history of the universe—but let me tell you something about football at this age. Ninety-five percent of the kids on each team played just like you'd expect someone younger than ten to play. In other words, they didn't have a damn clue what the hell they were doing.

Honestly, a quarter of them probably had no idea how they even got there. Their football-crazy dad slapped some helmet and pads on them, told them to go stand in the middle of some field and run around a bunch.

That meant for the 5 percent who actually *did* know what they were doing, who were big or fast or athletically advanced for their age, it was pure feasting time. The center would hike the ball, the QB would hand it off to Stais Boseman, and he would run past everyone and score. That was it. It was that simple.

That doesn't mean Stais Boseman wasn't legitimately, objectively amazing, of course. Dude went on to be named *USA Today's* number one football player in the *country* coming out of high school, *and* its number two basketball player. It's incredibly rare for someone to get that in both sports. Could've wound up with a bigger NFL career than me if he had stuck with football, but chose basketball instead. Played for USC, then a few years for the Houston Rockets in the NBA.

Me? That first year, Stais Boseman was so damn good they made me a fullback—not exactly a position known for its speed. Hell, I was *only* averaging about two touchdowns a week!

It didn't matter that I wasn't the brightest shining star though. Even in year one, football gave me something a lot more important than glory or touchdowns or stats—it gave me more of my dad.

It turned out he didn't only love watching his Cowboys on Sundays. He loved watching me play, anytime, anywhere. Like I said before, my dad had always been a big part of my life, but he liked to communicate through his passion for sports.

Now that I was playing football it was like we suddenly spoke the same language, a language we had all to ourselves, father and son.

He attended every single one of my games, and he even videotaped every damn one. We ain't talking about no old, clunky VHS dinosaur perched on his shoulder either. My mama may have been worried about sixty-five dollars for the league registration, but my dad spent that real money on a state-of-the-art JVC handheld so he could capture every moment, every play.

He wasn't one of those crazy dads you always see, yelling at the refs, bragging to all his friends, living vicariously through his kid's success. He never forced people to watch his son's "amazing exploits on the field"—those tapes were for me and him alone. Pop 'em in, watch 'em together, and chill on random nights at home. His own dad had passed away when he was young, so being there for my games, taping them, that was something my dad wanted to share with me.

I wasn't the only one who got a great deal either. The entire neighborhood started going to my dad for all their sports video needs, inviting him to every local baseball, basketball, or football game to capture their own kids in all their glory. The hood's resident director of photography.

At first my dad didn't have much to tape at my games, but after spending a year in Stais Boseman's shadow, I finally started putting out my *own* highlight reel. Partly because I got better, faster, stronger. But honestly, mostly because Stais was so damn good he skipped an age group and moved up to an older division. (Thank you, Stais!)

Without even knowing it, Stais gave me my shot, and I took it. I went from averaging two touchdowns a game my first season to four a game my second. And my third season? I could score five TDs in a single go.

You could even see the transformation in my old team photos, the ones all the players took before the season began.

That first year, the year I was behind Stais, there I was in my picture, wearing 44 on my jersey, for John Riggins, the legendary Redskins player. At that age, the only heroes I had in my life were my mom and my dad, but I knew Riggins was a fullback like me, and if I was gonna play I wanted to emulate the best. But the look on my face? I had this polite, shy little smile, all prim and proper and reserved. That ain't the face of no legend in the making!

Second-year photo, when I *knew* Stais wasn't coming back, I was wearing a new number, 35, same as an older kid I looked up to named Pokey, the star running back for another youth team. I was gonna be a star running back, just like Pokey, and now all of a sudden my smile in the photo wasn't so polite. I had a big old grin, a glint in my eye. Not too cocky, but an air of expectation, of suspense. I knew I could be good, but how good?

Then you hit that year-three photo. I chose number 32, because all the best pro running backs wore 32: Jim Brown, Marcus Allen, O. J. Simpson—*especially* O.J., not even because of his game but because my dad had bought me the official O. J. Simpson football. It was called "The Juice," its leather painted bright orange and his nickname written in bold letters on the side, so I *had* to be 32. By this point, my smile wasn't even a smile anymore—it was a smirk. My head was cocked to the side, and if my body language had anything to say, it was "I am the *shit*."

Turned out, though, I was getting too confident for my own damn good.

AS MY ATHLETIC path became clearer and clearer, the direction of the rest of my life got more complicated, a twisted-up Rubik's Cube I couldn't exactly figure out.

I knew my dad and mom weren't technically married. But we had a complete family experience, and that was important to them. They didn't want me and my sister to be some hood stereotype who grew up in a broken home. So they worked hard to create the feel of a happy, intact home life, and I thrived because of it.

But even though we looked like this perfect Universal Studios family, if you looked really, really hard, you started to see the set was made of plywood.

My dad was home every single night like clockwork. He helped provide for us through his job at the Post Office, and he was around almost *all* the time, but I also knew he kept another place on the side. Nothing big, just an empty spare room he rented in another part of the city. I didn't know what it meant, I didn't know what it was for. I remember being in his car as we did errands on the weekend, then parking once or twice outside a strange building so he could run in and pick something up.

"I'll be right back," he'd say.

"Where are we?" I'd ask.

"My other place."

How does a kid younger than ten even process information like that? He doesn't, that's how.

My mother, on the other hand, had one place and one place only. She was devoted to me and my sister as much as any mother could be. You talk about being a mother bear, she was a flat-out grizzly, ferocious in protecting and caring for us. I was one of the sappiest cubs you've ever seen, a big-ass mama's boy.

Every weekend, after my dad left early to go golfing—yes, folks in the hood do golf—I'd find my mom still curled up in bed, sleeping, and I'd snuggle up next to her, nice and warm and cozy. Sometimes I'd doze off, but lots of the time I'd lie there, staring at her, soaking her in—and protecting her myself.

See, both her dad and her grandma died from heart attacks at young ages, and I was scared I might lose Mama in the same way. If only I stayed close, I thought, if only I kept an eye on her, then everything would be okay.

Then after ten or fifteen minutes of me watching her like that, she'd always jerk awake with a start, flailing her arms.

"What you doing, Teddy Bear?"

"Just watching you, Mama!"

She finally told me to stick to my own bed when I reached thirteen.

Mama didn't just take care of us every single day, she focused relentlessly on our future too. All the rest of her family and friends were content to stay put in Compton, but not her.

When I was young, we moved over and over again until we finally found us an apartment right on the outskirts of the hood, off Slauson Avenue on Edgemar. Right on the border between the hood and more upscale black areas like Windsor Hills and Baldwin Hills. You heard of *Black-ish*? Well, this was *Hood-ish*. It was important, not just because the neighborhood was a little better, but because it got us access to school districts beyond Compton and South Central. As a former straight-A student herself, Mama wanted to make sure we got good educations. Even let friends of mine borrow our home address so they could get into better schools outside Compton too.

But as loving and nurturing as she was, there was something about that Rubik's Cube that seemed a little scrambled to me, even as a little kid.

At the same time she was helping us strive for something better, Mama didn't have a job. My dad did, but he and my mom weren't married, so she was still able to claim welfare benefits for the family. We got a welfare check for about $400 twice a month, on the first and the fifteenth. Food stamps we'd get on the third of the month.

Now, to give you some context, where I was from, being on welfare meant you were poor, but a normal level of poor. Being on food stamps, though? That meant you were poor as *shit*, like almost shelter-level poor.

And food stamps back then weren't like they are now, when you get this fancy electronic card from the government you can swipe like a regular debit card. Naw, back then food stamps were paper, came in a book, and looked like this funky colored money, like a foreign currency made especially for people from the country of Broke-Ass Motherfuckers.

One time I went by myself to the grocery store to load up on groceries—couldn't use food stamps to get any good stuff like candy or Cheetos back then—found everything I needed, and headed to the checkout line to pay up. As I was about to pull out my book of funny money, I saw a bunch of my classmates—and they saw me too.

Shit!

None of these kids were rich. Some of them were probably on welfare, and a few of them were definitely in the free school lunch program like me. But remember, food stamps were different. Those were for the poorest of the poor.

"Yo, what up!" I said to my friends.

They stood there expectantly, waiting for me to pay. I gulped.

"I, uh, think I forgot to get something in the back. I'll catch y'all later."

I got out of that checkout line as fast as I could. I hid behind an aisle, peeking out to make sure they'd left before I finally headed back to the register. Looking around the whole time to make sure there weren't any stragglers who would catch me with my Monopoly cash.

Don't get me wrong here. There's nothing to be ashamed of, inherently, when it comes to poverty. Sometimes people struggle, sometimes people need help, and there's nothing wrong with that. I get that.

But I didn't get why my mom wasn't working. My grandma—who also worked full-time, by the way—would tell me that Mama didn't work so she could focus on me and my sister. Alright, that's cool. But I knew plenty of kids whose parents both had jobs, and they seemed fine. My dad had a full-time job, and *he* was able to make time for us.

Hell, he was able to make time for a whole "other place," and he still worked. Come to think of it, how could he afford to rent a spare room somewhere, but here I was having to worry about buying shit with food stamps? What the fuck was up with that?

My life was punctuated with question marks, and no one seemed to have the answers. I'd watch the Cosby Show, and every episode would end with Bill in his sweater sitting with the whole family around the kitchen table, sitting and talking, explaining stuff, answering questions. (Of course, in real life Bill had a whole bunch of *other* questions he couldn't answer so easy, but we'll save that for a different book.)

No one did that for me with my family, so I was left to twist and turn that Rubik's Cube all on my own. It helped me learn the importance of thinking for myself, of always being inquisitive and challenging authority.

But it also meant I reached some very wrong conclusions as I found my way.

DESPITE ALL MY success playing football, when my fourth season came around I decided to quit.

Actually, check that. The irony was that I didn't want to quit *despite* my success, I wanted to quit *because* of it. My confidence had turned to cockiness, and that became complacency.

In three years of football, I hadn't lost a single game. Not one. And after Stais moved up, I had become the focus of our entire team—and of opposing teams too.

Before our games, I'd be walking to the field when all of a sudden, a bunch of parents would walk up to me, dragging their sons after them. These were people from the other team, people I didn't know, had never even met before.

The parents would stop their sons and point at me, physically point their fingers, and call out my jersey number.

"See 32?" they'd say. "He's the reason they always win. You gotta shut him down."

We were eleven or twelve years old. And it would happen before *every single game.*

And every single game, it wouldn't matter.

My team would hike the ball, they'd hand it off to me—"Sweep to Wiley!" the parents would shout. *"It's a sweep to Wiley!"*—running the same damn play every single time, and I'd sprint 75 yards past all the other kids and score. Just like that. Done. And I was sick of it.

Sure, it brought me and my dad closer together. He came to all my games, he taped them all, we'd watch them together. But he liked to hold in his enthusiasm, didn't communicate much more than "Alright!" or "Good play!" I don't think he meant anything by it. He just wasn't a big talker.

So one day, about a month into practice for my fourth season, I told my dad I wanted to quit.

"Why you wanna quit?" he said.

"I don't know, I'm tired of football," I said. "Every day all my friends are playing Nintendo or out riding bikes, and I'm stuck in this house putting on pads to get ready for a stupid practice when we always win our games anyway. Who cares?"

He looked at me intently. There was no drama, no hysterics. No "Don't you get it, boy? This is your ticket! You can make it to the NFL!" None of that. He wasn't that kind of guy.

"You start something, you finish it," was all he said. "Then, when the season's over, if you still hate it, you can quit. But finish what you start."

My mom, of course, had a slightly different approach.

"I paid sixty-five dollars to register your ass on that team!" she yelled. "You damn right you gonna play!"

My parents may not have been interested in explaining my family life to me, but that moment, when it really counted, they explained the importance of following through.

I stuck with the team, and like we did the previous three years, we made it through the entire regular season undefeated, with me leading the way at running back. When I arrived at the field for our championship game, though, I noticed something different.

This time, it wasn't the parents of the *other team* bringing their sons over to scout me before the game—instead, the parents of *our team* were taking all of us over to check out *their* star.

"See that guy? Number 27? Block him, and Marcellus will score, okay?"

I listened and I scoffed.

They got a guy? I thought. *Whatever, I ain't scared.*

I looked over at our opponents, the Orange County Piranhas, saw number 27—and I swear that twelve-year-old looked like Earl Campbell.

Oh shit! That motherfucker huge!

Now, technically, there's no way he could've been that much bigger than any of us. Everyone in peewee had to make a certain weight before the game, including me. But I swear to God above that dude was six foot two, 240 pounds—I don't care what the damn scale said.

No way they gonna block 27, I thought. No way.

And I was right. For the first time in my entire football career, I actually had to face legit competition on the other team's defense. He tackled me on every single play, all game long.

Tackle, 27! Two-yard gain! Tackle, 27! Nine-yard gain! Tackle, 27! Four-yard gain!

I picked up some yards, but I was never able to break one big, never able to find the end zone. Without me scoring, our offense couldn't do shit. But theirs couldn't do anything either—until with one minute left in the game, we fumbled the ball. They scooped it up, ran it back, and scored the very first touchdown by either team, going up 6–0.

Their fans went crazy, just *erupted*. Not only because they scored, but because that was the first time my team had even been *down* all season long! Game wasn't even over, but by leading at all, they felt like they had already won.

They hadn't. We got the ball back, with less than a minute to go and one last chance.

After the kickoff, we started with the ball at the 30-yard line. Tried the same damn play we always tried—the classic sweep to Wiley—and number 27 stopped it cold. Shit.

There were six seconds left on the clock, enough time for one last play. Coach says, alright then, we have to score. This is it. Right here, right now. So guess what? We gonna pass the ball to Wiley.

Pass? They hadn't passed me the ball *once* in almost four years of peewee football. They didn't have to! Run a sweep to Wiley, and we good.

Not anymore. Not this game. It had to be a pass.

We went out to the field. I lined up in the slot—I didn't even know what the slot was, but I lined up there.

Hike!

Our quarterback threw me a quick lateral pass—barely a pass, more like a fling—and I caught that thing and held on tight. Soon as it was in my hands, here came 27, barreling down on me like a twelve-year-old freight train.

Just like that, I decided to try something new: I stopped in my tracks.

Dude flew right by me.

I took off down the field, juking and weaving past the rest of their defenders like they were nothing. Past the 40-yard line, the 50, the 40, the 30. So damn easy!

Then the 25, the 20, the 10 . . . almost there! . . . when *BAM!*

Guess who tackled me on the 10-yard line?

Number 27.

He was so big, so fast, and I was so busy weaving and dodging the other mortals on the field, that this motherfucker actually caught me and dragged me down before I could score.

The clock ran out. Half the crowd went "Awwwww." The other half went "AHHHHHH!"

We had lost our first game of the season. I had lost the first game of my entire career. Other kids on my team started crying, moping, kneeling on the field, hanging their heads like we were at a funeral.

But me? With family members in the gangs, I had been to plenty of funerals—real funerals.

I jogged gracefully over to the award table, politely shook everyone's hand, and calmly accepted my second-place trophy as the crowd clapped respectfully.

We had lost. But it didn't make me mad, not at all. What it made me was determined, maybe even inspired. Over the last few years, I had forgotten what it meant to face adversity, to have to really strive to be better than your opponent. Now I knew, and I liked it.

My dad asked me if I wanted to quit now that the season was over.

Hell naw. I wanted to keep playing football. I wasn't going to think of quitting ever again. I was going to work my ass off, and I was going to get better.

To this day, I don't know who that number 27 was.

Dog, if you out there? Tweet at me.

Let's race.

I CAME HOME FROM school and walked into the kitchen. My mama was there, cooking up dinner.

"Hey, Mama," I said.

She didn't hear me, because she was talking on the phone, had it cradled between her ear and her shoulder so she could keep talking as she did stuff around the house. Fold laundry? That's cool, talk on the phone. Do some dishes? No problem, just talk on the phone. Watch TV? Hell, talk on the phone then too.

Talk, talk, talk. Usually to my grandma, sometimes to her friends. But always talking, all the time, it felt like.

I hated the phone.

To me, it represented everything I hated about living in the hood. Part of that was low ambition. Everywhere around me, it seemed like people didn't do shit. Sure, I liked to run my mouth as much as the next guy. I used jokes to get out of plenty of tough situations, and I loved being the class clown at school. But I didn't *only* talk. I backed up everything I said with *action*. Studying, getting As, playing football, winning MVP of my team. But aside from a few big exceptions, to me it felt like talking was all everyone else *did*. Talking on the phone, talking in the kitchen, talking in the living room. Complaining, gossiping, doing nothing with their lives. Not planning, not getting motivated, nothing. It was like a disease.

The other part I hated was the anger that the low ambition naturally gave birth to. When the people around me didn't take control of their lives, when they got frustrated with their reality, they'd get all this pent-up energy, all this rage, and sooner or later they'd explode — usually over the most trivial shit you could imagine.

I'd be at the grocery store, and someone would drop a water bottle accidentally—no big deal, slipped out of their hands on the way to checkout—and maybe, just maybe it would bounce on the floor and happen to hit a stranger's foot. Then suddenly, *pow!*

"Man, you better watch that, motherfucker!"

Just like that, you got a knife pulled in aisle four.

Even my own grandma, who I loved more than anything, who taught me so much about life, spent half her time on a razor's edge. One day, one of her sons decided to raise a hand to her, and how did she respond? She raised a gun—and pulled the trigger.

Next time I went to Grandma's house, there was a bullet hole in the wall, but at least it wasn't in him. Thankfully, she wasn't *trying* to hit him, she was trying to send a message.

Well, message received—by me, anyway. From an early age, I learned that the world of adults in South Central LA wasn't for me.

Thank God I still had my sister, right? In that crazy, mixed-up environment, Tiki was the one person who always had my back. Who always looked out for me. Yeah, she lived on the edge like a lot of the people around us. She wasn't exactly a peacemaker, but I knew why she fought—she fought for me, to shield me, protect me. She fought so I didn't have to.

Like me, she was a doer, not *only* a talker. Someone who wanted to get shit done, who wanted to get out of South Central.

At least that's what I thought.

That day in the kitchen, I watched my mom talking on the phone to my grandma, shook my head, and went to my bedroom. Like I said before, "bedroom" was actually an exaggeration. It was really more like a semiprivate nook, with three walls and a sheet we hung for the fourth. I shared that tiny space with my sister.

I walked in, and there she was, lying on the bed, talking on the phone too, sharing the same line as my mama and my grandma. The three of them gossiping away together. Talk, talk, talk.

Shit, I thought. They got Tiki too!

In my mind, my sister was gone. A talker, not a doer, like everyone else.

I decided right then and there that it was all up to me. *I* had to be the one who was different. *I* had to be the one who did something with his life. Something that would change our circumstances.

Whenever I went to church on Sundays, one of my favorite passages was from the book of Matthew: "Small is the gate and narrow is the road that leads to life, and only a few find it." To make it out of the hood, I had to be one of the few who followed that narrow path.

But I wasn't going to just follow my own path. I was going to carry my family down the road with me.

My fourth year of peewee football I realized how I was going to do it.

I was thirteen years old, and the better I played, the more attention I got. Local high schools even started recruiting me. Nothing super official—the kind of thing where an informal representative would approach me after a game and slyly ask if I'd considered going to Whatever High.

I'd finish cramming my hot dog in my mouth, and say, yeah, I knew exactly where I was going—Westchester High, which had a good football team.

Over the next four years, I was gonna use my skills to earn myself a big-time college scholarship, a great higher education, and my biggest dream of all—a spot in the NFL.

There was one problem. My body had different plans.

CHAPTER TWO

ONE MORE REP FOR JANET JACKSON

IT WAS A weekday, and I had just gotten home from practice at my new high school.

In the past, getting home wouldn't have been the end of the day—it would've been the beginning of the night. Maybe doing some homework or riding bikes with some friends. Maybe playing some video games. Definitely listening to music. Always listening to music.

But not tonight.

Tonight when I got home, I sat by myself on the floor, thinking. No video games, not even any music this time. Maybe the TV was on, maybe it was off. I really don't remember, and it really didn't matter. All I wanted to do was think—and ice my knees.

My knees, which seemed like they were constantly in pain, constantly aching, constantly slowing me down, whether or not I was actually practicing.

Tonight was different from before because this year was different from before. This year, my freshman year of high school, I was finally betrayed by the one thing that had *never* let me down once in my whole life—my own body.

It was the fall of 1988. I was changing, and the world around me was changing too. The hood had always been a place that the rest of the country either forgot or—more likely—intentionally ignored. We were poor, we were killing each other, and we were no one's problem but our own. Then, suddenly, rap groups like Public Enemy and NWA came along and woke America the hell up. They weren't only talking about girls or parties or whatever, they were talking about real shit. Life. They were smart, critiquing the racial and economic injustice that people in my city experienced every day—and, in NWA's case, sometimes even glamorizing it and the entire gangsta lifestyle.

The nation couldn't get enough, and neither could I. I didn't just listen to every album, I read them cover to cover, memorizing all the lyrics. I didn't fall for NWA's glorification of gangbanging, because my uncles had shown me the ugly reality behind the veil. But I was proud of the way South Central was getting recognized. We were officially on the map. Our music—*my* music—was finally being heard.

It was South Central's time—and it felt like it should've been my time too. I'm not a naturally braggadocious person, but the facts are the facts: up until that year, my athleticism had made me exceptional. I was faster than almost everyone else my age, and even most of the kids who were older than me. In track, I had anchored a relay squad on the famous LA Jets youth track team that set the national record in the 4 x 400-meter race. In football, I had big-time high school coaches trying to recruit me from my grade school league. Grade school!

And to me, all that had come naturally. I had practiced hard, sure, but my talent was mostly a gift. At an early age, I barely had to work for it.

I was never too pompous, never too full of myself—spending a month getting your ass beat by gangbangers every day after school does wonders for your humility—but athletic greatness was something I came to accept. Maybe even take for granted.

Then I got to Westchester High.

When I was little, my mama spent a year moving our small family around, positioning us just right so that my sister and I wouldn't have to settle for high school in Compton. We bounced from Compton to Lynwood to Long Beach and finally ended up at our Slauson and Edgemar apartment, just far enough west to give us some other educational options. Again, I'd call it *hood-ish*.

If I had wanted, I could've gone to Crenshaw or Dorsey High, nothing but a five- or ten-minute drive away. But instead, I took the bus at least thirty minutes to get to Westchester, two or three miles from the beach.

Now don't get me wrong—Westchester was still pretty gangster. It had a few shootings here and there, and gangs like the Rolling 60s and others. But compared with Dorsey and Crenshaw, it was a huge step up. Most important, their team was good enough for me to get noticed. For my plan to work—to use my football skills to get my family a better life—I needed to play for a good team that would get covered by the local press and potentially college recruiters.

Problem was, I also needed a little something called *knees*. And right when I hit ninth grade is when my body, and my knees especially, decided it didn't give a damn about my dreams.

My knees started killing me, and all my coordination, all my finesse, abandoned me. My movements felt awkward, tight. That would've been one thing if it had been packaged with a nice big growth spurt, but I was barely growing at all, stuck at about five foot nine and 150 pounds, which is fine if you want to play football as a hobby, but not if you want to reach the highest level someday.

I saw a doctor at Dominguez Valley Hospital in Compton, where I had been born and where my grandmother worked in supplies. He ran a bunch of tests and told me I had Osgood-Schlatter disease, a condition that affected my knee ligaments. It was intensely painful, and tended to occur in adolescent boys who were both growing and active in sports.

Well, I was definitely getting the pain, but the growing was happening very slowly and very steadily. All I could do, he said, was be patient and wait. But waiting felt like an eternity.

I still played ball of course. But I had expected—naturally—to play on varsity my first year. No way was that happening with my knees. Hell, I didn't even make JV. Instead I was relegated to the freshman team, or the B's, and they didn't even let me play my natural position.

If you're a running back with bad knees and a solid build in high school, congratulations—they're officially gonna make you an offensive lineman. So that's what happened. I went from being a superstar running back to a superfast, skinny-ass lineman.

From the outside, anyone would've still thought I was alright. I was still getting playing time, still having an impact on the freshman team. I don't wear fear or anxiety in public. Never had, never will.

But on the inside, I was devastated. I had gone from being the shit to being pretty good. That might not sound too bad, and I don't expect anyone to feel sorry for me, but at that age it was hard to handle. Football had been my identity. I had pegged all my hopes to it—not only mine, but my family's—and now it was gone.

My grandma always liked to say, "Don't let 'em steal your joy."

Well, my whole life I never had—till all of a sudden it was like grand-theft auto.

I spent hours on the floor, icing those knees, trying to save them up for practice, lost in thought. I'd turn my music on. NWA or Public Enemy's "Rebel Without a Pause." The soundtrack to my mind.

I knew I wasn't done. I didn't know how yet, I didn't know exactly what I was going to do. But I knew I had more to give. I knew I had more coming, more potential. I just needed to be patient.

Some might even say I needed to get a little . . . Nasty.

SOMETIMES I WOULDN'T only think in front of the TV, I'd actually watch. Usually *Transformers*—the old-school cartoons, not that crazy Michael Bay shit—and every now and then, *occasionally*, I'd watch myself.

Put in one of the tapes of my old games, sit back, watch, and study my game. Use them to get better. And hell, I'll admit it—sometimes reminisce about the fun times of the past.

Except one day I didn't find football on my dad's videotape—I found something a lot more interesting. Let's call it an unexpected scene from *nature*.

Get your head out of the gutter! It was honestly, seriously footage of my dad at the zoo. But I didn't see me or my sister or my mom on this little excursion, I saw him hanging out with a woman I had never met before.

Up until that moment, I had never really questioned my dad's life with us. He was there every night, every day, as good as married to my mom, and a very engaged father to me. I was aware of his "other place," but it meant nothing to me.

But suddenly, when I watched that video, something clicked. I twisted that Rubik's Cube and at least *started* to get all the greens on the same damn side. As present and stable as my dad had been, he had also somehow made time for a girlfriend too.

Now don't get me wrong. I never negatively judged my dad for having a life on the side. In a way, I actually respect the decisions he made. A lot of dads in my neighborhood got girlfriends and lied about it, or just left, no explanations, no nothing.

My dad didn't lie to my mama. She knew about his other place. He could've taken the easy way out, sacrificed all of us so he could have a brand-new life, no strings attached. But he stayed involved, stayed present, stayed there for us.

That doesn't mean it was easy on Mama.

A couple years before I started high school, she finally got that job, working for the Post Office out in Santa Monica, about twenty-five minutes from our place in the morning, before traffic got bad. She even got herself a car when my grandma gave her her old, huge-ass Monte Carlo—could've taken out a bus in a head-to-head collision.

I'm not sure exactly what triggered that push to self-sufficiency— another twist in the Rubik's Cube—but that's right around the time my dad started spending a little more time at the other place and a little less with us, staying late at "work" a couple hours too long.

Despite all that, it was important for Mama to maintain that facade, especially in front of the rest of her family.

We'd always have Christmas at my grandma's place, the tree and everything. Grandma wouldn't have a big gathering, just her kids and grandkids, but it was always important to Mama to make exactly the right impression. She was the oldest, and Grandma had no problem telling everyone exactly what she thought of her daughter.

"You motherfuckers all know what it is," she'd announce, pointing at my mom. "She's my favorite! That's the damn truth!"

Did I mention Grandma had a way with words?

But once I got to high school, Dad started showing up later and later for those holiday celebrations—Christmas, Easter, Thanksgiving, all of them.

"Where Charles at?" people would ask.

Mama would smile and make excuses, saving face as much as she could.

But I knew. I understood that our family was coming apart. And it only made me more determined to earn us all a better life.

"ALRIGHT, DOG!" JABARI SAID. "Now one more rep for Janet Jackson!"

It's true. Janet Jackson, the queen of hits like "Nasty" and "When I Think of You," was the key to my physical transformation in high school. She had just released her hit album *Control*, but pop star Janet wasn't my Janet. My Janet was "Charlene," a character she played in my favorite TV show, *Diff'rent Strokes*. Janet/Charlene might've been Willis's girlfriend on the show, but in my heart she was all mine. She—and my best friend, Jabari—helped me channel all my frustration about football, all my fears that I wouldn't live up to my potential, into action. Action that got me bigger, stronger, and better.

With all due respect to Janet, it really started with Jabari.

I had known Jabari since kindergarten. While I'd always been the class clown, Jabari was the pretty boy. No better way to put it. On the one hand, you had me, running around in all these no-brand clothes and shoes. On the other hand, you had Jabari with his blue-green eyes, always dressing super fresh with Le Tigre polo shirts and Diadora sneakers and shit.

He and I were the smartest kids in class, but he talked with a little stutter, had to go to speech therapy and the whole deal. Kids would tease him and clown him all the time for it, but he didn't care, he just kept talking. He never shut up.

No surprise then, I liked him immediately. And he stuck with me in high school, even when it looked like my star was starting to fade.

Like me, Jabari was on the football team at Westchester. He hadn't even made the cut for my peewee team back in grade school, but by this point he was actually better than me—both because he had improved and because I had fallen off so much. But like me, he still needed to get bigger, faster, stronger.

Every day after school, he and I would head up to the roof of my apartment building, out there under that big Los Angeles sky. We had these weights set up, old cracked pieces of shit made of concrete. If they said forty-five pounds, we were lucky if they were thirty-seven.

Didn't matter to us though. We bought our vitamins and amino acids from GNC, and we promised each other we'd work our asses off to be the best athletes we could be, to get buff and swole. And that's exactly what we did.

We'd go up there and curl, bench, and squat for hours. I'd get to where I could barely even move, and then I'd hear Jabari shout out those magic words.

"One more rep for Janet Jackson!"

I'd think of Charlene, and I'd lift the damn house.

We'd run from all over Los Angeles, practically. From school we'd run to the Pacific and back a few times, racking up five or ten miles. From my place, we'd run up Valley Ridge and into Baldwin Hills, sprinting up what we liked to call Throw-Up Mountain. If you got up that thing without puking at least a couple times, congratulations, you won.

When we weren't working out, we'd walk a block up Slauson to Yee's Chinese Food. (Which conveniently changed its name to Jim's during the '92 LA riots because of all the racial tension, then turned right back to Yee's afterward.) There were only two things I could afford there, the child's plate for $3.49 and the number one for $5.49, a plate of egg foo young and fried shrimp. Now good luck finding the shrimp in all that puffy batter, but I loved that stuff, and the food was only part of the experience.

We were talking, designing our lives, willing the world to be what we wanted it to be.

"What kind of girl you want to marry?" I'd ask.

"Well," he'd say, "I want her to be beautiful, but not too beautiful—cuz then she'd be dating too many dudes, and girls would talk shit about her."

"Right," I said. "She gotta be beautiful, but more beautiful to *us*."

"How tall you want her to be?" he asked.

"I don't know," I said. "Like five ten."

"Damn!" he said. "You ain't even five ten yet!"

"A man can dream, can't he?"

We were some inexperienced motherfuckers—I won't even tell you how old I was before I lost my virginity—but we talked, and we grew. As boys who aspired to be men, and as athletes.

And I mean that literally. I grew about an inch and about twenty pounds every year.

It was a trend that continued all through high school and even through college, till just past my senior year. I was a late, but very steadily transforming, bloomer.

As I got bigger, as I got stronger, my play on the field improved. I still hadn't reached my potential, and I had a long-ass way to go. But I spent less time sitting on the floor in front of a blank TV and more time focused on getting better. The team started playing me at my natural position, running back. Like most high school players, I played on both sides of the ball, and I began thriving on defense as well as a safety. When I was in grade school, my natural talent had been enough to make me stand out; now I had the work ethic, the *drive*, to match.

So when my next opportunity came, I was ready.

Even though Westchester had a good football team, by the time I finished my sophomore year I started to realize that their *program* was lacking.

See, to make it to a big-time college program back then, you needed to be more than just a great high school player on a good team. This was long before the days of social media. You couldn't DM your highlight reel to any coach or recruiter on Twitter and get an answer back five minutes later telling you if you were any good. You needed your high school coaches to *invest* in you, to push your profile to college recruiters, to make sure you got noticed and got your shot.

There were guys on my Westchester team who were a lot better than me, but for some reason, maybe because the coaching staff wasn't giving them enough support, those kids never got the big scholarship offers they deserved.

Everyone told me that if I wanted a shot at a big-time college, I needed to switch to a school that had a coach with demonstrated connections to major recruiters. Follow the well-worn, traditional path to stardom.

That's why I was putting in all those extra reps for Janet, right? To be the best! Well, why wait for college? The best could start right now!

Then my dad talked to exactly the kind of coach everyone said I needed, a guy by the name of Angelo Jackson. Jackson had a huge national profile. A good word from him could get you noticed by all the big schools. His programs served as the launch pad for tons of kids who went on to play for major colleges.

But to play for him, I'd have to do more than take a bus ride every day.

I'd be leaving behind everything I knew. I'd be leaving the public schools for the first time in my life, attending private school on an athletic scholarship. I'd be going to school in one of the wealthiest, whitest, most conservative parts of Los Angeles. A whole other world from Compton, or even Westchester, for that matter.

My junior year, I'd be going to Santa Monica.

ST. MONICA CATHOLIC High School was seven blocks from the ocean. The area around it looked more like a country club than a city.

Sure, South Central had its fair share of palm trees and green lawns, but look a little closer and it's Beirut with a few shrubs.

Not Santa Monica. Trees and parks everywhere, massive houses and fancy shops. People like to talk about the grass is greener on the other side? Well here, the grass was *literally greener*. Scrape away at the fancy surface, and you'd find more fancy surface.

The Catholic church the high school was affiliated with wasn't exactly Our Weeping Sisters of the Eternal Poverty either. To put it delicately, that congregation was rich as hell. Even Arnold Schwarzenegger went to church there.

Every morning, my mama would take me with her on her way to work at the Santa Monica Post Office, at the butt-crack of dawn. I'd wake up at 5:00 a.m., haul my ass into that tank of a car at 5:20, and be on the road by 5:21. Dropped off at the front gate of the school by 5:47 so she could make it to work by 6:00. Even LA had empty roads that early in the day, so we made good time.

"Damn, kid!" the janitors would say, watching me trudge onto school grounds. "What you doing getting here with us?"

Classes didn't start till 8:00 a.m., so I was the only student there. It was so early the building wasn't even open yet, so I'd set up camp by the stairs close to the gym. And when I say "camp," I mean it literally— I brought an old sleeping bag, green on the outside with pictures of action figures on the inside. I'd spread that thing on the ground and lie on my stomach, reading, studying, and doing homework.

Of course, me being me, I also had to have my music, so I'd bring my radio with me, a not-so-state-of-the-art Toshiba boom box, my pride and joy.

I'd work for an hour and a half, till 7:15, and right about then some other students would start showing up to get ready for class.

I figured out real fast that no matter what the neighborhood or church congregation may have looked like, a lot of the students were like me. Maybe even most. Black kids, Mexican kids, middle class or maybe on academic scholarship. There were some wealthier white kids too, sure, but St. Monica's mission as a school was to reach a broad, diverse group of kids of all socioeconomic backgrounds. St. Monica's didn't feel elitist—it felt normal, like a public school that just happened to be private.

So those kids who found me chilling by myself at 7:15 in the morning weren't much different from me. And by the time they showed up, let's just say I was *done* studying.

That's right. The books would be gone, and it would only be me, the newest hot football recruit, hanging, listening to music, and having fun.

First it was a cute girl coming by and saying hello. Then another, then another. Then all the guys started to realize that the stairs by the gym were where to go if they wanted to talk to the cute girls. And before you know it, it became a thing. The place where everyone *used* to hang, this tree in the middle of the yard that the seniors called their own, turned into a ghost town—and all the action migrated to *my* spot.

My very own Marcellus Wiley morning sleeping-bag party.

Of course, what none of them realized was that the only reason I had time to do all that laughing and clowning was because I did so much damn work before they even showed up. Not only studying once I got to school grounds, but reading in the car while my mama drove us. Then later in the evening, my dad would pick me up from school after his job, and I'd study even more on the long drive home in traffic.

Study, study, study, and party on the side. A few of my closest friends and I even formed our own posse we called FAY—as in "Fuck All Y'all." Except it wasn't a fuck-you to society, it was a fuck-you to all the hardcore bullshit of LA. My boys and I studied, we played sports, we made music. That was our "gang."

No matter what, though, I made sure to leave lots of time for my main love, *football*.

With my natural, slow-moving growth spurt, plus plenty of work-outs with Jabari and Janet, I grew my junior year to five feet eleven and 170 pounds. Still pretty damn skinny, but now strong as hell, with amazing conditioning after all our runs up Throw-Up Mountain.

My first year at St. Monica's and I was already a starter. Coach Jackson kept me at running back on offense and safety on defense, and I thrived. Helped our team to a dominant regular season and a run in the playoffs, all for a coach who had connections with major recruiters everywhere.

I was right on track for a breakout senior year and offers from the best college programs in the country. Couldn't have been more perfect if Jabari and I had planned it ourselves on a walk to Yee's.

Till all of a sudden, it wasn't.

MY SENIOR YEAR at St. Monica's, I went from being on one of the best teams in the city to being on the worst in the city. From going to the playoffs to losing every game.

Let me repeat that: I, who had never even had a *losing record* before, was on a team that lost *every single game*—all except one that we won retroactively because it turned out the other team had an ineligible player. No matter what the record books say, I don't even count a lame-ass win like that.

What the hell happened?

It's simple. I went from being on a team coached by Angelo Jackson to being on a team that wasn't.

That's right. Right before my senior year, out of the blue, Coach Jackson left St. Monica's and moved south to Inglewood High School. And almost all his hand-chosen players—we're talking about some of the best high school stars in the *country*—went right with him.

I say "almost" because there was one dude who stayed behind. Me.

"Daddy," I pleaded with my father, "you gotta let me go. St. Monica's only got *seventeen players*!"

"No," he said. "We did it before, but not again. You ain't switching schools."

In other words: finish what you started.

I had changed my entire life to play for Coach Jackson because everyone said it was the right thing to do.

Forget about Westchester, they all said. Forget about your old school and your old friends. Go with the flow! Focus on football! Head to where all the action's at, with Coach Jackson! That's your future, dog!

I had listened to what everyone said, and it came back to bite me.

I wasn't making that mistake again. I was going back to my original values of finding my *own* path. I was sticking with St. Monica's.

I played my senior year on a team that had only seventeen guys. Seventeen.

My junior year? We had fifty.

Think about that. In football, you got eleven players on the field for the offense, then another eleven for the defense, then of course you still got special teams. Now, most high schools might have *some* overlap between offense and defense, but we had almost *all our guys* playing the whole damn game, offense, defense, and special teams, without any rest at all.

A lot of our positions didn't even have backups if someone got injured, which—duh, it was football—of course they did.

I was still the star, sure. But what good is being the MVP of the Bad News Bears?

Besides which, even though I was growing, my body was really taking its time. My senior year I grew to six feet but stayed 170 pounds—my usual inch of height, but not my usual extra weight.

I was strong, but still skinny as hell compared with college play-ers, even incoming freshmen. College coaches could see that I had a hell of a frame, but I was still building my house, and I was a long-ass way from being a mansion.

So all that high-profile college recruiting I was counting on in my "breakout" senior year? All those shots at starring for an elite team that would catapult me to the NFL? Most of that was destroyed.

I'd talk to my boys who'd gone to Inglewood, and they'd start going on about all the letters they got, all the visits, all the calls from the huge premier programs of the day.

"Yo, Marcellus, should I do that Michigan trip?"

"Hey, man, I just got a call from Lou Holtz!"

"What you think of Florida State, dog?"

Me? I didn't get any interest from the major football factories. Instead, I had more questions, more doubt, more wondering when I'd get the chance to display my full physical potential. I had more nights sitting on the floor of the living room, thinking by myself.

What would I do? Had I made a mistake by following my gut, by listening to my dad and staying at St. Monica's? Had I been wrong to go against the grain and find my own way?

The answer, to me, was obvious: hell naw.

And if people were shocked by my decision to stay with St. Monica's, they were gonna shit themselves over what came next.

I'D NEVER EVEN *heard* of Columbia University till my senior year. One day, one of our new assistant coaches came to practice wearing light-blue shorts with white block letters on them.

"Columbia," I said. "What's that?"

He made this face like he'd taken a swig of some rotten milk.

"That's where I went to school," he said. "Ivy League. Don't even *think* about going there. It's the worst football school in the country."

I found out later that he was dead-on, at least when it came to football. Columbia and my best sport did *not* go well together. If they were known for anything, it was how bad they were. Only a year before my coach told me about them, they had finally, mercifully, ended what was known nationwide simply as "The Streak"—the longest losing streak in the history of NCAA Division I football.

Forty-four losses in a row, from 1983 to 1988, plus three ties just to rub some salt in their wounds. These dudes were almost as bad as my high school team!

But if my coach wanted to get me to do something, the *last* thing he should've done was tell me not to do it. I was officially in full-on, find-my-own-path mode. When I got my recruiting letter from Columbia, I didn't tear it up—I opened it even quicker.

Did I want to make it to the NFL someday? Absolutely. But if my experience with Coach Jackson taught me anything, it was that finely laid plans didn't mean shit.

I knew there was a good chance I'd never make it to the pros—those were simply the odds. And even if I did get paid to play football, I knew that sooner or later that would end, and I'd be stuck in the real world like everyone else.

The real world ain't gonna grade you on your 40, it's gonna grade you on your 4.0. I had too much responsibility on my shoulders to ignore that fact, which is why I spent all those secret non-socializing hours studying, reading, and getting good grades. So much so that I ended up graduating as one of the best students in my class. As far as I was concerned, if I didn't make it in life, my family was doomed. They were depending on me, and only me, to get us all out of South Central.

So before I cared about a college's ranking in the BCS, I cared about its ranking in *U.S. News & World Report.* And according to *U.S. News,* Columbia blew my other options out of the water.

I may not have been getting calls from Florida State, but to their credit, my high school coaches had been working their butts off to get me noticed by a bunch of other colleges. Both for my sake and because if my coaches wanted to recruit and build a strong team, they'd have to prove that young hot players would have a future at St. Monica's. Get me into a big program, and I'd be exhibit A that my coaches knew how to lobby for their players. I got letters from a bunch of schools, but I narrowed them down to four aside from Columbia.

First there was Colorado State University. They were offering a full ride, but they weren't high in the BCS *or* the academic rankings. Next.

Then there was St. Mary's College, outside San Francisco. Good academics, but way too small when it came to football. Next.

UCLA offered me too. Now they had the football and the academics, but I didn't want to go to high school again. I went on my campus visit, and I saw people I already knew, buildings I already knew. I wanted to go away from home, grow up *and* out, test my wingspan.

I also didn't want to sit on the bench. A program like the Bruins' is recruiting players as good as or better than you every single year. I was good, but I was also realistic. If I was going to put everything I had into football—basically a full-time job *plus* a full load of classes— I wanted to see the field. Next.

Finally, there was Cal. And that was a whole other story. Berkeley obviously had the academics, which was most important to me. Their football team played in the Pac-10, one of the biggest stages in the country for college ball, so I knew I'd have a chance to get noticed by pro scouts. But the Golden Bears weren't so elite that I'd always be looking over my shoulder, worried about my spot. Plus a few of my buddies were thinking of going there, so even though I'd be away from home, I'd still have a little bit of a support system with me.

Then the head coach who was recruiting me left and went to Arizona State. He kept recruiting me at ASU, but my hopes for attending Cal were gone.

I still hadn't made up my mind what to do when I went on my visit to Columbia, my first time in New York City.

As the plane landed, I wondered how different it was going to be from everything I had seen on TV and heard in my favorite music. The raw sound and break dancing in the movie *Beat Street*. The b-boys in the dance crew Rock Steady. The burning buildings in the Bronx. I had as many preconceptions about New York City and Columbia as anyone there could've had about me, maybe more—and I couldn't wait to challenge them.

I didn't have to wait long. A porter in the airport grabbed a few of my bags and, before I knew it, sped off through the crowded terminal faster than I—a major football recruit—could keep up. And what did he say to me, a potentially tipping customer?

"Fuck, hurry up!"

He didn't even turn around. It was like getting dropped on a treadmill with no stop button. And I loved it.

Outside it was snowing, some of the first snow I had ever experienced in my life. I was wearing nothing but a T-shirt and shorts. And I loved it.

We got to campus, and I ran down the icy paths, soaking up the cold, laughing. Eventually I changed into jeans and a jacket, but this was no Triple F.A.T. Goose winter coat—we're talking something barely thicker than a windbreaker. I passed by varsity athletes walking around like they were the shit, and I loved that too, because I knew if I came here, I'd be better than all of them. If I came here, I was gonna destroy this place.

But more than anything else, my big decision came down to a single sentence spoken by the Columbia head coach, Ray Tellier.

Coach had a lot of work to do to build Columbia into a winning—or even semi-decent—program again, and he knew it. (He also had help from a very talented staff—both Chip Kelly and Dan Mullen served as his assistants, though Kelly left right before I got there.) Coach Tellier had only been at Columbia for three years, and he was trying to recruit players with a national profile that the Lions had no right to compete for. Some of us were from the city, some of us were from the country, but we were all smart, and we could all ball. One of those players was me.

On my visit, he took us on a little field trip—to the Empire State Building. It was a small group, about eight of us. We went up to the top and felt like we were standing in the center of the universe. His point was clear. Columbia may not have offered the best football program in the country, but it offered something no other college could—the world, right at your fingertips.

"Men," he said, the Statue of Liberty in the distance, "if you go somewhere else you can carry the torch. Come here, and you can light the torch."

It was like sweet nothings to a contrarian's ear. Let everyone else go to the big schools, the USCs and the Alabamas. Let everyone else listen to the crowd like a pack of mindless football zombies. I was gonna do my own thing. I was gonna light that torch.

I was going to Columbia.

CHAPTER THREE

THE GAME WITHIN THE GAME AT COLUMBIA U

HEADED INTO THE campus eatery and grabbed a tray for my breakfast, just like any other freshman student at Columbia University. Except for one not-so-small thing—I was six foot one, black, and straight off the streets of Compton.

Other than that? No big deal.

It was the fall of 1992, and after a couple weeks at school I was starting to get used to most of it—the clean, walled-off campus, closed off from the rest of New York City. The perfect green lawns and the trimmed, pristine shrubs. The redbrick walkways and the massive ornate buildings with their pillars and domes. I was a long way from home, yeah, but my new surroundings didn't faze me. Hell, I had never *wanted* to live in the hood, so I liked being on the quad.

But what I still wasn't used to was the people. Specifically, the diversity.

In South Central LA, practically the only people I knew, the only people I grew up around, were black and Mexican. Even when I got to St. Monica's, most of my good friends were black and Mexican. It was the only thing I knew. I had my boys from other parts of the country tell me horror stories about running into racist white people who called them the N-word. But sometimes I think what I had was worse, because I wasn't exposed to any white people at all, racist or otherwise, until I was thirteen years old.

Not that that was an intrinsically bad thing. These were all my friends and family, the community I knew. But it also left me completely unprepared to deal with the rest of the world.

Now here I was at an Ivy League school, in the heart of the most international city in America, surrounded by every kind of person the world had to offer—Indians, Asians, Arabs, Sikhs, Muslims, and Jews. These were kids who had dreamed of coming here their whole lives. Whose fathers had gone here, whose grandfathers had gone here. Who expected to go here—and then expected to inherit their daddies' empires.

Unlike me, a kid on need-based grants and loans—no sports scholarships in the Ivies, remember—who had only heard about Columbia a year ago.

"Damn, these some hard, big-ass donuts," I said to a white girl standing behind me in line.

"Are you kidding?" she said. "That's a bagel."

"So why is it all hard like that?"

"Because," she said, before moving away very quickly. "It's a bagel."

Bagel? How the hell was I supposed to know? Until a few weeks ago I had never even met a Jewish person! I went with bacon and eggs, and searched for a spot to sit down.

But if the other students were foreign to me, I was just as foreign to them—maybe more.

I wasn't even on the varsity football team yet—Columbia actually had a freshman team that year, the last year they did—but I already had a reputation. On a campus that has only about six thousand undergrads, it's not hard to get a rep as a big-time athletic prospect, especially with a football team as historically shitty as Columbia's. Getting a major talent from Los Angeles was news.

Past that, I was big and black and from Compton, it was that simple.

The funny thing is, I wasn't even all that big yet. Going into my freshman year, I was just over six feet tall and 185 pounds, with skinny legs and baggy jeans, a big T-shirt and inverted shoulders. I looked like some dude from Ethiopia who needed a dollar a day from Sally Struthers to save my life. Hell, my own mama was bigger than me by sixty-five pounds. They should've signed her!

Back at home, I was called every name in the book—nerd, sissy, fag. Anything that meant "soft" back in the '80s, I was called it.

But here at Columbia? I was straight-up gangster. Sure, there were a handful of other black students, but most of them were upper-middle class. Straight out of Connecticut, not Compton. I was the closest thing to hood anyone there had seen—and they weren't shy about letting me know.

"Mind if I sit here?"

I looked up from my bacon and eggs. I was sitting at a pretty big table with more than a few empty seats, but my fellow student—an Asian kid, no older than twenty—gestured at the spot right across from me. He was smiling, part nervous, part friendly, very eager.

"Go ahead," I said, smiling back.

He sat down awkwardly. He also had eggs. No bagels.

"So," he said, "what's your name?"

Alright, I thought, *here it comes.*

It had only been a couple weeks, but I had already had a dozen of these conversations. Chances were he already knew my name, he already knew I was a football player, and he definitely already knew where I was from.

See, I had learned that there were three lanes of students at Columbia when it came to me. Lane One was the kind who didn't really care. They knew who I was, or at least knew that I was some kind of savior for the football program, but it didn't really mean shit. It's like how I knew about Duran Duran back in the '80s. Yeah, I knew who Duran Duran was, I knew they were big, but what the fuck did I care? These students had their life, they had their studies, they had no opinion.

Lane Two was the kind who had an opinion, and it wasn't a very good one. They'd look at me and think, Oh, here comes the inner-city reclamation project. A stereotypical poor black dude who gets in because of affirmative action or some shit. They didn't bother to find out that Columbia doesn't offer athletic scholarships, or that I was one of the top students at my high school, and frankly, I had no interest in telling them. If someone doesn't like me, that's their problem— I ain't even gonna waste my time. I only count people who are with me, not against me.

And then there was Lane Three. For Lane Three, I wasn't a threat, I was an opportunity. Don't forget, this was the early '90s, and LA was officially the shit. We're talking Snoop, we're talking Dre, we're talking *Menace II Society* and *Boyz n the Hood*. To Lane Three, that's what I was. A curiosity from another world. An exotic wild animal they had only seen before on TV, and now they finally had a chance to experience the real thing in their own personal zoo. There weren't even any cages or moats to separate us—only a cafeteria table, and the comforting knowledge that we were inside Columbia, and nothing bad could happen to anyone in here.

How did I feel about that? Well, Lane Three was exactly who was sitting across from me right now.

"Wow," he said. "So you're from Compton? *The* Compton? The one I see in all the movies?"

"Yep," I said, between bites of scrambled eggs. "That's the one."

"Wow," he said again, and I could tell he was working up his courage. "I hope you don't mind me asking but . . . is that really what it's like? I mean, you know, I don't know, like with the shootings and the drugs and everything?"

"Yeah," I said, trying to play it off. "I mean, it ain't like all that happens every single night, like they make out in *Boyz n the Hood*, but yeah."

His eyes grew wide.

"So you've been, like, shot at?"

"Oh yeah."

"Wow. Like, where?"

"All over. Got a bunch of shots fired at us when we was playing a football game."

"No way!"

"You could see the dust coming off the field from the shots and everything."

"No fucking way!"

It was true. A game I was playing in for Westchester High my freshman year really had been broken up when a bunch of shots suddenly hit our field. They came out of nowhere, never even caught the guys responsible. That shit was scary as hell.

But at the same time I had to laugh. Impressing these dudes at Columbia was so damn easy. Like walking into the army academy and they give me three stripes on my sleeve just for showing up. I hadn't done a damn thing besides having the incredible luck of being born in the hood. I had never wanted to be poor. I didn't want to get by on two welfare checks a month and government cheese. That's not cred—I needed credit.

But honestly? I had no problem with other students asking me questions, because I had so many questions of my own. I mean, shit, until a few minutes earlier I didn't even know what a damn bagel was!

In my life, I was used to playing a very specific game with a very specific set of rules. There were no mysteries about football. Get the ball into the end zone, and you scored. Get more points than the other team, and you win. Simple. Same goes for the rules of my hood. Study hard, keep your head down, listen to your mama, and try to get the hell out. Done.

But now that I was finally out, I realized that out here at my new university in the real world, there wasn't just a game, there was a game within the game.

I'd only been on campus a couple weeks, and I'd already met more people from more cultures, religions, and skin tones than I ever even knew existed. I'd explained to what felt like a hundred people that, yes, bullets really did fly through the air in South Central, just like in the movie *Boyz n the Hood*. I'd talked to individuals who were worth more money than I'd ever dreamed of—and those were my fellow students!

In this new world of Ivy League expectations, nothing was

what it seemed, and no one would simply tell you the rules—you were expected to already know them. Everyone around me already knew how to fit in. They had spent years preparing for Columbia, going to prep schools, taking special courses, and getting individual tutoring. They already knew what it meant to come from privilege, what it meant to have money, to succeed in a world that wasn't all black. They had never known anything different. This was their world.

But if you were like me, and you didn't know? It was up to you to find the answers and figure shit out.

Which is why as soon as my new best buddy stopped interrogating me, I flipped the script.

"So now that you know about me, what's up with you?" I said.

"Uh, what do you mean?" he replied.

"You said your dad works on Wall Street, right? Like, he's an investor, right? So he investing his money or someone else's? How much he make in a year? We talking more than athletes?"

He looked at me.

"Finance," he said. "You sure you want to know all that stuff?"

"Hell yeah! I want to know it all, big dog!"

I smiled and took a bite of bacon. This was going to be interesting.

MY FIRST MATH class at Columbia didn't even have any numbers in it.

Now I ask you, what the hell kind of math class is that?

My adviser, Jackie Blackett, had tried to warn me. Jackie was, and still is, an athletic director at the university. In charge of, among other things, helping student athletes like me with the student part of it all. But she was really more than that.

As far as I was concerned, she was my godmother, the one who watched over me and helped translate my new environment into a language I could understand. Who tried to teach me the unspoken rules to this brand-new game.

There was one problem. My skinny freshman ass was too dumb to listen.

"I want to be an aerospace engineer," I told her as we sat in her office, planning my schedule.

Jackie peered at me patiently—and a little skeptically—through her square-frame glasses. She had short hair and a big, caring smile. She had grown up in Brooklyn, but she was from Barbados originally. She was black like me, so there was a trust and ease there that I didn't have with the rest of the staff. She viewed the world through the same lens as me, and I could tell.

"Alright," she said. "Do you know what level of math that takes?"

"Yeah!" I said, nodding my head enthusiastically. "Science and math!"

"Right," she said. "We'll start you off with the math requirement."

"Cool!"

"I'll see you in two days."

I walked into that math class the next day. Now, I had taken AP Calculus my senior year in high school, so math—*advanced* math—wasn't foreign to me. But a few things jumped out immediately.

First, there was no one of my particular *hue*, out of about twenty students.

Fine, I thought, I'll be the first black aerospace engineer in the history of Columbia University.

Second, as soon as I sat down, everyone around me covered up their paper. I looked around and realized it wasn't a reaction to me—everyone in the whole class was covering up their paper with their elbows, making sure no one else could copy their notes. That's right—this wasn't a test or even a quiz. They were worried someone would copy *their notes*.

Third, one of the students—students!—was wearing a three-piece suit.

I soon realized that "Three-Piece-Suit Guy" would be a recurring character in *all* my classes at Columbia. And I'm not talking about the same person—that would actually be relatively normal—I'm talking about a type. A type of student who took shit so seriously they wore a damn suit to every class. Or maybe they were constantly going to job interviews, I don't know. But there was one of these guys in almost every class, even math.

The professor walked in, he welcomed us all to class, turned around, and started writing on the white board. No explanation, no instructions, no nothing. Just writing.

I looked around, and I realized everyone else was writing too.

So that's it? I thought. Do I just write, or what? He's gotta turn around, right?

So I wrote. I copied every damn word he put down. Copy, copy, copy. Write, write, write.

And just like that, class was over. It didn't feel like he turned around once. I looked down at my notebook and started flipping through the pages. I had filled up about half of it, and I swear, there were no numbers. No numbers in a math class. Not one nine, not one seventeen—just words and symbols, Greek letters and triangular matrices. This shit didn't look like math, it looked like an eye-chart test!

I went back to Jackie and got the hell out of that class. It took two days, exactly like she said.

That was my official "Welcome to Columbia Academics" moment. But it was only the beginning.

Every one of my classes was like an experience in intellectual warfare. And I'm not talking about my professors coming after me—I'm talking about other students going after the professors.

Where I came from, if you raised your hand, it was to ask the teacher a question. But at Columbia, students raised their hands to make statements. To challenge the teacher and show how well prepared they were.

The professors might have a book to support whatever they were saying, but if they deviated from that book even by a millimeter? Well then, someone was going to start an argument, and Three-Piece-Suit Guy would usually be the one leading the charge. The students knew they were paying the teachers' salaries, and as far as they were concerned, they were going to get their money's worth, and the professor had to take it.

The classrooms were more competitive and combative than anything I had ever seen on the field, and I had no idea what to make of it. In football, if you start going after the coach too much, he won't stand there and listen politely, he'll look at you and say, "You wanna play next week?"

Sure, I got good grades in high school, so I was no idiot. But the kind of intelligence I had always valued was *practical* intelligence. I wanted to know how something applied to *me*, how I could use it now and in the future. Heated debates about theory and history and fiction felt like a waste of time. They were like intellectual sightseers, and I just wanted to get the hell out of the jungle.

I took the whole core curriculum, logic and rhetoric, contemporary civilization, art humanities the first semester, and music humanities the second, which I thought might be better until I realized rap wasn't exactly considered a "humanity." We would be assigned a nine-hundred-page book to read in two days, and these kids would walk into class acting like they had memorized every damn page and ace the test. I had no idea how they did it.

Everyone else had a computer. Me? I applied for every credit card I could get my hands on my first day at campus and treated myself to a new stereo—and a brand-new word processor. That's right, a state-of-the-art electric typewriter, one of Brother's finest.

Where I'm from, no one had a word processor. So I'm thinking, *I'm gonna kill these papers! A's are coming my way!*

Uh, no. No, they're not.

My essays were coming back bleeding red ink. I'd get an A for content, for the substance, but they'd tear me apart for the grammar and structure. This while Three-Piece-Suit Guy was churning shit out on his autocorrect computer, applying everything he'd learned in his college-prep writing courses, and getting an A in all categories every single time.

I started to get disillusioned. I had no natural interest in academics simply for the sake of academics, but I knew I had no choice. These same obnoxious, overdressed overachievers in class were gonna go on to lead Fortune 500 companies.

The advantages they had weren't just about the next test, the next report, the next grade. They were about life.

I was back to playing the game within the game. And I needed to figure out these rules—fast.

BUT FOOTBALL? THAT was a game I definitely knew how to play, and—not to be braggadocious or anything—I was very good at it.

Now I know what you're thinking. I was playing for the worst team in the Ivy League. You hear "Ivy League," and you immediately think *wack*. Like because we're a little smarter and we're not on athletic scholarships, we must suck. And look, I get it. I played in the pros, and it's not like the Buffalo Bills were filled with dudes from Dartmouth and Cornell (though their fans might feel otherwise sometimes).

But the Ivies don't suffer because of their quality; it's a matter of quantity.

A great player in the Ivy Leagues is as good as a great player in the Big Ten or Pac-12. But on an Ivy team, you might have two of those great players, maybe four. You never see eleven *great* players on the field all at the same time the way you do in the major conferences.

The Ivies have had their share of good players in the NFL—guys like Chad Levitt and Seth Payne, both out of Cornell, or maybe the best of them all, Matt Birk, who graduated from Harvard and will get elected to the Hall of Fame someday. They might not have been drafted high, sure, but they went on to have standout careers in the League.

Was it still a little, shall we say, *different* playing football at Columbia? Of course it was.

I had a teammate whose family had a lot of Texas oil money. I heard the dude had a monthly stipend of $25,000. That's right—$25,000 *a month*. That was more money than my family would see in a year! The guy got dropped off near campus once in his own private *helicopter*.

But as far as I was concerned, it was just more motivation. I might not have that Texas oil money, but I was gonna get rich my own way—by making it to the NFL. Not that school wasn't critical of course, but to me, that was always my safety net. My high-wire act would be, I hoped, playing in the NFL.

At this point in my life I hadn't even thought of playing defensive end yet—don't forget, I was only 185 pounds when I got to campus. In high school I played both safety and running back, and out of all the colleges that recruited me, Columbia was the only one that was gonna let me keep playing offense, another reason I went with the Lions.

So on the freshman team, I played running back and kick returner. I may have been a tiny bit nervous at first—there's something about the transition from the gym to the field in that very first practice that always gets me—and I of course wanted to prove myself, live up to the hype. But honestly, I'd always been the guy who went into a new situation and knew he was going to start. And that's exactly what happened at Columbia.

I was also joined by my own little crew of other scrappy new recruits with outsize aspirations. That's right—I wasn't the only one who had to take the subway to get around town instead of a helicopter.

We had an athletic little wide receiver named Jim-Jim Jones who came from a high school in DC that didn't have one white dude in the whole place. I saw his yearbook, and every single person from front to back—all the students, teachers, administrators—was black. Another guy from New Orleans named Ralph Hudson, who owned a ferret, was smart as shit, and was so country I couldn't understand a damn word he said. And Johnny Harper from Cleveland was big as hell and funny as shit.

Last of all, there was Matty Lenzen, our quarterback and one of my best boys. Matty L was white, from a heavily Latino part of Los Angeles, and we bonded immediately over music. Tribe Called Quest, Cypress Hill, De La Soul, all the rappers who weren't only performers but were exceptional musicians too. As deep as I was in my rap game, I gotta admit—Matty L knew even more obscure, underground rappers, a bunch of shit I'd never even heard of. (Though I like to pretend I discovered Lauryn Hill, who was just a fellow student at Columbia when we used to rap battle over the phone. Guess that wasn't good enough for her—she left college and her career blew up.)

All us young players came together, a band of brothers, starting out on our own small freshman-year team, and going 4-2 in a shortened season. That might not sound like much to you, but at a program as historically shitty as Columbia's, it was something to be proud of—a sign that better times for the varsity program were on their way.

And me? I won the award for freshman team MVP. I *knew* better times were on their way for my skinny-ass too.

IN COLLEGE THE most important currency is social. And thanks to my increasing football stardom, socially I was a young Bill Gates, except tall, black, and good-looking.

Of course I still had the same novelty I started out with—me, the relative nerd, was suddenly a bona fide representative of LA gangsta culture. I'd always have that at Columbia, no matter how many years I was there, no matter how many games I played and yards I racked up.

But now I didn't just have football potential. I was a football reality, a known quantity, a legitimate celebrity on a campus that barely spanned ten blocks.

Everyone knew me, and if they didn't know me, they got introduced to me. As soon as I went anywhere new, someone would shout, "Marcellus!" and run up and give me a hug. If I showed up at a frat party and spotted a girl I wanted to talk to, I didn't have to say, "Excuse me, lady, what's your name?"

I'd start walking up to her, and out of nowhere some guy would throw his arms around both of us and shout, "Do you know who this is?"

Before I could say a word, this guy, my own personal Wikipedia page, would spit out every possible fact about me, all of them portraying me in the most flattering light.

Did it get old? Maybe for some people it would've, but not for me. My ego loved that I was never anonymous—and I loved spreading the wealth to my friends even more.

I was about to head to the first Black Student Organization party of the year. I was looking for pretty black girls, so what better place to check out, I figured, than their official organization? But I wasn't going to do it alone. I went and found my best white buddy, Matty L.

"Matty, we going to the BSO party," I said.

He didn't even flinch.

"Let's do it."

When we arrived, everyone came up to me like we were best friends, hugging me, the whole deal, like usual. Then they saw Matty. I wouldn't say there were racial tensions, exactly, but there was this kind of vibe of "Come on, man—can't we have *one* party just for *us*?"

For once, I got to be someone else's personal Wikipedia page— Matty's.

I introduced him, talked him up, and that boy turned that party out. I warned them not to let his "paint job" fool them, because this mother knew more about some of the underground rappers we were listening to than we did. The whole party he was all in, doing the same dance he still does to this very day—spinning in a circle with his drink over his head. He wasn't trying to be black or down. He just liked what he liked. All I could do was watch, just crying laughing.

That was the power of being a football star at such a small school—it got you and your friends access to anything, anywhere. It was one of the few new, unspoken rules I learned easy.

By the time we called it a night, my white friend Matty L had more numbers than I did. For me, that was the definition of success.

I STARTED LEARNING SOME of the other, harder rules behind the game within the game too.

After week one of my sophomore year, I got called into the dean's office. Now why, you might ask, would that happen. Bad grades? Skipping class? Cheating on tests?

Nope.

It was noise complaints. Exactly 107 noise complaints. Which I had received in a single week.

"Are you serious?" I said to the dean. "Are there even a hundred and seven people in the whole dorm?"

I was angry as hell. Not because of the music—hey, if they didn't like Snoop and Dr. Dre, that was their prerogative, I wasn't gonna take it personally. But because, except for one little dude from India at the beginning of the week, no one had the guts to come knock on my door, look me in the eye, and simply ask me if I could turn my music down.

When it came to football, these were the people who praised me—who seemed to *worship* me—to my face, but if they had a problem with something as stupid as my music, they couldn't come and talk to me about it?

To me, the problem wasn't that my music was loud. Hell, I heard some of *them* playing loud music at night too—it just wasn't rap. The problem was I was big and black.

One of the first things I did after leaving the dean's office was take a trip to see my godmother and explainer-in-chief, Jackie Blackett.

"I hear you, 'Cell," she said, in that calming tone that only she could master. "But let me ask you: Have you been playing your music loud?"

"Well, sure," I admitted grudgingly. "I guess."

"And how late are you usually playing it loud?"

I shrugged sheepishly.

"I mean, you know, maybe two in the morning? Maybe?"

What could I say? It was Snoop and Dre! The same stereo I had bought the year before with my brand-new credit cards, paying it off ever since!

"But that's not the point!" I protested. "They don't even have the nerve to say nothing to me. They gotta go behind my back!"

"I know," she said. "And maybe they need to do a better job learning about you and who you really are. But you have some learning to do too. You need to learn that environments are unique, nuanced. Not everybody is like you. You're used to coming in and being 'the guy.' That can be intimidating for other people, even if you're not trying to intimidate them. You have to learn to meet them halfway."

I listened to what she said. And from that day on, I went from Snoop and Dre to Whitney Houston in *The Bodyguard* soundtrack— I was addicted to that shit. Was I perfect? Nope. I kept playing my music loud late at night. But once I cut the rap, the complaints stopped. It wasn't a volume issue at all—it was a cultural issue.

But it was a start.

I applied some of the same tricks to my academics too. Not changing who I was, necessarily, but adapting, learning, meeting the system halfway.

Was I ever gonna be some pseudo-intellectual who got off on wearing suits to class and arguing abstractions with his professor? No, and I had no desire to be that.

But I chose a major, sociology, that had some very practical applications. I got to study human nature, all the patterns of our behavior, how our commonalities were so much greater than our differences. I learned that even if we didn't realize it, all the decisions we make are socially influenced, whether it's what we buy, what we eat, or what clothes we wear. Every choice we make is impacted by our environment, by the people and items around us. Now *that* was interesting.

And as for my other classes, the more time I spent among the scholarly wolves, the more I learned how not to be a sheep.

All those guys who acted like they memorized the nine-hundred-page book in two days? They hadn't read a page. It was CliffsNotes, plain and simple. So I bought myself a bunch of little yellow books and started to at least sit a little closer to Three-Piece-Suit Guy in class.

On my papers, I didn't have the technical advantage my wealthier classmates had with their autocorrect computers and college-prep writing courses, so I worked harder. I learned from all that red ink on my pages, figured out more sophisticated sentence structures, and started getting better grades.

I learned all the different methods, how to interpret information quickly and concisely with a high level of intelligence. In short, I wanted to balance my studies with my athletics, get my degree, and get out. I was here to get ready for life, not to philosophize.

I even figured out how to connect with my hallmates. I decided the people in the dorm needed to get to know the real me—not just the football star, not just the Boy from the Hood. But me, Marcellus Wiley.

The answer wasn't Whitney Houston—it was typing.

That's right, my technologically obsolete word processor ended up being cutting-edge when it came to connecting with people, and making a little cash on the side.

Back in the eighth grade, I wasn't just a killer when it came to peewee football, I was also one of the fastest typists in the nation. No joke. I literally won the national typing championship for my age, maxing out at eighty-two words a minute with only a single error on the test. I *told you* I was a nerd!

Well, I'd never lost my gift. Everywhere I went, I would look at street signs, magazine covers, T-shirts, you name it, and secretly type out every sentence, word, or letter I saw, silently moving my fingers over an imaginary keyboard. Still do it to this day.

At Columbia, my skill finally found its purpose.

You live down the hall and got some notes or longhand you need typed up for class today? Hand it to me, come back in ten minutes, and this shit will be done.

I'd sit down at my desk, flip over my keyboard cover, have my cord all plugged in, and—

Badabadabadabadabadabadabow!

Done! That'll be five dollars, please.

People would come to me panicked, on a deadline, and I'd just laugh. No one else knew my history—I didn't tell a soul—but I knew that I could churn out whatever they gave me in a matter of minutes.

Badabadabadabadabadabadabadabow!

Done! Hmm. This time let's make that ten dollars, please.

Word got around the dorm. One person worked up the nerve to ask me, then another did, then another and another. Before I knew it, I had my own cottage industry of paper-typing going on, making as much as fifteen dollars a pop. And when you can barely afford a new pair of track shoes, every little bit counts.

But as nice as the money was, as much as I legitimately loved to type, those aren't the main reasons I did it.

I did it because I wanted to soften the edge of the stereotypes they had about me. If we were gonna live next to each other, I wanted us to get along. I wanted to bond with people in a real way, beyond being perceived as the black guy from South Central who's really good at sports.

My short Indian dude hallmate may never have spoken to me again after the music complaint, but, oh, what do you know? He needs to clean up this paper, and I can type real fast and even show him where the home key is on a typewriter.

Holy shit, he thinks, Marcellus is a nerd, just like us—he just likes playing rap music loud!

In that single five-dollar exchange, you're gonna start to get to know me, and I'm gonna start to get to know you. Not as an object or a cliché, but as a person. We're gonna meet each other halfway, on common ground, just like Jackie said.

I wasn't just learning how to play the game within the game anymore. I was making up my *own rules*, and convincing everyone else to play along.

THEN, RIGHT AS I was finally mastering that game, the other game—the one that had always seemed so simple, so easy and straightforward—suddenly got a lot more complicated.

Football.

My sophomore year I played well, sure. Given the overall level of competition in the Ivies, it would've been weird if I hadn't. But I was playing *Columbia-level* good. I wasn't playing *NFL-level* good. I wasn't great.

Now, I was still just a sophomore, so I had two years to go, but I was already feeling the pressure. Did I embrace the challenge of getting noticed by NFL scouts at a school that was known for anything *but* football? Of course. But I wasn't stupid. I knew that trying to go pro out of the Ivy League was like trying to beat the odds in Powerball.

Des Werthman, a Columbia guy who played both sides of the ball, was one of the most dominant, multidimensional players I've seen at any level. He wasn't tall and he wasn't superfast, but this dude could do it all, putting up crazy numbers in rushing and tackling. Des graduated in 1993, right after my freshman year, and what did he do? Never drafted, never made it past tryouts in the League.

I don't care what your numbers look like—making it to the NFL from the Ivies is not easy. And my sophomore year, we went 2-8. That wasn't even all that great by Columbia standards.

My junior year needed to be more than a breakout, it needed to be flawless. I had to build that NFL résumé, and fast.

But instead of going for a thousand yards as a running back, my coach gave me a nice little surprise—he didn't want me to be our featured back at all anymore.

Heading into my junior year, we got a new recruit, Jeff Byrd, out of Rancho Alamitos in Orange County, California, a few miles from where I grew up but a whole different world. I nicknamed him "Butter" for his golden, Coppertone cocoa butter skin.

Butter showed up on campus with a letterman's jacket full of patches, and they weren't bullshit. This guy had won the California rushing title his senior year, broke the all-time record for yards in a season in Orange County. Now California is a big-ass state, and Orange County plays a lot of football. Those were some impressive patches.

My first thought was simple: *Aw, shit, you better start working out.*

Next thing I knew, Coach was coming up to me in spring training for "the talk."

"You know, Marcellus," he said, "you're one of my best players. I need you on the field."

Damn, I thought. *What does this mean?*

"Jeff's looking pretty good at running back," he said.

"Yes, he is," I agreed.

"You ever thought about playing D-end?"

D-end?? That was *real* football, going in and hitting dudes every play, every day. I was usually trying to run *away* from guys.

But when a coach asks you a question like that, it's not really a question. He already knows the answer. I had turned down UCLA to avoid exactly this kind of problem, and here it was biting me in the ass anyway—at Columbia!

I had to admit, though, it kind of made sense. See, I wasn't a skinny little freshman anymore. By the start of my junior year, I was six foot three and 240 pounds. I was almost as big as my own mama, and I was getting bigger every day. I had outgrown being a running back, but as a defensive end? I'd be big, but more important, fast as hell compared with everyone else.

So I accepted the change—and I struggled. I was physically gifted, yes. Strong as shit, I could run, and my will was unbreakable. But I was brand-new to the position. My technique wasn't great, and I was getting double- and triple-teamed on every play. I was good at stopping the run—all I had to do was get off my blocker and attack the runner coming at me. But pass rush was harder. It requires moves, specialized technique to torque around offensive linemen.

Our team ended the year at 5-4-1. Better, but still not good.

The irony is that our star running-back-in-waiting, Jeff "Butter"

Byrd, ended up transferring *that season* to try his luck at Stanford. So after all that hype about him taking my place, I still wound up playing running back part-time—*and* D-end full-time. Playing both sides of the ball might be common in high school, but it ain't in college. Only one other player had done it at Columbia in recent memory. That distinction had its advantages—*Sports Illustrated* named me Player of the Week that season, getting me some of my first national press. But playing that much was hard on my body, especially as I was trying to adjust to a completely new position with a completely new skill set. I was still far from operating at an NFL level.

To add to my worries, suddenly academics became a problem again. The school put me on academic probation. Not because of my grades—I'd figured out my system, and it was working. No, this problem was actually harder to solve. I wasn't on track to graduate in time.

See, I was taking about thirteen credits a term, a full load but about two credits less than average. That was perfectly normal for a college player at a major program—like I said, playing football was a full-time job. At most D-I schools, a football player is allowed five years to graduate, sitting out one of those years for his redshirt season and playing the other four.

But here's the catch: at *other* universities, players had athletic scholarships that would cover their tuition as long as they were in school.

There were no athletic scholarships at Columbia. I had enough grants and loans to cover most of my tuition—but not all—for four years only.

If I needed five, I was shit out of luck. Tuition alone would cost me $40,000, and that's not even including living expenses.

A lot of guys who played football at Columbia actually quit the team to focus on their studies and graduate on time. Happened constantly. Now I damn well couldn't do that—I still dreamed of making it to the NFL. But paying for a fifth year? That wasn't an option either. As you'll recall, I was dirt poor.

So there I was, facing another season playing a position I barely knew and a bill of $40,000 if I wanted to graduate, and lo and behold, who comes knocking but a suitor I hadn't heard from in years. My first love. The one who got away.

Cal Berkeley.

That's right, the school I would've gone to if it wasn't for a coaching change was calling again, and they were interested in what I had to offer as a D-end.

I had friends who played and studied at Cal, guys I had known back in LA, all trying to convince me to transfer, telling me I was better than anyone they had on the team. With all my boys on campus with me in California, I wouldn't need to spend all this time explaining my world to strangers, trying to figure out secret rules to the game within the game. I could just be myself. I could just live.

And the education? The thing that had been most important to me from the beginning? Berkeley was close to Columbia, and forget about paying forty grand. I wouldn't have to spend a dime.

The choice was clear. I knew what I had to do.

I had to see my godmother, Jackie Blackett. If I had learned one thing by my third year in college, it was that when I didn't have the answers—and most of the time I didn't—Jackie did.

I went to her office and told her everything. The ins and outs, the pluses and minuses, the conditions and caveats. After I finally finished talking, she looked at me and said one thing:

"'Cell, you don't run away from your problems. You attack them head-on."

It took me back years and years, to when I was on the verge of quitting peewee football before the season even got going. My dad had looked at me calmly and spoken almost the exact same words. *You start something, you finish it.*

It was all I needed to hear.

I told you she was my godmother. The universe sent her to me.

I chose to finish my education at Columbia. But I also chose to do it on my own terms, writing brand-new rules to my very own game within the game.

After I finished the first semester of my junior year, I went back to Los Angeles and spent a full year at home, taking extension courses through UCLA, catching up on my credits at a hundredth of the cost of Columbia. It was like my own personal redshirt.

When I wasn't studying, I was eating and working out, following a training regimen given to me by my Columbia strength coach, Mark McAllister. If I was going to have a shot at the NFL, even a *chance* to make it pro, I would have to come back to Columbia for my last year of eligibility and play the best football of my life.

And I was gonna have to be yoked to do it. I needed to become a prototypical D-end, completely embrace my new position. That meant a frame of about six foot four and 280 pounds—which pro gurus considered big enough to stop the run but not too big and slow to rush the quarterback. And *that* meant I needed to add two inches and forty pounds. I called up Jabari—my boy was a genius studying math at Cornell, an Ivy League guy like me, and he was still my ace. That summer, the two of us got to work, like back in our high school days, hitting ten reps, then adding one more for good ol' Janet J.

I wasn't thrilled to leave my dreams of being a running back behind. I had grown up playing that position, it was like second nature to me. But I knew what the NFL was looking for—and it wasn't a 240-pound running back who could run a 4.8. Playing

D-end was my last best chance to make it to the League. So that redshirt year, I committed myself to developing the body—and the mind-set—to do it right.

It worked. By the time I went back to Columbia a year later for my last season of college ball, I was six four and 260 pounds of chiseled granite—and still getting bigger. I was laser-focused on dominating as a D-end. And best of all, I was right on track to graduate on time.

I was ready to finish what I started. And just as I'd hoped, it was the year that would change my life forever.

CHAPTER FOUR

BWAAA! ALL THE WAY TO THE NFL

WHEN I GOT back to Columbia's campus in January, in a weird way it was like nothing had really changed.

Same buildings, same teachers, even most of my same teammates. My coaches were happy to have me back to train with them, of course, but they had been planning my workouts over the past year, so none of them were too surprised by my transformation. I saw some old acquaintances who never knew why I left in the first place, and a few who'd never even realized I was gone.

"Oh yeah!" they said. "I guess I haven't seen you in a while, have I? So, like, where have you been?"

Then they'd pause, their eyes opening wide.

"And how did you get so big?"

I'd just laugh. Columbia may have been the same, but I felt

completely different—and not only physically. It was cool being back at school, fun reclaiming my old social status, but most of the novelty had worn off. I just wanted to get my work in, academically and athletically. Studying and training. I was pinpoint focused on two goals: graduating and making it to the NFL.

By the time finals rolled around, my boy Matty L—same guy I took to that hilarious Black Student Organization party—would go with me to the library almost every day. He was about to graduate, after all, even though I'd still be coming back for one more year. We'd unload all our books and spread out a bunch of food on the table, eat our fill, then dive into studying, reading up on astronomy or fulfilling the science requirement for my sociology degree.

I'd work as fast as I could, flipping through one page after another at hyperspeed, sitting on the edge of my seat and thinking about the prize that awaited—as soon as we finished, as soon as I'd read that last paragraph or Matty would finish his last problem, we'd sprint to the computers to check the internet for my name and next year's draft.

"Try out 'Marcellus Wiley NFL draft projection,'" I'd say as he typed. "See what they got!"

Of course, this was back in the '90s, so the computers felt like Commodore 64s, and we weren't even using Google, but Yahoo still got the job done alright.

"Uh," Matty said, hitting the Return button. "I think they pretty much got nothing."

Okay, so Yahoo wasn't *that* effective. When we first started searching ESPN, seeing what draft gurus like Mel Kiper had to say, it was clear they'd never even heard my name. I wasn't even an afterthought on their lists.

At the end of spring camp, an NFL regional scout finally came to campus to work us out, and I thought I finally had my chance, even convinced my girlfriend to spot me some money for new track shoes so I could fly on that turf. The scout showed up looking all official with his clipboard and glasses perched on the tip of his nose. He timed us, weighed us, measured us, poked and prodded us. I thought I did pretty well too—until I went back to that library.

Clack, clack, clack away on Yahoo.

Nothing. No Marcellus Wiley.

What the hell was I gonna do? Finishing out at Columbia sounded all well and good, but I still needed to find a way to *break out*. To make a noise so loud that the big-time scouts couldn't afford to ignore me, even if my shout was coming from the heart of the Ivy League.

And then I found my shot—in New Hampshire.

For our preseason scrimmage, we traveled up to Dartmouth to play against the Big Green. And I had to go up against hands down the best offensive lineman in the Ivies. Brian Larsen was a big, tall motherfucker at six foot six and 290 pounds. He had NFL size, and the technique to back it up. Unlike me, the dude had already been noticed by the pros, and draft boards definitely knew *his* name— pretty much unheard of for an Ivy League player in those days.

Guy was smart too. He came from a long line of doctors, wasn't even sure if he wanted to go pro at all, thought he might want to be a neurosurgeon. In fact, a few months later, that's exactly what he decided, picked up a scalpel and hung up his cleats for good.

Me? Right now, I knew what I wanted. I wanted to beat Brian Larsen's giant, neurosurgery-studying ass.

There was one problem. As big and as fast as I was, I had only been playing defensive line for a year. One year. To put it in technical terms, I didn't know what the *fuck* I was doing. And here I was about to go against one of the best O linemen in the country.

Not just in a game either. Because this was a preseason scrimmage, we did drills too.

They put me up against Larsen. One-on-one.

I'm not a naturally nervous guy, but there's something about one-on-ones that always puts me on edge. They're nothing like real games. During a game, you're working with a whole group of guys, depending on each other, pushing for each other, carrying out very complex, precise plays. During a one-on-one, it's pure technique. No one to collaborate with, no one to count on. Nothing but a simulation.

Then there are the crowds. During a game, people have a lot of shit to focus on—dozens of players on the field, the music blaring from the speakers, the popcorn in their hands. During a one-on-one, all the focus is on you. During a one-on-one, it's you and your opponent, man against man.

The entire world goes still, watching, waiting.

I lined up directly across from Larsen, put my hand in the grass. Positioned between us, someone held the ball to simulate a snap. As soon as that ball moved, it would be go time.

As the defensive player, my goal was simple: get past the other dude and hit a tackling dummy that stood in for the quarterback. But when the other dude is six foot six and 290 pounds, that goal gets a lot more complicated, and I'd only have two chances to get by him. That's it, two.

I studied Larsen's stance, and my brain went crazy with all the different ways he could block me. I don't know, it looks like he could stab me . . . But what if I'm wrong? He could easily do a kick-out instead . . . Or maybe he'll . . . Ahhhhhhhh!

Fuck it, I thought. *I'm gonna run around the motherfucker.*

Snap! Suddenly the ball twitched.

Larsen moved, but I moved faster.

Vrooom!

He may have touched me—barely—but all I heard was the sound of wind in my ears as I plowed through that lawn, whooshed right by him, and touched the bag. My teammates exploded, cheering me on.

Alright then, I thought. *Alright. One more.*

We lined up again. His boys were shouting, trying to get him pumped up.

"Come on, man! You got this!"

"Let's go! Get up!"

But this time I'm ready. I know he'll expect me to attack from the outside this time, so I decide to go inside instead, but I gotta sell my move if I want it to work—fake outside first, *then* go inside.

Snap! The ball twitched.

I take off. I fake outside, then go inside—*fuck, I don't know if he bit on my fake!*—I hesitate, then surge inside after all.

Bam!

He hits me, but just half of me. I stretch out my hand and the bag is mine.

Hell yeah!

The rest of the scrimmage went by in a blur. I got past Larsen, a top NFL prospect, not once but twice. Two for two. Nothing could beat that. Nothing.

As my team walked off that field and back to our bus, an older black guy, maybe in his fifties, approached me. I had never seen him before. So many people in the stands, hard to pick anyone out, you know?

"Hey, Marcellus," he said, sticking out his hand for me to shake. "I just wanted to introduce myself. Name's Bird."

"Bird?" I said. "That's your *name?*"

"Yeah, Bird," he said, like it was the most normal thing in the world. "I'm a scout for the Arizona Cardinals. We here checking out another prospect"—he didn't have to tell me who—"and I love what I saw from you today."

"Really?" I said, brightening. "Thank you!"

"Uh-huh," he said. "And let me tell you something. I got a big mouth. And I'm gonna tell *everyone* about you."

To this day, I haven't seen Bird once since he told me about his big mouth. Don't even know what his real name is. Hell, for all I know, his mother actually named him "Bird." But whoever he is, wherever he's at, much love to that man.

Because after that scrimmage, our little gym at Columbia became a must-see destination for NFL scouts. Our games became a hot spot for coach after coach and general manager after general manager. All of them coming to check me out.

And one day, soon after that, I sat down at those old-school library computers once I finished studying. Matty had graduated by this point, but I kept the faith, searching with whoever I happened to be studying with or just checking myself. I went to Yahoo and typed in my name. I waited five minutes or however damn long it took the internet to work back then, and there it was:

Marcellus Wiley, Columbia, Senior—Potential Sleeper

"Holy shit, man!" I said. "HOLY SHIT!"

I was listed as someone to watch, an outsider looking in, not even projected to go for certain in any of the seven rounds. But it was exactly the start I needed.

The NFL finally knew my name—and I'd make sure they'd never forget it.

"WHAT YOU GOT to do?" I said.

"Bwaaa!" my teammates all yelled back at me.

"I can't hear you!" I shouted. "WHAT YOU GOTTA DO?"

"BWAAAAAA!"

My boys on the team were *hyped*, ready to draw blood, practically foaming at the mouth and howling at the moon.

Unfortunately, we were right in the middle of astronomy class, leaving our professor highly irritated and the other students absolutely baffled. But hey, sacrifices must be made for team unity, right?

Going into my last year of college ball, I still had a losing record at Columbia. Now, this being Columbia, nobody really cared *that* much, but I didn't want to go out like that. As co-captain of the team, I wanted to make my mark, create a real legacy. And if I really wanted to impress all those NFL scouts who started coming to our games, I couldn't just perform in drills or the weight room—I needed to win. I needed all of us, the entire team, to *win*.

That was no easy task at a place like Columbia. Don't get me wrong—our coaching staff was top-notch, and we had some dudes who could ball, more than in an average year. But even though football is a game of skill, it's a greater game of *will*. And the hardest thing to do at a place like Columbia, a place that has a literal *tradition* of losing, is inspire that will.

Somehow, someway, I needed to take that same attitude, that same energy I was bringing to my NFL dreams, and translate that to all my boys. And not only the great players either, not only the star recruits like me.

See, on any decent Ivy League team, you're gonna find a natural division. There's gonna be guys like me, brought in *expressly* to play football, sports scholarship or no. Players like my boy Rory Wilfork, our hyper-talented linebacker and co-captain who I helped recruit out of Miami.

Then you'll have everyone else, usually the majority of the team, who are just, well, pretty normal dudes. Smart guys who happen to be a little more athletic than most, a little better at football, so they're playing football at Columbia. Basically, jock-nerds.

(And in case you were wondering, a lot of the marginal guys were black dudes, and tons of studs were white. This was about football, not color.)

Each of those parts is critically important in its own special way. The studs bring the flair, the special sauce—the muscle. The jock-nerds provide the backbone, the foundation. And if you want your team to win, if you want to be truly successful, you need to bring both those sides together with one unified, electrified mind-set.

You need *BWA.*

That's "Ball with Attitude," pronounced "bwa," rhymes with "spa." I swiped it from my favorite group, NWA, then made it slightly more palatable for an urbane, Ivy League audience.

Once I got a couple cats on the team saying it, it spread and grabbed hold of all of us, black and white, studs and jock-nerds, till it became our team's battle cry wherever we went.

In the middle of a frat party.

"What you got to do?"

"Bwaaa!"

During study hall.

"What you gotta do?"

"Bwaaa!"

Or walking through campus.

"Bwa!"

"Bwaaaa!"

"BWAAAA!"

It was a secret language that only we understood—and that left everyone else absolutely mystified. We weren't just a team, we were a club, a special fraternity that only football players could join. I even came up for a name for our secret society.

The Bulgarian Brothers.

"Bulgarian" because when I watched the '96 Atlanta Summer Olympics, I saw some huge, swole-ass Bulgarians competing in weight lifting. Well, me and my teammates were swole-ass motherfuckers too, so obviously we must've all been from Bulgaria.

"Brothers" because Hulk Hogan always called *everyone* "brother" on TV, and I loved to do my Hulk Hogan impression, get my voice all deep and gravelly like his.

Hence (in my best gravelly Hulkster voice), the Bulgarian Brothers.

What? That don't make no sense? Fine then, damned if I care.

Bwaaaa!

See, it was exactly that attitude, that us-against-the-world, fuck-all-y'all mentality that brought us together that year, that made us a team, that helped us truly believe that even though we were Columbia—hell, *because* we were Columbia—we were gonna win.

Then we played our first game of my senior year. Suddenly I wasn't sure if that attitude meant a thing.

We were at home against Harvard. We'd played 'em tight all game, sure, and the score was tied at 13 with seconds to go on the clock. But Harvard had the ball, and they lined up to kick what looked like an easy field goal. Three points. That's all it would take for us to lose the game and start the season the way Columbia always started the season—as losers.

Me and my Bulgarian Brothers lined up on defense to block the field goal. Ready, waiting, our hearts pumping as much damn BWA as our bodies could handle.

The ref blew the whistle. Harvard snapped the ball. Their kicker's foot connected with leather, seconds from putting away the game—and I jumped, stretching my arm out as far as it could go, my fingers barely reaching the ball.

Blocked!

In overtime, David "Rah-Rah" Ramirez caught us a touchdown, and we—Columbia, *the* Columbia, *that* Columbia—won our first game of the season 20–13. The Bulgarian Brothers exploded in celebration on the sidelines, absolutely bewildering the home crowd by screaming "Bwaaa" over and over again at the top of our lungs.

That win was like a flame meeting the gas of everything we had built up, everything we had worked for, everything we believed.

We never looked back.

We went 8-2 on the season, which is a hell of a year for any team. But for Columbia? That was like winning the Rose Bowl, the Sugar Bowl, and the Super Bowl all in one. No other Columbia team could even match it, until last year, 2017, when a new band of brothers also went 8-2.

Pretty good—but not a better record than ours.

Bwaaa!

IT WAS NOVEMBER, the end of our season. We went out on a two-game win streak, finishing up with a 31–27 win over Brown on the twenty-third.

I was back at it in the library, and I had clicked "refresh" on the internet browser about five times. I didn't care if it was fifty.

I looked at the draft projections. It didn't matter how many damn times I checked, the results were always the same. Marcellus Wiley, stuck in the seventh round, the very last round of the draft.

"Fuck!"

It had been a hell of a season, both for my team and for me. The scouts, coaches, and GMs kept coming to our games, we kept winning, and all of a sudden, I wasn't only getting messages from cute girls left on my dorm-room phone. Just a few months ago, I'd get home at the end of the day and that red light might be blinking two or three times. Now? That shit looked like Rudolph at Christmastime, flashing like crazy.

I'd run into ladies on the way to class, pouting and giving me the business.

"Why haven't you called me back?"

"Aw, I'm sorry," I'd say, as sweet and sincere as could be. "I have so many messages to get through, I didn't even see yours!"

Funniest part was, it was true.

Now that the season was over and I didn't have to follow NCAA rules anymore, I had even found myself an agent. Well, "found myself" is a little bit of an exaggeration. I got calls and letters from too many agents to count, and five of them visited me on campus, all trying to sign me. But I didn't want a dude who just knew me from the draft board, who was just trying to land me because I was hot. I wanted a guy who really knew me, who had followed my career, who I could trust.

That guy was Brad Blank—yes, that was his name. Brad was an Ivy guy like me, graduated from Brown, so he knew our league and the whole New England region. Plus, he'd already repped a few legit players like Herman Moore with the Lions, Jeff Lageman with the Jets, and Mike Mamula with the Eagles.

If that didn't do it for me, the trip to meet him in his Boston office did. Brad put me up in this hotel that was like the King Jaffe Joffer suite at Waldorf Astoria in *Coming to America*. A whole damn suite— felt like I had to round five different corners just to make it to the bedroom. Soon as I opened the door to the place, what did I see but a baby grand by the window, looking out over the city.

"Oh shit! I get a piano in my room!"

But even with all that attention, all that success, I hadn't budged from the seventh round in the draft projections. Don't get me wrong—seventh was a hell of a lot better than nothing at all, definitely better than being outside looking in, but still, I wanted more certainty. Doesn't take much for someone projected to go in the seventh to not get selected at all.

Thing is, as well as I had done over the season, as bright as I had shined in those preseason drills against Brian Larsen, I still played for Columbia. I might've been named All-American, but I was All-American in the Ivy League. The overall level of competition wasn't as high as in a conference like the Big Ten or the SEC.

Pro scouts knew I could dominate against the athletic accountants of Princeton and Cornell, but how the hell would that translate against the big ballers of Ohio State and USC?

In January, I showed them. I played in the East-West Shrine Game—an annual all-star game for college players on their way to the pros—at Stanford University in California. In the week of practice before the game, scouts got to watch me compete every day against elite players from the top programs in the country, and I more than held my own. I continued to perform well in the game itself, even sacking Arizona State's star QB Jake Plummer. But after sixteen plays, I dislocated my finger and had to head to the sidelines. By hanging with the big ballers, I gained a ton of cred with the scouts. But there were still a lot of questions left unanswered.

I needed to prove I belonged on an objective level. I needed to pass every test the NFL could throw at me, mental, physical, and psychological. And I needed to do it all on my own, without any brothers—Bulgarian or otherwise—to back me up.

I needed the combine.

I couldn't fucking wait.

THE 1997 NFL Scouting Combine took place in Indianapolis in February over several days, like it does every year. The combine is a battery of tests including the bench press, the vertical jump, the 40-yard dash, plus position drills and virtually anything else they could measure, time, or weigh.

Only about three hundred players in the entire country get invited to it each year, so in a sense even getting asked to the dance was a triumph. But showing up wasn't going to move me out of the seventh round of the projections. I needed to perform—and as a guy from Columbia, I knew they'd be grading me against a curve. A big one.

Six weeks before it began, my agent set me up with Mike Boyle, one of the top athletic trainers in the nation, a guy who had coached Mike Mamula to a record-setting combine performance two years earlier. A performance that rocketed him from a projected third-round draft pick at best to the seventh pick in the draft overall. Not seventh *round*—seventh *pick*.

Mike Boyle was the first trainer to prepare his athletes for each specific event they competed in, something that's par for the course now. And I soaked up everything he taught me, repping each event over and over again.

Forty-yard dash. Bench. Vertical.

Forty-yard dash. Bench. Vertical.

And on and on for six whole weeks.

So when finally I got to Indianapolis that winter, I knew I was ready. But I also knew that performing in practice was a whole other world from performing under pressure.

I got to my first day in Indy, hyped to get going—and had a solid day of medical exams. Physicals, questionnaires, hooked up to a bunch of wires, poked and prodded by all the League's specialists.

I'm not getting drafted because of my blood pressure, I thought. I need to get out on that field!

Day two, my time finally came.

I was so anxious to go, so pumped on adrenaline, I was trippin'— it was almost too much.

Other players who played against each other in their big-time conferences had all grouped together, forming their own little ecosystems on the sidelines, trading intel and gossip.

"Shit, dog," they'd say, nodding toward one highly touted athlete or another. "Look at him. He like ten times fatter in person than he was on TV."

"Slow as hell," someone else would mutter.

"Overrated," someone else would say, nodding knowingly.

What would they say about me when I competed? Why the hell did I even need to *do* this? I already *knew* what I could do. I had run a 4.6-second 40 a million times when I was training.

Why did my entire future come down to just two attempts right here, right now, in front of a bunch of judges I didn't even know? What if I slipped? What if my hamstring tightened up right at that critical moment? All that training, all that preparation, would be for absolutely nothing.

Everything came down to this moment. My lifelong dream of playing in the NFL, my mission to finally get my family out of the hood. It would all be decided here, now.

But if that was the way the game was played, I'd play it. I had no other choice.

I went on to run a 4.91 for my 40. Good enough to put me in the top ten for defensive ends, but still. I knew I could do better. *I knew it.*

More than that, I knew I *had to* do better.

For my vertical leap, I jumped 35.5 inches. Still not nearly as good as I was capable of—but the top score in my position group. Bench press? I did 28 at 225 pounds, again the top score out of all the defensive ends. And the broad jump and 10-yard shuttle? Forget about it. I killed motherfuckers in those. Ran a 1.58 in the 10-yard, and that's where a D-end really makes his money because most of our plays don't go any longer.

Ultimately, out of all the D-ends in the combine, I came in first in two events, second in one, third in another, then sixth and tenth in two more. I didn't just kill it in my own position either. Across the board my numbers were well above average for all the competition at the combine.

I crushed it, exactly when I needed to most.

That should've been enough, right? I had aced test after test, put up fantastic numbers, given the scouts and GMs exactly the kind of *objective* proof they were looking for.

But that wasn't all.

I also had to go through what some called the beauty pageant and others called the slave auction. I liked to think of it as the NFL's own personal swimsuit competition.

They had each one of us, all 330 athletes, walk onto a stage in front of a packed house of scouts, coaches, GMs, and draft gurus—in nothing but our drawers. Not to weigh us, not to measure us, nothing scientific in any way. Literally just to look at us in our underwear.

For some guys, that might mean a pair of loose-fitting boxers, something close to a swimsuit, or shorts, maybe spandex.

Not me. My underwear was *underwear*. High-cut, tight-ass briefs. I was practically wearing a G-string up in that place.

And let me tell you something—I looked *good*.

You don't even have to take my word for it. I could actually hear these motherfuckers talking about me in the crowd like I wasn't even there.

"Amazing physical specimen."

"Fantastic muscle tone."

And my personal favorite:

"Look at that butt!"

Now, critics would say that this shit is sick, an objectification of us as human beings, even an eroticization calling all the way back to slavery in the Old South. Hence referring to it as a "slave auction." And on one level there is a definite parallel. These NFL dudes might as well have been opening our mouths and checking our teeth, they were inspecting us so carefully. It was a meat market, no question. And let's be honest—most of them were white, and almost all of us were black.

But for me personally, the comparison doesn't resonate. One, because by definition "slavery" was never a matter of choice. Slaves *had* to be there, they were forced. We, on the other hand, didn't just want to be in the combine, we'd dreamed of being in the combine. Two, look at the different outcomes. If you were in a slave auction, your next day was gonna be pure hell. Unpaid hard labor. But us? We were potentially setting ourselves up for millions of dollars, and in my case a lifestyle I could barely even imagine. That's far short of slavery.

Besides, if I'm being honest, I also have to admit that it definitely helped my stock. I was cut, chiseled as hell. Six foot four inches and 271 pounds of hard muscle. And I was proud of it too. Why you think I did all those extra reps for Janet Jackson? Because they *weren't* only for Janet Jackson—they were for exactly that moment.

Say whatever you want about the eye test—I aced it.

When I finally got back to Columbia, I rushed to the library, said forget about the studying, and went right for those Commodore 64s. I had already heard people talking at the combine, gotten a lot of pats on the back, already been given a glowing review by my agent, but it wasn't real, wasn't *official*, till I found it online.

I typed away on that keyboard, waited for that old-ass search engine to work its magic, and there it was. Reviews on Marcellus Wiley from Mel Kiper and every NFL draft guru who mattered, with analysis like *raw but talented, athletically gifted*, and *a project, but worth the investment*—though unfortunately nothing about my butt.

Most important of all, there was the draft projection. That little number that said exactly how high all the experts said you were gonna go. I looked at that and knew that I had finally broken through. My own path had finally brought me to my chosen destination.

According to the draft projection, I was going in the first or second round. And I believed it.

ON COLUMBIA'S CAMPUS, all of a sudden it seemed like I wasn't the only one who followed Mel Kiper religiously. Everyone seemed to know I was gonna be a top pick in the draft, which was coming up on April 19. Everyone.

Life got very, very interesting.

I had always stood out from the crowd there, literally. Always been popular, almost never needed an introduction. But even by those standards, shit got weird.

I started noticing people following me in the grocery store, at the cafeteria, on my walks to class. I'd spot them once early in the day, then they'd keep popping up again in the weirdest places, like I was living in a low-budget movie that couldn't afford to cast enough extras. Then all of a sudden I'd be about to buy my textbook, and they'd be right there next to me.

"Hey, Marcellus! How are you! I heard you did great at the combine!"

Half the time I wouldn't even really know these people. They were another face on campus who wanted to brag to all their friends that they had the guts to talk to Columbia's national football sensation. Never really bothered me, though I did want to say, *Honestly, couldn't we have done this at ten in the morning when you saw me the first time?*

Then there were the women, and about *that* I will not complain. No matter how big I had been before, I always had to make the first move when it came to girls. Not anymore. Now they were asking *me* to go out on dates, to the point where I had to actually turn attractive women down—a very, shall we say, novel experience for me.

Not only students either, but successful bussinesswomen too, bussinesswomen I'd meet at Columbia. Suddenly ladies in their thirties and forties who had always patted me on the head before started patting me on the butt instead. Who could blame 'em? If it was good enough for NFL scouts, why not them?

These were highly attractive, highly educated women I had known for years offering to take me out to fancy dinners I *still* couldn't afford on my own. Hell, I was still living in the dorms, sleeping on a thin old mattress without a box spring, and *Star Wars* sheets! *Those* offers were something I *definitely* wasn't turning down.

One night, around eleven or twelve, I was back in that same dorm room, chilling and listening to music, when I suddenly heard a knock at my door.

I opened it up, and standing there was a girl I'd seen around campus but never really had the guts to talk to. She was Puerto Rican, a year or two younger than me, and stunningly beautiful.

And right then she was in my doorway in a black leather trench coat and heels, like Robin Givens in motherfucking *Boomerang*.

"Uh," I said with a gulp. "Hey?"

She smiled, kind of tucked in her chin, and laughed, like she knew this was crazy but she'd made up her mind and now she was gonna do it.

She undid the belt of her coat and slowly opened it up, revealing absolutely nothing underneath except my jersey number painted on her chest.

"Is number five here?" she asked.

Wow, I thought. She found paint in Columbia blue and everything. Impressive!

I babbled something that was far less witty than my usual material, and next thing I knew, she took me to a galaxy far, far away on my *Star Wars* sheets.

As my life threatened to blast into hyperdrive, I did the best I could to stay grounded. Whatever the projections were, I was still far from being rich. So to earn some extra cash I started training other students at the school gym in my spare time.

It was the perfect setup. These guys had plenty of their daddies' money to spend, and I had all my old workouts from Coach Boyle to use. These cats could barely bench fifty pounds, but they loved the idea that they were using the same plan as an NFL draft prospect.

Who cared if they never even finished? They got to quiz me

about what it was like competing in the combine, and I got to make one hundred dollars an hour—a hell of a lot better than typing, and more money than a lot of professional trainers make even today. It was nice spending cash as I got ready for what I hoped would be a far bigger paycheck in the League.

At the same time, I was still going to see my godmother, Jackie Blackett, no less than once a day. If my life was on high-octane gasoline, she was always the brakes. Everyone else would congratulate, and she would moderate, keep me focused, always reminding me that my job wasn't done yet, that I couldn't let this temporary success go to my head.

And she was right, because I still had one massive hurdle to get past before the draft—the Columbia pro day later in March.

All big-time college football programs, and even many smaller ones, have pro days. Basically mini combines they hold for their own players, including the ones who weren't invited to the official NFL combine. Pro scouts, GMs, coaches—they all get invited, and depending on which players are actually competing, you can get some pretty important League reps in the crowd.

Now, Columbia had had scouts stop by to check out players in past seasons, of course. But they hadn't had a full-on pro day like this. This year they had me, my boy Rory Wilfork, and a few other guys to show off, and there was a packed house to watch us perform.

Given what I had done at the actual combine, you might wonder why I'd even bother. But I still had a chip on my shoulder, still had something to prove.

No matter how well I had done in other people's eyes, I knew I could do better—especially in the 40-yard dash. I even had a slightly diabolical plan for how to make my results look even *more* impressive, no matter what my time was.

Everyone knows that running fast is even more impressive when a big-ass dude does it than when someone small does it. Like if you hear that a 200-pound guy can run a 4.6-second 40, you'll shrug and say, "Whatever." But if you hear that a 350-*pound* guy can run a 4.6-second 40, well, shit, give that guy a contract.

At the combine, I had weighed in at a solid but trim 271 pounds. At my pro-day, I decided to game the system.

That morning—and for days in advance—I chugged gallons of water. I mean gallons. Right down my throat.

Glub, glub, glub!

To top it off, I ate as many raw potatoes as I could manage. That's right, raw. I first tried raw potato back when I was a kid, and I used to make my special french fries at home. I swear people came from all over the hood to try them. I'd slice up these nice big steak-cut fries and cook 'em till they were golden brown. One time, I popped a little raw end in my mouth. Delicious! And a great source of starch when I wanted to put on some weight. So before my pro day, I went into the local grocery store, bought myself one of those big mesh bags of pota-toes, and bit into one after another. Piled them into my stomach until they were sitting there like a giant starchy rock in my gut. Went to my pro day, got myself weighed, and smiled a big, wide grin when I saw the scale.

I had gone from 271 pounds to 282 in less than a month. Over ten pounds!

Sure, four pounds of that was probably raw potato and water, but I got rid of most of it about a minute later, when I rushed my bloated ass to the bathroom, triggered my acid reflux, and regurgitated it back out, followed by a shit for good measure.

A few minutes after that, I went out to the track and ran 4.61. Three-tenths of a second better than I ran at the combine. My vertical went from 35.5 inches to 39.5. Bench press from 28 at 225 pounds to 35. And all at a weight that seemed to be ten pounds heavier.

I put an exclamation point on everything I had already achieved. Scouts came up to me one after the other when it was all over.

"We knew you were good," they'd say. "But we didn't know you could do this."

"Just you wait," I said. "I promise there's more."

WEEKS LATER, ON Saturday, April 19, I was selected by the Buffalo Bills in the fifty-second pick of the NFL draft, in front of my family, my friends, and a CNN camera crew in the small South Central apartment I had grown up in. After years of preparation, of struggling and dreaming, I was chosen in the second round, one of the highest picks from the Ivy League in the modern era.

It was one of the most rewarding, most surreal moments of my entire life.

Then we had my draft party—and I started to realize how my life would change now that I was in the League. How the people around me would change. Not always in a good way.

The party was later that night, a massive bash for hundreds of my closest family and friends, plus dozens of girls all clamoring to become the future Mrs. "My Husband Plays in the NFL."

Before it started, I stopped by the local mall to buy myself a head-band to match the Columbia jersey I was going to wear for the occa-sion. This is a store I had been to a thousand times before, and the owner had never said a word to me past "Hey." Got treated like every-one else.

But now, barely thirty minutes after the draft? It was like everyone was jumping off the walls with excitement, congratulating me, wishing me well. The owner came out from behind the register to give me a big hug, act like he was my best friend, and boss around his employees to have him take a picture of us so he could put it up on the wall, next to his snapshots with dudes like Kobe, Shaq, and Nick Van Exel. Other blood brothers of his, I bet.

And they say we change after we get drafted.

I made the phenomenal error of allowing my parents to organize the whole party, which meant it was held in a suite on the dark, completely horseless Hollywood Park Racetrack, and the entertainment consisted of a middle-aged white dude named J.C. who my dad worked with at the Post Office and did magic tricks on the side. Magic tricks I'd grown up loving.

This cat stood up in front of hundreds of young ladies and the dudes just itching to mack on them, and he did card tricks, turned dollar bills into dimes, and pulled a few birds out of his hat.

"This, ladies and gents, is what it sounds like when doves . . . *fly!*"

All my old "friends" came up to me, all my distant family members, all my ex-girlfriends I could barely remember, and they all told me, one after the other, how they always knew I would make it. How they always knew I would be the one.

Then the girls would say, almost on cue, "You ain't gonna know no one out there in Buffalo. You want me to come visit?"

They'd arch their eyebrows suggestively, squeeze my arm a little bit tighter, and I'd laugh, shake my head, and move on to the next flatterer.

I knew what they had really thought. That I was crazy when I went to Columbia. That I was a fool when I stuck with St. Monica's my last year of high school. That I was never going to amount to shit.

But honestly? I had never cared what other people thought. It didn't bother me, didn't even affect me, I just let it roll off my back. They were welcome to come to my party, eat the food, and roll their eyes at J.C.'s doves.

As far as I was concerned, that was the best damn magic show I'd ever seen.

IT WAS GRADUATION day back at Columbia, a day as important to me as the draft.

I was about to head to the ceremony. Unwrapped my elegant, dignified cap and gown. Took a deep breath. And decided to put on a T-shirt, a pair of sweat shorts, and my black-and-turquoise Space Jam Air Jordans first.

The cap and gown could go on top. No one would ever know what was really underneath.

Part of it was the LA in me. I had to go out with that same glee, that same joy, I came in with, when I first visited campus and got into a snowball fight in nothing but my shorts. Part of it was me having to always be the contrarian, always go my own way, make my own path.

Everyone else I knew was going formal, jacket and tie, or some fancy dress like they were on their way to the prom. For what? No one could even tell what they were really wearing underneath. Hell, I shoulda gone in nothing but my skin-tight Speedos from the draft's beauty pageant, one final fuck-you to Three-Piece-Suit Guy and everything he stood for.

My dad flew into New York for the ceremony. So did Mama and Tiki. Not my grandma though.

"I ain't flying all the way across the damn country just to hear someone say your fucking name!" she said with that glint in her eye. "Y'all tell me how it is."

The rest of my family was excited to go to New York—and ended up being completely underwhelmed by the size of the campus. After all they had heard about Columbia, they couldn't believe how tiny it was.

"This is your *college*?"

Back in LA, you got a school like USC or UCLA, that thing takes up a few square miles, each campus practically its own city. Columbia? The main quad was two or three blocks. And my graduation was right smack-dab in the middle of it.

I knew I needed a high safety net if football didn't end up working out. After all, getting drafted was only the beginning—who knows what would happen next year in Buffalo? And now I had the highest safety net an education could give you.

From here on out, it wouldn't just be Marcellus Wiley, kid from Compton. Or even Marcellus Wiley, NFL player. It would be Marcellus Wiley, Ivy League graduate, Columbia alumnus. No one could take that away from me.

The last week of class, the student newspaper, the *Spectator*, published a list of all the graduates, along with their projected place of employment and estimated first-year salaries. (You thought *athletes* were competitive? This was *Columbia*.)

The list was filled with the names of rich kids, going off to follow their family in business or finance or investing. They had all worked hard, yes, but they had also been born with an advantage, inherited their privilege, and now here they were, about to make $80,000 in their first year out of school at Lehman's or Chase or whatever.

With one exception. Right there at the top of the list, number one, was me, Marcellus Wiley. Company: Buffalo Bills. First-year salary: $500,000.

I smiled when I read it. My diploma was forever. But the money was pretty damn nice too.

I couldn't wait to get to Buffalo.

CHAPTER FIVE

"WILD STYLE" AND THE STORY OF BRUCE SMITH'S SHOES

I WALKED INTO BUFFALO'S Rich Stadium for the very first time. The home of my brand-new team.

It was May 1997, and I was right off the shuttle from the airport, with a few other rookies and a team administrator. I felt like a big, jumbled bag of emotions. Eager, nervous, scared. And most of all, wanting to prove to everyone—including myself—that I belonged.

Other first-year players from big programs like USC and Alabama weren't just used to a higher level of football than me—although they were. They also already had friends in the League. Guys they had played with or against for years. A built-in community. A brotherhood.

I was from the *Ivy League*. One of a handful in the entire NFL. I didn't have any of that.

This moment was the culmination of fourteen years of dreams—

dreams that started when I was a kid in peewee football. Dreams that only got stronger when I struggled to get noticed at Columbia and made a name for myself at the East-West Shrine Game and the combine. Dreams of playing at the highest level of the game. Competing against the best of the best. And someday, hopefully, being counted among them.

Now, suddenly, here were their names and numbers on all their lockers, right in front of me.

Shit! To my left, I saw "THOMAS 34" in big block letters. Thurman Thomas, one of the top running backs of all time. I'd grown up watching him on TV.

Oh fuck! There was "REED 83"—Andre Reed, the Pro Bowl receiver. That dude would definitely make it to the Hall of Fame.

And there, right there, was the name of the biggest and best of them all. SMITH 78. The one, the only Bruce Smith, the greatest defensive end of all—

Whoa, now. Hold on a second. What do we have here?

I gulped. Heart skipped a beat.

I wasn't looking at Bruce Smith's name anymore. That shit was old news. I had eyes for one thing, and one thing only.

His shoes.

A huge pile of shoes. A giant stack of shoes. A literal *wall of shoes,* right there inside his locker.

And not just any shoes, no. These were Nike Air Veers, *the official Bruce Smith shoe.* Best of all, they were all owned *by Bruce Smith himself!* These were Bruce Smith's very own Air Bruce Smiths!

Bruce didn't know it—he couldn't have, I hadn't even met the guy yet—but his shoes and I had history. Growing up poor as dirt in Los Angeles, I had dreamed of those shoes. Plush black leather with a big white strap across the top, covering the laces. I would watch this commercial with Bruce and Dennis Hopper on TV, Hopper playing a deranged fan obsessed with Bruce and his elite footwear, and I would feel Dennis Hopper's pain.

I wanted those shoes. I coveted those shoes. I dreamed of those shoes. I had even asked my mother to buy me those shoes.

Bad move.

"How much they cost?" she asked, a suspicious look on her face.

"Just, uh, $79.95," I said sheepishly.

"Boy, please!" she said.

Now, here I was, years later, staring at six or seven pairs of them, owned by *the* Bruce Smith, in *the* Buffalo Bills locker room.

Except this wasn't just the Buffalo Bills locker room, this was now technically *my* locker room. And it wasn't just *the* Bruce Smith, this was now Bruce Smith, *my* brand-new teammate. Not only one of the best defensive players in the history of the game, but the man I had been brought in to back up and one day replace.

I looked at Bruce Smith's shoes, and I saw my chance.

Sure, I could've just bought a pair for myself. I could afford as many of those bad boys as I wanted on my NFL salary. Hell, I could've bought some and asked Bruce to autograph them for me.

But I didn't want to just own the shoes. I wanted more than a fashion statement and support for my arches. I wanted to prove to myself that I was one of the guys. That I was part of the fraternity. That I really did belong on this team with all the other greats.

Growing up back in LA, the gangs all had initiation rites. Surprise, surprise, they were always illegal. Rob someone, kill someone, do something that proved to the other guys that you would put yourself on the line, even go to jail for them. I had never been in a gang before, but to me, this team, the Buffalo Bills, this was my new gang.

So to me, the answer was clear. If I wanted to belong, I couldn't ask. I had to take them.

I had to steal Bruce Smith's shoes.

No chance for that now. My new teammates were right behind me, not to mention a member of the Bills' staff. Even I wasn't that crazy.

So first, I had to figure out how.

MY ROOKIE YEAR in the NFL, Wild Style was born.

"Wild Style" was a nickname given to me by Gabe Northern, a linebacker who went by "Zoo," because he was even crazier than I was. Drop the "y" from "Wiley," add "Style," then you got me—Wile Style. (I add the silent "d" so Columbia doesn't think I never learned to spell.)

But Wild Style was more than a name, or even a style—it was a whole way of life.

The year before I got to the NFL, my last year at Columbia, I had actually gotten engaged. That's right—me, engaged, and still in college.

I wasn't even in the League yet, hadn't even been drafted, but I had heard all the stories about what happened once guys like me came into money. Spending sprees and groupies, women coming after you who were only interested in getting a few bucks for themselves, the works.

I didn't need that shit. I had already sewn my wild oats in every available field during my college days. I was gonna play it safe, just get commitment out of the way and slide right into years of peaceful, responsible living.

I had been dating a girl in LA long-distance for about a year. How much different could that be from a lifetime together, right? Let's do this shit up.

Before the draft, my agent gave me an advance of $10,000. Perfect. Just enough to get my girl an engagement ring while leaving a whole lot left over to spend on my family. I walked into a Zales, found something nice but not too gaudy for about two grand, and proposed over Christmas. Done and done. My plan was working perfectly.

Until we had a little talk about the rest of that $10,000.

"So what you think you're gonna do with the rest of it?" she asked me innocently over the phone.

I was already back in New York for my final semester, but what the hell did I need $8,000 for as a student? I had gotten by with almost nothing for close to five years. I knew exactly where that money was going.

"Oh," I said. "I'm gonna send a check to my mother."

She didn't miss a beat.

"Your *mother*??"

I know she didn't just snap on my mama. That was the end of that bullshit, right then and there. No more engagement, and she could keep the ring.

That was the end of something else too—my whole philosophy of embracing slow, dull, geriatric living in the NFL. Fuck that! My engagement lasted about two months, and that was about how long the boring Marcellus lasted. I was gonna be rich and single, and I was gonna *live. Eat, eat!*

As soon as I got the first installment of my signing bonus, I took the check to my neighborhood Bank of America on Crenshaw Boulevard. I waited quietly in line like everyone else, and handed my ninety-nine-thousand-dollar check to the teller without a word.

She looked at it, did a double take, and promptly lost her shit.

"Ahhhhhh!" she screamed, turning to another teller. "Marcellus is rich, girl!"

The staff in the back practically exploded with excitement.

"I always knew that motherfucker was getting big! I knew it! I knew it!"

"We on Crenshaw, girl! You better calm down!"

"You say you got drafted? Drafted to what? Where? Like football?"

"I *knew* he was getting big! I *told* you, girl!"

First thing I did with my paycheck was take care of my family in a big way—exactly what my former fiancée did *not* want me to do.

Growing up poor, my mama, my sister, and I had always had to take the bus. Now, complaining about the bus might seem a little stuck up to you, and don't get me wrong, we had lots of bigger problems—welfare checks every month to get by, kids making fun of me when I bought stuff with food stamps, you name it. But in a city like LA, having to take the bus as a kid brought its own unique indignity.

Back in grade school, we had track practice at Crenshaw High. My sister and I would finish up late, at 8:00 p.m., and Mama would meet us at the school. It was already dark. We'd all go to the corner of Crenshaw and Fifty-Seventh Street and wait for the bus. And wait. And wait.

And wait.

At least forty-five minutes. At least.

I'd stand on that corner and watch every single car go by. They'd stop at the red light, then keep going as soon as it turned green. They didn't have to wait for nobody.

I'd see a big-ass Oldsmobile pull up with its chrome rims, a single person driving, and the rest of the seats completely empty. I'd think, *Man, they could fit me, my sister,* and *my mama in there, plus two more, and we'd all be home in five minutes!*

Instead we'd have to wait. Useless, wasted time.

Once we finally got that bus we'd still have another ten minutes from all the stops.

So that was a minimum of fifty-five minutes spent watching the world drive by and leave us to rot in the dust. Fifty-five minutes that could've been five.

My first NFL contract was for $2.1 million over four years. None of us would be taking the bus ever again.

I got my parents out of the hood, bought my mom and my dad their own houses in Ladera Heights, the black Beverly Hills of LA. They had stopped living together once I graduated high school and moved to New York, their mission—to dutifully raise their kids in a stable two-parent household—officially accomplished. They had done their part, and it was time to move on. My dad married his longtime companion once I finished college, the same woman he'd been seeing since way back when I was in high school, while my mom embraced her independence. But they stayed on good terms with each other, and their houses weren't that far apart. As for my sister, over time I helped her leave her insurance job so she could come work with me, something she does to this day.

For myself? One of the first things I got was a gold medallion in the shape of an NFL shield, studded with tiny diamonds, the works. I'd wear it around my neck, like a sign to everyone that I was *not* engaged: "Hey, ladies! Check it out! NFL!"

Now I realize it was cheesy as hell, even though all the players had them back then.

But more than anything else, more than even *real* jewels, the proverbial jewel on my crown was my brand-new truck. Over the summer, before I moved to Buffalo, I bought a brand-new Ford Expedition—the first of many new cars—burgundy on the outside, cream on the inside.

My corny-ass even put two Buffalo Bills flags on that thing, drove it around the hood, parading for everyone to see.

And once I got to Buffalo, Wild Style did everything big.

My first year I wasn't playing that much, so I had plenty of time to live right. I got a house of my own in a neighborhood where a few other players lived. Single, and I had my own *house*!

It wasn't a mansion or anything, just a pretty ordinary house. But to me, a guy right out of college who grew up in the hood, everything that was ordinary to my older teammates was absolutely extraordinary to me. My own private Disneyland.

We fly on our own planes to games? *What?*

We got flight attendants who'll serve us as much steak and shrimp cocktail as we want? *Double what??*

Meanwhile, all the veterans would be looking at me, shaking their heads and sighing like, *Yeah, that kid is wild alright.*

I had a gun, a little .380 the guys at the shop called a Baby 9, and the first one I had ever owned. Bought it after my LA friend got jacked at gunpoint for his own truck, a hooked-up Yukon, while he was in front of his own house. He figured if he could get robbed in a damn Yukon, I'd be even more at risk in my big new ride, alone in a strange new city.

That piece was so small it fit in a wallet-style holster that I could slip right in my front pocket. I carried it everywhere I went, into bars, into restaurants, into the locker room—even though guns were banned there—everywhere. Other guys on the team may have had rifles for hunting, even guns they kept at home for protection. But to carry it around with me? That was something new for the Buffalo Bills.

"Where you think we live, Wiley?" my teammates would say. "Calm the fuck down!"

I even bought myself a little dog to be my wingman, a white Boston terrier with black spots I called Moo-Moo because she looked like a tiny cow. Took her everywhere, including team meetings and the locker room—the second thing I brought that was banned. The other players loved her. And it *definitely* didn't hurt that women loved her. But don't tell the coaches—they never found out about my dog or my gun.

A lot of the other first-year players were pissed that they ended up in Buffalo. Not the team—the team was great back then. But the city? They wanted a Miami, a Chicago, an Atlanta. Anywhere but *Buffalo.*

Well, none of those dudes went to Columbia University. Compared with the old campus party scene, Buffalo was like the Vegas strip.

In town there was one place we all went, Birchfield's, and its specialty was cheap, strong drinks. It's closed now, but back in the day it got silly. On the first Friday of every month, the drinks got even cheaper and stronger, and it would be crazy packed with all the cutest girls from around. Which was basically about seven in Buffalo, but who's counting.

Or if we were feeling adventurous, we'd head to Toronto or Niagara Falls to hit up the naked ballet, which is my highbrow way of saying "strip club."

If we got really lucky, Bruce would come out. He was married, so he just chilled, but the rest of us could play his bodyguards, running interference on his many female fans.

"Oh my," the girls would say. "Are you here with *Bruce*?"

You're damn right we are! Now can we please have your number? Like, all y'all's numbers?

I went out with a few women every week, and I must've had about fifty numbers I could call for any given situation. Dinner, drinks, show, or what I liked to call "horizontal hanging."

As one of the few single dudes on the team, I was a very popular man—not only with the ladies, but with my fellow teammates. Most of the cats on the team were married or engaged or had some kind of significant other. Hell, more than a few of them already had kids, even the rookies.

They needed an excuse if they wanted to go out at night, a loophole to get their ass out of the house. That was me—the human loophole.

All the wives and fiancées knew I was single, and best of all, they trusted me. If I said I needed their guy to be my wingman at Birchfield's, they were happy to give their blessing. Or if I said the guys and I needed to watch film at my place, they'd let us go "watch film"—which usually meant chilling, playing cards, and having ourselves a time.

Of course, as big as I was living, compared with other players I still had a ways to go. I mean, I wasn't on NFL welfare—that would be the practice squad guys, who could barely afford apartments. But I didn't have even close to the biggest house on my block.

Fortunately, I was ready to learn from the other players, even if they didn't always realize what they were teaching me. Like one day, after practice, when I got a ride home from Ted Washington.

That morning, we'd had our first snowstorm of the season. I woke up early, looked out my frost-covered window, and saw trucks plowing the streets.

Great, I thought, *I'm all set.*

Got in my Expedition in my garage and pushed the button to open the garage door.

Grrrrrrrrrrrrrrr. The gears ground as the door slowly raised.

I looked, and all I could see was snow, snow, snow, blocking me in.

Damn! I thought. The streets were plowed. You mean they don't do your driveway too?

"No, they don't do your damn driveway!" Ted told me at the end of the day as we got in his truck, a sick Hummer that had no problem handling the snow. I hadn't even been able to get my car out of the garage that morning.

We called Ted "Mount Washington" because this dude was huge. A nose tackle, six foot five, already in the League for six years. Must've been about 365 pounds, but he'd actually get defensive if anyone asked him how much he weighed.

"No one knows!" he'd say. "I don't need to weigh myself, dammit!"

He was so big and strong he didn't have to be fast on his feet to get a guy. All he had to do was stretch out his long-ass arms—*punch!*— and he'd get you. Didn't even have to move.

As massive as his Hummer was, Ted was so damn big he barely even fit in it. And it was dirty as shit, with crumpled-up McDonald's wrappers everywhere—the floor, the seats, everything—because a man as big as Mount Washington does *not* diet.

"Oh, throw that shit on the ground, man," he said as I tried to find a place to sit.

I shoved the trash to the side, and realized some of it wasn't trash—there was an envelope from the Buffalo Bills, his name on it in bold black letters, already opened.

"Ted, where you want me to put this?"

"Throw 'em in the glove compartment," he said.

Too late. Me being the rascal I was, I had already reached inside.

Stuffed inside, I found two uncashed checks—and those two checks almost totaled more than I'd make in two years.

"Ted!" I said. "These your game checks, man! You haven't even cashed them!"

"Wiley, those ain't my game checks, those are my off-season bonuses. Just put it in my glove compartment, man!"

Off-season bonuses?? That meant this dude had been sitting— literally—on hundreds of thousands of dollars in uncashed checks for *months*! He had almost half my entire four-year contract balled up in a bunch of McDonald's wrappers in his damn car.

Did that make me jealous? Not in the slightest. It made me even hungrier—and not for fast food.

Ted was a skilled, experienced veteran, making veteran money, a lot more than a second-round-draft rookie like me could expect. To me, those checks were like an arrow sign on the side of the road saying, *You on the right road, man.*

Keep getting better, earn your way, and all this will be yours someday.

BUT IF I was going to get there, I couldn't just be Wild Style. I had work to do—on my game.

I found out just how much in my first week of training camp, in one of my very first practices as an NFL player, doing one of my least favorite things—pass-rush drills.

These were the same kind of drills I did against Dartmouth's Brian Larsen back before my last season at Columbia. The same kind of drills that first got me discovered by Bird, the mysterious NFL scout. And they were the same kind of drills that still made me weirdly nervous, even now that I was in the NFL.

Hell, even more so, because now I really had something to

prove—and everyone on my brand-new team watching to see how I would do.

Best of all? This time, my competition was a *little* tougher than a great O lineman from the Ivy League. This time, I was in a one-on-two drill, up against John Fina and Ruben Brown. John was six foot five and three hundred pounds, Ruben was six foot three and three hundred pounds. They'd been playing on the O line their whole life. I'd been a defensive end for about, oh, three years.

Fina was good, but Ruben was a star. He'd already been to the Pro Bowl once, and he'd go on to make it eight more times in his career. For the uninitiated out there, that means the dude could *ball.*

We were on the side of the field, near the fence, but it felt like everyone was watching. After all, I was the Bills' number two draft pick, I was the heir apparent to Bruce Smith, and I was straight out of the Ivy League. Don't see that every day.

I lined up across from them for the first rep. I'd already decided to go inside, which would take me right at Ruben.

I got in my stance, put my hand in the dirt. The ball was between us, at the end of a stick held by a coach, mimicking a real game-time snap. As soon as that ball moved, I could go.

I looked at that ball, I looked at that stick. I knew if I wanted any shot against Ruben, I'd need to jump that snap, react to the very first *hint* of motion, and take off.

But which should I look at? The ball or the stick?

I suddenly realized I didn't have a damn clue—and that was *exactly* when it happened.

I shot forward, out of my stance. Ruben was fanning out, holding his giant hands out like two defibrillators about to shock me in the chest.

I tried to hit him with a swim move, my favorite move from

college, old reliable, but old reliable was dead in the water against a guy like Ruben. He punched me and drove me back, and when I say he "drove me back," I mean I got in that car and went for a *ride*.

He slammed me right into the fence.

"*Oooooohhhhh!*" the crowd erupted.

Ruben busted out laughing, jogged back to the huddle.

I was embarrassed, but only for a second. Honestly, outside of the theatrics, it was still just a block. I had been blocked before, I'd probably get blocked again. No big deal, right?

Until *I* tried to jog back to the huddle—and I couldn't.

My jersey was caught in the damn fence. I struggled, I squirmed, I did everything I could, but I was stuck. So not only did I mess up my first rep, but I couldn't even *line up* for my second rep.

I had to wait for Rusty the equipment dude to run over and unstick me. Rusty, a five-foot-seven guy with a big-ass tool belt who was always running everywhere, always hustling, always jogging, never walking. Thank God for that, because I felt so damn humiliated that what took Rusty about five seconds to do felt like it took five hours.

Standing there, stuck to that fence, something hit me even harder than Ruben Brown at full speed. All the skills, all the moves and technique that worked back at Columbia, I had to toss all that out. I had to start over, reconfigure everything.

The basic goals were still the same, of course—as a D-end I had to stop the run when they ran the ball, or rush the quarterback when they passed. My run game was still acceptable, because that came down to power and strength, and I had plenty of that. But my lack of pass-rushing experience was finally catching up to me. Don't forget—I'd only been playing this position for two seasons, and at an Ivy League school. Most of the other D-ends in the League had been doing this since they were eight, and they had played at places like Florida State, where the competition—and the training—was at a much higher level. I had a ton of raw physical talent, which is why I'd been drafted so high. But as for technique, I had a long way to go. And more than the run, technique was essential for rushing a quarterback.

There were two critical elements to good pass rushing: using angles and technique to get past blockers, and timing your jump on the snap. And I needed to work on both. The same way I needed to figure out the rules for a whole new game within a game when I started college, that's what I had to do now—but with football. I needed to find my CliffsNotes.

Problem was, just like when I was back in New York, I didn't have any good friends I could go to for lessons. If I had come from a Florida State, if I had been a part of one of those unofficial college fraternities in the NFL, I could've gone to one of my brothers and talked to them. But I was still building those connections, still finding my way and proving I belonged. I didn't even have a godmother like Jackie Blackett.

So I did the next best thing. I went to the best. I went to Bruce.

I started by simply observing. Studying the moves he used to get past guys. Bruce's go-to was what they called the "swipe." Bruce would charge a lineman, swipe his arms like a couple windshield wipers, and knock the guy right out of the way.

Honestly? Thing looked exactly like "wax on, wax off" from *The Karate Kid*. Seriously, I think he stole his big move from Daniel-san. Which was all good by me, because now I could steal it from him.

My second year, I also went to our D line coach, John Levra. My man was like a connoisseur of the top pass-rush moves in the NFL.

He'd scan game footage and collect everything he could find, from Reggie White to Richard Dent, collate it, and put it all on tape for me.

Dent's signature move—club down and rip—ended up being my favorite. He'd engage with a defender, bring his hand down sharp like a club, then rip it right back up, go right by the dude. No Daniel-san there—the technique was so unique they actually called it the Dent move. But I studied it and had no problem swiping it for myself.

But for the last part of my rush game, I knew I had to go back to my teammate.

Perfecting my jump on the snap was the single most important thing I could do for my game. Every extra tenth of a second I could gain on the O line would be a huge advantage. If there was a trick, I needed to learn it and master it. If there was a trick, Bruce would know.

This time, I got up the nerve to talk to the man himself. I caught him after practice, sitting in front of that same wall of Nikes that had sent my mind reeling.

"Hey, Bruce," I said, smiling my brightest, most charming smile. "Got a question for ya."

He looked at me.

"Yeah."

That was encouraging.

"Dude, you get off the ball faster than *all* of us. What's your secret?"

Bruce thought for a second.

"What you looking at before the snap?" he said.

"The ball."

"Where on the ball?"

"The tip."

"Which tip?"

"The top tip," I said.

"That's your problem," he said. "I'm looking at the guy's pinky finger and the *bottom* tip."

Oh shit. It was like a lightbulb went off in my head.

Bruce Smith, the best D-end of all time, had just given me the first CliffsNote I needed to reach the next level.

Now I *really* couldn't wait to steal his shoes.

I WAITED A FEW weeks before I finally struck. Planned my attack. Studied the mannerisms of my target.

Here I was supposed to be *filling* Bruce Smith's shoes, and all I could think about was *stealing* them. If I was gonna do it, I was gonna do it right.

Bruce wasn't as big as you'd expect for a devastating All-Pro D-end, but somehow that only made him more physically intimidating. He was about 260 pounds, but his arms looked like they weighed 310. He always covered them in Vaseline to keep them warm in the Buffalo weather—and probably because it made them look cut as hell. It had the desired effect. This was not a guy you wanted to make angry, not on the field or anywhere else.

Luckily, he barely spent any time at his locker, and he owned so many damn shoes there was no way he'd ever miss a single pair.

Finally, one day after practice, I made my move.

I looked right, I looked left. The coast was clear. I casually strolled over to his locker, leaned down like I was putting something back that I had forgotten to return, and instead picked up my very own, truly authentic pair of Air Bruce Smiths.

I sauntered back to my locker and shoved them deep down at the bottom of all my stuff, where no one would ever, ever find them. I was now a criminal mastermind and—most important of all—I felt like an official member of the Buffalo Bills. Almost like I'd won a trophy for the childhood me.

There was just one little detail I didn't count on: Thurman Thomas.

Our future Hall of Fame running back had seen the whole damn thing.

AS I GOT used to life in the NFL, I realized there was a flip side to being Wild Style—being lonely. And I hated being alone.

Freedom was great and all, but at the end of the night, if I wasn't on yet another date, it would just be me and that big, empty house of mine. Ask anyone and they'll tell you, I'm a talker. I love to talk. Love to be around people, engage, feed off their energy.

But Buffalo could get very, very quiet.

I had hoped that my dog, Moo-Moo, would help fill some of the void in my empty house, but the only thing Moo-Moo was good at filling it with was boo-boo.

In fairness to Moo-Moo, I was a horrible trainer. It'd be snowing like crazy outside, and I'd give her the sternest look I could possibly manage as I got my coat and her leash ready.

"Moo-Moo, I know it's snowing outside, but you gotta pee-pee boo-boo!"

And she'd look back at me with those big brown eyes, and I swear it was like she was talking to me.

"You crazy? It's freezing out there! I'm gonna pee-pee boo-boo right here."

And that's what she'd do, pee-pee boo-boo right there on the floor. I tried white pee pads, blue pee pads, I tried it all. She didn't care. She'd shit wherever she wanted—as long as it was the last place *I* wanted.

At the end of the season, I brought Moo-Moo back with me to Los Angeles. We got to my mama's house, Moo-Moo found a spot in the sun, rolled on her back, stretched out, and took a nice, long nap. Mama had her potty-trained in less than a week.

That was the clearest statement she could make—Moo-Moo was dumping my lonely ass for LA's sunny weather. I went back to Buffalo alone.

My relationship with my other constant companion—my Baby 9 gun—didn't go any better.

The longer I carried my "extra wallet" around with me, the more I felt like it changed me. One night on my way home from a club, I was driving home at 3:00 a.m.—alone, again—when I passed over a small bridge. I rolled down my window and started shooting into the night sky.

Blam! Blam! Blam!

Shouted "Yeah!" from the adrenaline rush.

Then I got home and thought, *What the hell was that about?*

A short while later, it was another late night at the exact same club. Again, I was heading home, all by myself, to my big empty house.

I pulled up at a red light and noticed a guy walking closer to my car. He stopped in front of my car, looked right at me. Turned and came over to my window.

This wasn't a good neighborhood, and there was no one else around. My hand moved to my "wallet." I had my gun right there, ready for anything.

He knocked on my window.

Shit, I thought. *Am I prepared to shoot someone?*

I rolled down the window.

"Hey, man," he said. "Do you know where Chester Street is?"

I took a deep breath. I had been a split second away from potentially taking someone's life.

As I drove home, I passed over the same small bridge where I had fired my Baby 9 in the air a few weeks earlier. This time, I slowed down and tossed my gun into the water. Haven't owned one since.

More than anything, though, I just needed people. Conversation. Not drinks, not clubs, not chilling. Talking, plain and simple.

On the road I had my roommate. Road games were even less glamorous than Buffalo, honestly. Just me and a big dude named Pat Williams, a defensive tackle who was six foot three and 320 pounds, sitting there in our hotel room, ordering room service, relaying farts back and forth, and checking the hotel cable box for new releases.

Big Pat told me the trick ending of *The Sixth Sense* in the first five minutes I was watching it, and he snored like crazy, but other than that? Good company.

Back in Buffalo, though, I needed more. So I started cakin'.

When my boys and I went out, there might be ten or twenty of us, all hollering at the same seven cute girls at the club. It was Buffalo, after all—the pickings were slim. By the end of the night, we'd all be sitting there comparing stories, saying, "Wait—you got her number too? Shit!"

Afterward, all the other guys might follow up, asking to get a drink, seeing if the girls wanted to chill.

Not me. When I called someone up for a first date, I actually invited her out to dinner and the whole deal. Food, conversation, quality time—known as *cakin'*, because it meant I ended up spending real money, or "cake," to wine and dine my date.

It drove the other guys crazy, because the ladies would always choose me.

"Man, Wiley, why you be cakin'?" they'd say. "You wasting your time when you could be out with a dozen different girls!"

I'd laugh.

"How many girls you fools need?"

But the truth is, I *liked* cakin'. I didn't do it for the girls, I did it for me.

I didn't want to be sitting at home alone, cooking some bland-ass chicken and rice with my pooping dog. I wanted to be with someone.

So I didn't care if it was a first date. I didn't care if I barely knew her name, or if she was looking for a free meal from a pro football player, which of course some of them were. She needed to eat, I needed to eat—let's go eat dinner together!

Maybe I'd see her again, maybe I wouldn't. But for that one night I'd have someone to talk to over dinner about life, about my day, about whatever.

The Wild Style in me could still get very wild, don't get me wrong. But I was also starting to realize that I wanted—needed—more in my life.

THERE WAS NOTHING like walking out of the tunnel in an NFL stadium onto the field before a game.

There was literally a light at the end of the tunnel. You walked toward it, shoulder to shoulder with all your teammates, and it was like you were being reborn, the excitement, the energy is so intense. The tens of thousands of fans, the roar of the crowd, the sheer size of the stadium—all of it was awe-inspiring.

But more than anything else, I remember the cleats.

All forty-five active players wearing their cleats with their hard, plastic soles, and the way they sounded on the concrete as we marched toward that field, echoing, rhythmic.

Clack clack clack clack clack!

Like clapping thunder or chiming cymbals, getting louder and louder with each step.

Until suddenly we'd hit that soft turf and our footsteps would go silent, just like that—and just in time to give way to the screams of the fans.

It was epic, magical. And finally, in week seven of my first season, I played well enough to live up to that magic.

As a team? Not so much. We were playing the Patriots on their home field, and they kicked our butts, ended up beating us 33–6. But for me, our collective ass-whupping was an individual opportunity.

I was Bruce's backup, and even though my pass rush was still struggling, I had only been getting better at stopping the run. Once New England started putting the hurt on us big-time, two things happened: first, our coach didn't want to wear down our star D-end too much in a game we'd most likely lose, and second, the Patriots started running the ball like crazy to run down the clock.

This was my time.

As soon as I hit that field, my adrenaline started flowing like crazy. Since practice had started, I'd been suffering from plantar fasciitis—an inflammation of tissue in my foot, which felt like fire but never slowed me down—and that shit vanished in the excitement. I was pumped as hell, lava running through my veins.

On the Pats' line, I'd be going up against Bruce Armstrong, a six-foot-four, 300-pound tackle who had already been to five Pro Bowls in his career. Five. Let's put it this way: if Ruben Brown had managed to drive me into a fence, Bruce Armstrong could drive me *through* one if I wasn't at the top of my game.

As good as Armstrong was, though, I was the one who could bench 495 pounds and squat 695. And when you're trying to stop the run, power matters—a lot.

Of course, it also helped that I was fast as hell.

New England ran that ball, and I took off, dodging dudes, turning on those jets—*vroom! vroom! foom!*—tackle!

They ran it again. Tackle!

And again. Tackle!

I could feel my confidence growing one tackle after another, feel it all come together. Feel it click right into place. Like I had my own personal cheering section in my mind, in my heart, screaming at me, pushing me, egging me on.

Aaaaaaah! Aaaaaaaaaah!

I finished the game with four solo tackles and seven assists. My dreams were becoming a reality. I could play the run at football's highest level. I was ready for more.

With Bruce still killing it, I didn't have many opportunities to rush my first year. I stuck with the run, honed my skills, bided my time. But my second year, the coaches finally gave me my shot to go after the quarterback.

My defining moment had nothing to do with big stats or even a single sack. It all came down to a look and a phrase.

It was week six, and we were up against a Jacksonville team with an offensive line that featured Tony Boselli and Leon Searcy, who had a combined weight of 637 pounds. I had one sack in my entire NFL life. I was only going up against Searcy—thankfully Bruce had a rivalry with Boselli and wanted him all to himself—and this motherfucker was good, a six-year vet who went on to be a Pro Bowler.

Now, I ain't no punk, but before the game even started, I was thinking that if I didn't play, that'd be fine with me.

But I had been making progress in practice, was finally getting good push against our O lineman on a regular basis, so the coaches put my lucky ass in.

I was lined up across from Searcy on the left side of the field. He and I both knew the next play was gonna be pass. The Jaguars had a left-handed quarterback, Mark Brunell, which meant that if I managed to get by Searcy, I'd be attacking from Brunell's blind side—an easy target if I could just get there fast enough.

I got down in my track stance, kept my eye on that ball like Bruce taught me—looking at the snapper's pinky finger and the bottom tip. As soon as that thing moved, as soon as it even twitched, I was off—

Foom!

—put a move on Searcy—

Aaah!

—and went right by him.

Just in time to see Burnell get off a quick pass to a receiver.

Fuck!

No sack for me.

Then, as I was heading back to the huddle, I heard Searcy say something.

"Damn, dog, you fast as shit," he said. "Good move."

I laughed to myself. I had used Bruce's Daniel-san–style swipe move. It had worked perfectly.

Just like that, I knew it—I had finally developed both components of my game, the run *and* the pass. My confidence shot sky-high from then on out, ignited by that one moment, that single phrase. I got 3.5 sacks that year, 5 the year after that, and 10.5 the year after that.

Not too bad for a guy from the Ivy League.

––––––––––

FLASH BACK TO my very first year on the team—and my grand theft of Bruce's shoes. A few weeks had gone by since I successfully pulled off my heist, the single act that had proved to me—if no one else— that I was a full-fledged member of the Buffalo Bills.

Bruce, Thurman Thomas, and I were in the locker room. The evidence was still buried under a pile of my clothes and gear—and I was certain I had gotten away with it. Until suddenly I heard Thurman say something, and I realized he wasn't only the best running back in the League.

He was also our team's biggest snitch.

"Hey, Bruce," he said. "Check your shoes. You might be missing some."

I froze, my heart pounding. I had gotten to know Bruce by that point, and he was a great guy. We'd chilled together at Birchfield's, hung out in Toronto, and I'd gone to his place in Virginia for the holidays. I'd gone to the dude for help on my game, asked for advice on jumping the snap, even adopted his signature swipe move (which, in my defense, he'd also adopted from *The Karate Kid*).

But still, I was just a rookie, not even a starter, and these were Bruce Smith's very own pair of Bruce Smith–branded Nikes!

I stared at him. I didn't say a word because for once I couldn't think of a thing to say. Finally, after what felt like ten full minutes, Bruce laughed the way only Bruce laughed.

"Ay-ahhh, no one better be messin' with my shoes."

And that was it. He let it slide. Never said another word about it.

I accomplished a lot those first couple years in the League. Earned my first big paycheck, helped take care of my family the way I'd always dreamed, worked my ass off to take my game to the highest level. Even snatched a pair of shoes from the greatest D-end of all time.

But none of it felt as good, felt as *real*, as when Bruce shrugged and gave me a pass. It was official. I was part of the gang.

I had what it takes to make it in the NFL.

CHAPTER SIX

AT THE TOP LOOKING DOWN

I STOOD AT THE bottom of the sand dunes in Manhattan Beach, staring up at the peak.

For everyone who worked out there, that climb was a motherfucker. The ultimate prize. The unachievable goal. The dune itself was a hundred feet high or so, but it was so steep it felt like a hundred miles. Ten times worse than running up Throw-Up Mountain with Jabari in Baldwin Hills back in the day, because at least that was winding and paved. The dune was pure, shifting sand, and nothing but up. Like when I say I was staring up at the top, I mean I had to stare *up*, like straight up, like head-tilted-fully-back, crick-in-my-neck up.

It didn't matter what sport you played, if you made it to the top of that thing without stopping, you were ready to ball out. And in nine years of trying—trying since *high school*—I had never made it to the top without stopping. Not once. I'd made it halfway, sometimes three-quarters, sometimes even seven-eighths. But sooner or later, I'd always have to stop and walk to reach the peak. Always!

Not this time though. This time would be different.

See, I had a little extra fuel. I was about to hit my contract year.

It was the off-season before my fourth year at Buffalo, the last year of my contract with the Bills. After the upcoming season, every team in the NFL would be able to bid on my services. And I wanted to send those bids *through the roof.*

My first three years had been solid—especially for someone who was classified as an athletically gifted but unfinished "project" coming out of the draft. I had improved in each of my years in the League—from zero sacks my first season to 3.5 my second and 5 in my third. But the past doesn't mean shit when you get to a contract year. What matters is what you do *now.*

Kind of like if you got to the end of a class only to find out that your final is 95 percent of the grade. You've been busting your ass on paper after paper after paper, then you get to that last test and your teacher is like, "Yeah, none of that really mattered. The only thing that matters is *this.*"

Now that's a lot of pressure, but it's also a lot of potential. If everything goes right, that fourth year can turn into a magical-genie bottle. Rub that thing in *just the right place,* and all of a sudden that fat blue genie pops out and every single wish is yours.

If you're a young D-end like me, "just the right place" means sacks, plain and simple. Forget about tackles, forget about being a team player. If you get double-digit sacks, you've had a great contract year, and you're about to get paid.

Best of all? I was gonna be a starter. Buffalo had released the best D-end of all time, Bruce Smith, who went to the Redskins, leaving a big hole for me to fill in the lineup. I was about to go from being the greatest's heir apparent to having a shot at being one of the greatest myself—and a chance to get rich in the process.

So that off-season, training for my contract year, I put the cape on again. If I thought I gave 100 percent before, somehow I found another 20 percent I never even knew existed. I worked my ass off like you would not believe.

And I was gonna make it up that damn hill in Manhattan Beach.

I started running full steam, practically going straight up that dune. My long legs churned, but the sand was so loose and slippery every step I took felt like half of it was coming back.

Vru-vru-vru—wooop!

But I kept going. Passing people left and right, people who had given up and started walking, just like I had done all those times before.

To make it up this thing, you didn't only need conditioning and stamina—you needed will. Like I said before, football is a game of skill, but it's a greater game of will. This run was the exact same way. To beat the hill, you had to *believe* you could beat the hill.

And this time—this one time—I finally believed.

I made it to the top. Huffing and puffing, sweat streaming down my face, I stared out at the blue sky.

Down below me, Rosecrans Avenue stretched east. It went all the way to Compton, almost right to the front door of my grandma's house, where I had spent most of my childhood. That same Rosecrans Avenue came to an end right below me, near the beach—and luxury condos I could now afford to buy.

Two different worlds. Same street.

I was gonna keep working, and I was never moving back to the other end of Rosecrans.

In June, when I got to Buffalo's spring conditioning, I was in such good shape that the coaches didn't put me with the other D linemen. They wanted to give me a challenge.

"Wiley, you on some other shit right now," Coach said. "You running with the DBs and the linebackers."

In football practices, you're always with your position. You eat together, you lift together, you go to team meetings together. It's like segregation according to skill set.

For me to break out of those boundaries? For a guy as big as me to race against smaller, faster DBs and linebackers? It wasn't taking Physics—it was taking AP Physics, with a dash of vector calculus on the side. Like I had moved past my grade and was hanging with the honor students. I was on their turf, and I had to prove I belonged.

That's exactly what I did. About ten of us lined up for 40-yard wind sprints, and I was doing more than keeping up. I was coming in third or fourth place against dudes two-thirds my size.

"Man, Wiley, you keeping up!" they shouted.

"Oh, you know he trying to get paid!"

"He gonna eat!"

Shit, running a few 40-yard dashes was nothing compared with making it to the top of the Manhattan Beach sand dunes. I wasn't just gonna hang with these dudes, I was gonna *beat* 'em. Bring it the fuck on.

And then, right as I was lining up at the start for another sprint, I noticed something. My shoelace was untied.

Oh, I thought.

I went to bend over—and I couldn't.

I couldn't move an inch.

"Stop stalling, Wiley!" the guys shouted, laughing. "We know your big ass getting tired!"

I could feel my muscles straining, struggling to move.

Come on, I tried to command my body. *It's simple! Tie your shoe!*

Nothing. I was a cement block. The only part of me that could move was my eyeballs. Looking panicked at my teammates, then back down at those fucking shoelaces, which I couldn't tie.

Suddenly, the laughter stopped.

"Wiley? You alright, dog?"

My teammates laid me down on my back. The trainers rushed over. I wasn't alright. Not even close.

An X-ray and an MRI later, I found out I had ruptured two disks in my back. I would need surgery, followed by months of rehab.

Forget about keeping up with the LBs and the DBs. Forget about making it to the top of the dunes at Manhattan Beach. Two months from the most important season of my life, I couldn't even move. I'd be lucky if I was able to run at all by the time it started.

My first contract had allowed me to get my family out of the hood, but don't forget how fleeting success in the NFL is. The average career length of a pro player is 3.3 years. *Total.*

Guess what? I had just finished my third year. We're all just a single injury—a single untied shoelace—away from never playing again. From the rich side of Rosecrans Avenue back to the *other* side of Rosecrans Avenue.

Suddenly, I was back at the bottom of the hill, and the top looked farther away than it ever had before.

NOW THE STAKES were even higher, because I wasn't only fighting for my mama, my dad, my sister, and my grandma. I had a baby daughter too. My own life. My own responsibility. My own flesh and blood.

Her name was Morocca. I was desperate to give her the opportunities I'd never had growing up.

I met Morocca's mom in the off-season before my second year with Buffalo. I was back in LA for the summer, went with a couple of my boys to a reggae festival at UCLA.

Now, I like reggae, but let's be real here—Bob Marley ain't dropped a record in thirty years. You think I'm really going for the music? Hell naw! For reggae fanatics, that place was Rasta heaven. For me and everyone else, it was a mackin' fest.

I was making the rounds, dealing with all the pretenders who suddenly realized they had gone to high school with me, or knew me from back in the Crenshaw days when I'd work out at a gym called Black Diamond.

"Oh really?" I'd say politely, creating my own custom version of Andre 3000's iconic "Elevators" song. "Yeah, yeah, of course."

They may have had my ears, but they didn't have my eyes. The whole time I'd be scanning the crowd, looking for someone I *really* wanted to talk to.

That's when I spotted an old acquaintance of mine.

"Oh, hey, Jen, what's up?"

And *that's* when I spotted her friend, who I had never met before. "OH HELLO!"

Was it me, or was I talking too loud, even for a reggae festival?

Kim had an artsy vibe, pretty, with mocha-brown skin and curly hair. But most important wasn't what she looked like but what she had to say. We talked for a second and it was like she knew how to check off every single box I was looking for.

She was from up north in Palo Alto, a different, intriguing place that was off the beaten path.

Check.

She was in college, not some wannabe LA model or actress or something.

Check.

Her parents were together and had been happily married thirty years and counting.

Ooooh! Double check!

It felt like I had met a Huxtable. She represented not just everything I wanted in another person, but everything I wished I *could be*.

See, as much as I liked dating—and yeah, I did love to date—it was never just about hooking up. I was a die-hard romantic, always searching for my soul mate, always wanting to fall in love, and fall hard. My boys liked to call me a sucker for love, always wanting me to play hard to get, make the girls chase it. But what was the fun in that? I *liked* being in love!

I *liked* that feeling like you always wanted to be with someone, like they were the most important thing in the universe, like you lived and breathed only for them. I liked it back in Buffalo when all my teammates would make fun of me for cakin' with the ladies, taking them out for long dinners and conversations instead of drinks and partying. And I liked it back when I got engaged my senior year at Columbia, thinking—briefly—that all I wanted was to commit to a single special person before my NFL career even began.

And recently, I'd decided I liked something else too—I liked the idea of having a kid. A couple of my good friends from high school had just had kids themselves. Neither one of them was married, but fatherhood had changed them in amazing ways. Matured them, deepened their relationships with everyone around them, made them engaged with life on a whole new level.

And, I mean, if these knuckleheads could do it, so could I, right?

All I needed was the woman to have one with. Someone who checked all the boxes—both as a companion and as a future mother for my child.

So when Kim walked into the restaurant for our first date wearing this perfect white tennis-skirt outfit, it was over. I know, I know. Sounds crazy, right? But think about it. Kim in that outfit symbolized everything I had always fantasized about growing up. I ain't talking about sex, I'm talking about being with someone normal, someone stable. She was the picture of the dream woman I had conjured up on my walks to Yee's with Jabari.

Seeing her that night felt like a fairy tale. Inner-city boy meets suburban tennis girl. *We gonna fall in love and she gonna teach me to ride horses!*

And that's exactly what it was at first—minus the horses, unfortunately.

Even for a guy like me, who admittedly loved falling in love, I fell *hard*. I started having to go back to Buffalo for OTAs, Organized Team Activities, and I asked Kim to come with me. That was a *big* step, and we both knew it, so we took it slow. Not moving in permanently at first, but to give it a try, just to see how she liked it.

Being in school, she was at a time in her life when she was trying to figure out what came next. For me that transition had been pretty simple—I got drafted, and my life was opened up to an amazing new world. But she didn't have a path laid out for her like that. She had to find that world all on her own. Having someone you love to find it with—me—made that process a lot less scary.

Right before my season started, she moved out to Buffalo for good, leaving school behind. We had some great times in there, don't get me wrong. But we were young, and, to be perfectly frank, I had no idea what the hell I was doing or how to handle it, and it showed.

Over the past year, I had grown really used to my ways. I'd practice, I'd work out, I'd come home and listen to my music. Now when I wanted to listen to music, Kim would be there. Maybe she didn't want to listen to music, maybe she had a headache.

Alright then, I guess I'll listen to music on my headphones.

Headphones? Why aren't you paying attention to me?

Oh, so now I gotta pay attention to you? I thought you had a headache?

My forty-year-old self would've known how to handle stuff like that better. My forty-year-old self learned that even when it feels like you've won an argument, you still lose—because the other person in the relationship ends up feeling like crap.

Not my twenty-three-year-old self. To him, this was another Rubik's Cube he didn't know how to solve. Instead of learning to adapt, he was pulling off the stickers, trying to reconfigure the whole puzzle.

Instead of changing myself, I tried to change her.

I was so eager to be in love, so excited to have that suburban dream, that I moved too close too fast. And she was way too far from home, far from her parents, her friends, her center of gravity. Stuck in Buffalo, where if you were black, the first question was always, "What player you dating?"

She was isolated, the relationship was crumbling, and—to top it off—she was pregnant.

In February, soon after the end of my second season, she gave birth to Morocca. By then, Kim was already back home in Palo Alto with her parents. I flew there for the birth of our daughter. It was a

NEVER SHUT UP   141

strange feeling, a blend of the most pure joy and love I had ever experienced when our daughter was born—and the knowledge that my future with her mother was uncertain at best.

But any doubts I felt, any drama, melted away immediately the moment I saw our baby girl. She was big and gorgeous, a beautiful butterball. She was perfect. She had my mother's eyes.

And all I could think was that everything I did, from here on out, I'd be doing for her. Everything I'd ever wanted when I was growing up, I would provide her. Any way I had been wronged, I would make right for her. All the struggles I had been through, I would channel into wisdom, into hard work, to give her the life I'd always wanted for myself.

Then, right on the cusp of my contract year, my back injury threatened to take it all away.

AFTER THE SURGERY, it felt like someone sawed off the lower half of my body, then stitched it back on with ragged edges. The pain was dull but constant, and it felt like the signals from my brain were disconnected from everything waist down, like someone hung a sign up on me that said "Service Interrupted."

The doctors told me not to move my legs, but I didn't really have a choice. Every single one of my signals was turned off, a bunch of wires just cut.

I had the surgery in Buffalo, far from my friends and family on the West Coast. My boy Matt Lenzen, my old buddy from back in the Columbia days, worked in Pennsylvania in sales and marketing. He had been out of football for a few years, but he'd had back surgery before. The biggest operation I'd ever had was a tonsillectomy, and at least that got me some ice cream when we were done.

"Dude, I'm coming," Matty L told me on the phone. "I'll work from your place, maybe I can commute, whatever. I'm gonna get you through this rehab."

I wasn't about to say no.

We started the process as soon as I got home—with my stairs.

"Alright, dude," he said. "First things first. We gotta get you up those steps to your bedroom."

With one hand I held on to the railing, with my other I held on to him. Every inch, every centimeter was a battle. Those ten steps felt like they took thirty minutes to climb.

When I got to the top, I started to cry.

"Don't worry," Matty said. "We're not even on day one. It'll get better."

"It's cool," I said, catching my breath. "I'm fine."

I wasn't. I started crying again.

"Don't worry, man," he said. "We got this."

I stood at the top of those steps and looked down to the bottom. Not exactly the sand dunes of Manhattan Beach. A few days ago, I could've taken all ten of those at once, jumped right from the top all the way to the bottom without thinking twice. Now? Those tens steps were my whole world.

The headlines in all the papers said, "Bruce Smith's Successor Has Back Surgery."

That was *me* they were talking about. The papers acted like they didn't even know my name, but I was right on the verge of being my *own* Bruce Smith, making a name for myself that no one would ever forget. And now this? Why was it happening now? Why not six months ago, way before my contract year, when I would've had all the time in the universe to heal and get stronger?

Maybe success wasn't in the cards for me. Maybe this was as good as it was gonna get—me, leaning on my friend to barely make it to the top of ten steps.

I gave myself the day to feel sorry for myself. The next day I got into rehab and back to work.

My parents, my sister, my baby girl—they were all counting on me to nail my contract year. With less than two months to go before our first game, that meant I couldn't just work hard, I needed to work fast too.

I couldn't afford to be satisfied making "progress"—I wanted it all, like one of those old game shows with the shopping cart where you get a few minutes to fill it up with whatever you can get your hands on. You ain't happy with a few bags of chips and a couple toys—you want *everything*.

On my first day of training camp, I hobbled into the training room past about ninety cut-up, swole dudes. A lot of them didn't even have contracts yet, and many of them would end up getting cut from the final roster. But they were healthy, they were getting better in practice every single day.

Me? I was hurting.

Fuck it, I thought. *Gotta keep going. Gotta get everything.*

The trainers had to help me sit down and open and close my legs. They started me on the most elementary exercises ever. Nothing but a rubber ball that weighed less than a pound between my legs.

"Can you lift it?"

Meanwhile, out on the field there are helmets clashing, bodies crashing, dudes balling out left and right.

"Good! Maybe we can move up to a three-pound ball next time!"

The first day they actually let me train outside was like my own personal Super Bowl, I was that damn excited. Just because I got to go outside! They took me to the sidelines, far away from the action on the field. I was in tennis shoes, everyone else was in cleats, but still—I was outside, this was real progress.

"What are we doing?" I asked the trainers.

"We want you to walk."

"Walk?"

"Yeah. See if you can make it to the end zone."

Shit. Of course I made it to the end zone. Did I have to stop a few times along the way? Absolutely.

It was painful, it was frustrating, but every single day I improved. Thirty yards without stopping turned into fifty yards turned into a hundred yards. A walk turned into a baby jog turned into a run. Slowly your nerves start to wake up, your muscle memory gets sharper, your ankles and knees say, "Oh, you want to use me again after all these weeks!"

That first day they let me put my cleats back on, that was like music. The clacking of the spikes against concrete, it was like the song from *Jaws*.

Duh-nuh. Duh-nuh. Duh-nuh . . .

You know that giant shark's about to attack. Hit the grass, everything goes quiet, and if you're in that water, you better swim like crazy to get out of my way.

Even as I got better, even as I got faster, every now and then I'd step and feel a jolt of pain shoot from my leg right up my back, like a bolt of electricity through my sciatic nerve.

"How you feel?" they'd say.

"Oh, I'm *gooooood*," I'd lie.

Just get me balling on that damn field, I'd think, that's all I want.

Did I feel 100 percent? Absolutely not. It still felt like my spark plugs were dead, like I'd try turning the ignition and instead of the roar of the engine all I'd hear was a click, click, click. But it didn't matter. Everything was riding on this year. Everything. It was now or never.

Finally, after weeks and weeks of step after step—walking, then running, then putting my cleats on, then putting my uniform on, observing practice, limited practice, hitting the sled harder and harder and harder—with a dozen days to go before our first game of the season, I heard those magic words from my trainers.

"Wiley's full go!"

"Handcuffs off!" the coaches shouted.

"Aw shit," the players said. "Wiley's back!"

That's right—my back was *back*.

I put my hand in the dirt. I looked up. I was lined up across from the big boys again. They empathized with what I had been through, sure. But this was business. Now they wanted to kill me all over again.

I wouldn't have it any other way.

SOON AFTER MOROCCA was born, I had brought Kim and our new baby back to Buffalo. It was spring, I had just finished my second season, and we decided to give living together one more try.

We glossed over our past and gave into our love for Morocca. We thought she could be the glue that held us all together.

But there was more than that. When I said I wanted to give my daughter an ideal childhood, I was talking about more than material wealth or living in the right neighborhood. I was talking about stability. My parents had done everything they could just short of being legally married to give me a steady two-parent home to grow up in. They sacrificed their own personal freedoms to give me and my sister an upbringing that most people in the hood never had.

And now here I was, with more financial resources than my mama and dad had ever dreamed of, and I couldn't make things work with my own daughter's mom?

To hell with that. I owed it to Morocca to do everything I could to stay with Kim.

Unfortunately, everything I could do wasn't good enough.

Late at night, after another argument with Kim, I'd be up on the phone with my sister, still insisting it wasn't over.

"I don't care what it takes, Tiki," I said. "I don't care if I gotta be miserable for the rest of my life, I'll be with Kim forever. That's it. I can't lose my daughter."

"I understand, Teddy Bear," she said, using the same old nickname she'd had for me since we were kids. "I know you wanna do the right thing. But Morocca won't be happy if you and Kim ain't happy. You gotta think of her."

Tiki was right. This wasn't the Huxtables and riding horses together with Kim in her white tennis outfit. This was real life.

In May, Kim moved back to her parents' house in California— and took our daughter with her.

I was devastated. I didn't know how, I didn't care what it took, but I had to be with my daughter.

THE FIRST GAME of my contract year, the biggest season of my life, in my very first start in the League, all the hard-earned confidence of my rehab ran into a big-ass mountain of reality.

His name was Eddie George.

We were playing the Tennessee Titans at home on *Monday Night Football*. Third damn play. They were deep in their end zone, we were all lined up, and I saw their center's finger twitch, just like Bruce had taught me.

Bam! I took off, came around the corner, past their tackle, heading straight for their quarterback, Steve McNair—when Eddie chip-blocked me. Now an ordinary chip block is no big deal—just a quick hit by a running back to stall you before they keep running their route downfield.

Except this was no ordinary chip. It was a solid granite boulder.

Eddie was six foot three and 235 pounds, a giant for a running back, and he knocked my first-year-starting, back-surgery-recovering ass all the way into the twelfth row.

Blah-dah!

As big as he was, before the injury I would've been able to brace myself, fight the block, shake it off after. Not now. It was right back to Service Interrupted. I picked myself up off the ground, and I played the game—but I was flooring it with no gas left in my tank, just trying to keep the lower half of my body stitched together with the rest of me.

In those first few weeks, I had only one sack. One sack. At that rate, I'd be lucky if Buffalo re-signed me at the end of the season, much less trigger a bidding war across the NFL.

In my sixth week, Ted "Mount" Washington finally confronted me as we were boarding the team's plane.

"Wiley, what the fuck is wrong with you? We didn't get rid of Bruce for *this*."

Now Ted, the same gigantic dude who kept $900,000 worth of checks tucked away in McDonald's wrappers, was the sweetest, kindest guy ever. But he'd also talk the truth to you right to your face, same as my grandma, and he gave me his own kind of Ted Talk.

"You over here moping all the time," he said, shaking his head. "Fix your face and fix yourself!"

He was right, but I didn't know what to say—or what to do. Over the next few weeks I kept trying to improve, to get healthy, but if anything I felt like I got worse. My body still wasn't right, my spark plugs still weren't firing, and my confidence was suffering because of it. I was normally a positive, confident person, but I started to drag. Like flashing back to those dark days sitting in my living room, thinking, when I was a freshman in high school.

Finally, I decided to turn to the team's other starting D-end, Phil Hansen. Not only did he play my same position, but he was a veteran. In the League for nine years, he'd been through it all—and I knew he wouldn't clown me the way Ted liked to. Phil was patient, a good listener. With him, I could be honest, even vulnerable.

We were sitting next to our lockers after practice when I decided to take the plunge.

"Phil," I said, "I don't feel like I'm getting better."

"I hear ya, man," Phil said. "You wanna sit down and watch some extra film? Let's do it."

"Thanks, man," I said. "But it's my back—it's my body."

I hated the way I sounded when I said that. So sorry, so pathetic. Like every kid who ever whined that they "would've made it" if it weren't for X, Y, and Z. Like I was full of nothing but excuses. But Phil didn't judge me. Not for a second.

"Right," he said. "I totally get it."

Then:

"You know what? Come by my house after practice. I got a guy. He'll make you better."

Shit, I thought. That took a turn.

"A guy? What you mean, Phil?" I said. "What guy?"

"Yeah, trust me. Just don't say anything, okay? You can't tell *anyone.*"

Motherfucker. Was this some Lyle Alzado shit? Was he gonna hit me with some steroids?

No way. This was *Phil.* He wasn't into any of that stuff . . . Was he?

I got to his house after practice, knocked on his door. He opened it slowly, looked out at me.

"Don't say *anything,* you got me?"

"Look," I said nervously. "I won't say anything, okay?"

He nodded, stepped aside, and let me in.

Standing at the end of the hall was a white guy, lean and muscular with perfect posture. The kind of guy who used to play Division II basketball and currently dominated his rec league. Phil's guy.

"I got my own PT."

Holy shit. Phil had a physical therapist. Not just *a* physical therapist, but his *own* physical therapist.

Now, that might not sound like such a big deal today. These days, everyone has their own guy they train with during the off-season—or even during the regular season. Everyone has an expert, everyone has a guru like Alex Guerrero, a swami they could never live without. But back then, in 2000?

That shit was totally taboo. I mean, maybe not steroids-level taboo, but still. Each team had its own guys, and you were supposed to use *those* guys, end of story, no second opinions allowed.

Well, I needed a second opinion. I had been walking, I had been running, I had even been tackling, but it still didn't feel like *me.* It felt like 70 percent of me.

This guy—Phil's guy—took that 70 percent and turned it into

110. He went beyond all the generic meat-and-potatoes stuff I got from the Bills, all the standard building your mass and adding flexibility, and added a bunch of alternative stuff I had never even heard of before. Working on nerve sensitivity, my proprioception and movement in space.

Did I keep doing the normal stuff with the Buffalo staff? Sure. But then I'd do a hand-off and head right over to Phil's guy.

And I kept my word. The Bills never knew.

In week ten, after more than half the season had already slipped through my fingers, I finally got my second sack of the year in a 16–3 win over the Patriots.

Let that sink in a second. In the biggest year of my professional career, the year I was supposed to finally inherit the mantle from Bruce Smith and prove to the NFL that I deserved a big-time contract, by my tenth game of the season I had recorded only two sacks. Two. That's it.

But you know what? That's all it took. After that second sack, the floodgates opened.

Over the next seven games, I racked up an additional 8.5 sacks. That brought my total on the year to 10.5. That was more than *double* my output the year before. Best of all? GMs around the League knew I had started the season recovering from a back injury, so the fact that I turned it on later in the year only confirmed that once I was healthy, I was unstoppable. The raw physical potential I had brought to the League four years earlier seemed perfectly primed to explode.

Just like that, I was one of the top young D-ends in the NFL.

After all the drama, the injury, the surgery, and the slow, painful recovery, my contract year was a smash success. There was one small issue.

I still had to *get* a contract.

Free agency started at midnight on March 1. The clock was ticking fast, and it only sounded like one thing in my mind:

Cha-ching!

MY THIRD SEASON, after what felt like never-ending legal battles, I finally managed to bring Morocca back to live with me in Buffalo—at least for a few months.

The summer without seeing her every day had been hellish. Of course I had the back surgery and my recovery—but to also have my own baby girl living thousands of miles away from me, not even knowing who her dad was? It was a nightmare.

I spent days crying in bed, talking on the phone to Tiki, to Jabari, to my honorary godmother from Columbia University, Jackie Blackett.

"I'll get back to her somehow," I'd say through my tears. "I'll figure it out, I *have to*."

Then, suddenly, fate smiled on me.

Kim had met someone new, and things were getting serious. She decided to move from her parents' place in Palo Alto to live with him in Baltimore. As she got established, it was decided that Morocca would come stay with me.

In September, my daughter came back to Buffalo, and back to me. During the week, I was like the NFL's very own Mr. Mom. I'd wake up first thing, feed her, get her ready for the day, and drop her off at daycare on my way to practice. After practice, I'd pick her up and bring her home, where her nanny would help me take care of her until we finally put her to bed.

Sometimes I'd handle chores around the house while the nanny played with Morocca, sometimes the nanny would do the cleaning up while I played with my daughter.

On weekends, though, when I wasn't playing in games, it was just the two of us—just me and Morocca.

My boys from the team would come over to chill, and I'd be sitting there feeding her applesauce in her high chair.

"What's up, Wiley?" they'd say to me. Then to my daughter, "Hey, Monky Monk."

At that point, Monky Monk—or "DJ Monky Monk," as I liked to call her—would typically fling her applesauce onto the floor for my three cats to fight over.

"Man," my friends would say, shaking their heads. "You all in, brah."

They were right. I was all in. It was one of the greatest times of my life.

By the time the season was over, Kim was settled in Baltimore and engaged to be married. DJ Monky Monk went back to live with her mom, and the legal battles—over money, over custody—continued, not ending until Morocca was eight years old.

Not having her with me was devastating, but that wasn't the death blow. What absolutely killed me was having to accept that she'd end up calling someone else "Dad." Kim's new husband. A great man, a great role model. But not me.

I would've done almost anything to change that, to not have to share that name with another guy. But my absolute priority, beyond everything else, was making life easier for Morocca. And if that meant I wouldn't be the only "Dad" in her life, I'd agree to it. I'd take a bullet for Monky Monk, I really would.

Through it all, I'd think back and remember those four months with my baby girl. Picking her up from daycare, wiping food off her chubby little face, holding her close to me. And I'd wish I could've stayed there, with her, forever.

THE NIGHT OF the start of free agency I was chilling at my teammate Sam Roger's mansion in Marina del Rey, one of LA's most gorgeous and exclusive beach communities.

First, because we were watching a Pay-Per-View fight on TV together.

Second, because he was cool about the whole free-agency thing. None of the giggling, nervousness, and wide-eyed wonder of my old friends back in the hood. No ex-ex-girlfriends and long-lost cousins showing up out of the blue hoping to collect on your big payday. Just some relaxed people who had been through the same exact free-agency experience themselves, getting ready to welcome me to the family.

Third—do I like this house? Because I'm about to get me something like this.

As soon as the clock struck midnight on the East Coast, the feeding frenzy—or what I *hoped* would be a frenzy—would begin. Any and every team in the League looking for a young, explosive D-end about to reach his prime would dial up my agent, Brad Blank, same guy I had when I graduated college. And Brad would promptly tell them I was gonna cost *a lot*.

Of course, even with my breakout contract year, there were no guarantees. A few nights earlier my entire career flashed before my eyes at Jerome Bettis's birthday party in Los Angeles.

I had driven my tricked-out stretch Excursion there—when I make up for taking the bus as a poor kid, I *really* make up for it, alright?—and when I got out of the party, the valets seemed to have conveniently removed all the TVs from inside my truck.

That put me in a little bit of a quandary.

Normally, I would've made a big fucking deal out of some dudes jacking all my TV sets. But this was days before free agency. Teams don't only look at your skills and your stats, they also look at your character. Or more specifically, "Is this the kind of dude who's gonna embarrass our whole organization by getting into fistfights at clubs?"

So I played it cool, told the nice valets that I was simply gonna sit back and wait until my televisions were kindly returned to me. Unfortunately, though, a few other cats who also got robbed weren't that chill.

Before I knew it, a crowd had formed, fists were flying, and sirens were wailing in the night.

"Officers, I didn't do a thing!" I told the cops. "Not a thing!"

Didn't matter. They cuffed me and tossed me in the patrol car.

Now I was thinking two things: One, where I came from, a cop cuffs you and takes you in, you don't know *what* they gonna do to your sorry ass. Two, whatever they did, I hoped to God it didn't show up on the news, because I would be *fucked*.

We arrived at the station. The cop looked at me, shook his head—and took off my handcuffs.

"Don't worry—you're good," he said. "When we see a celeb caught up in something that wasn't their fault, we try to pull them away from the scene before it becomes a thing."

He patted me on the back.

"Welcome to the Hollywood Division, where we have seen it all."

Fuck that—now *I* had officially seen it all. A cop helping me get *out* of trouble? Forget about the game within the game—I was officially playing in a whole other league.

Now, a couple days later at my friend's mansion in Marina del Rey, I was finally right on the cusp of joining that league—literally—for a whole lot more money.

My agent called. Just minutes before 9:00 p.m. LA time—
midnight on the East Coast.

"You know the rules," he told me. "Keep that phone on, and let's
get going."

"No problem," I said.

The clock hit 9:01.

Bbrrrrrrrriiiiiiinnnnnnng!

I rushed outside and picked up.

"I already got three calls," he said. "San Diego, Oakland, and
Pittsburgh."

"Heck yeah!" I shouted.

"Alright, I'll call you back."

The clock hit 9:08.

Bbrrrrrrrriiiiiiinnnnnnnnnnnng!

"Alright," he said. "You're getting on a plane to San Diego first
thing in the morning. After that you're going to Oakland and Pittsburgh."

The trips didn't mean I was signed. It didn't even mean I had any
offers. It was part of the free agency dog-and-pony show, meeting
with the coaches, taking a tour, smiling, nodding, and shaking
hands—all as, behind the scenes, the teams were making offers and
jockeying for position. And hopefully bidding each other up.

"Don't worry," my agent said. "The numbers are gonna be good.
This is gonna move fast. You know what? I don't even think you're
gonna make it off the West Coast."

San Diego, I thought. So close to home. If I ended up there, I'd
barely be a two-hour drive from all my friends and family. But Oakland wasn't too far either—and if the money was right . . .

I got to the Chargers facility bright and early the next day. They
gave me the same tour they'd give a fan who won a radio-station

contest. *This is the locker room, where the players change. This is the weight room, where the players lift weights.*

Man, I don't give a damn about your weight room, I thought. *I'm trying to take care of my family! I want an offer!*

I met with the Chargers' general manager, John Butler—the team's official dealmaker, who had also been *Buffalo's* GM when the Bills signed me four years earlier, and the very first guy I'd spoken to on the phone after I got drafted. This dude didn't just dig me, he had a *history* of betting on me.

I kept my poker face on the whole time. I did the smiles and I did the nods and I handled my business.

And still—no offer.

Then just like that, they put me in a car to the airport and told me to enjoy my trip to Oakland.

Shit!

As soon as I got to the terminal and away from any San Diego spies, I gave my agent a call.

"They didn't even offer me!" I said.

"I know," he said. "That's them on the other line. I'll call you back."

He called me back.

"They offered twenty million dollars."

"Let's do this!!!" I shouted.

"No, no!" he said. "Come on, we're not taking the first offer. This is a negotiation! You're getting on that plane to Oakland."

"Alright," I sighed. "If you say—"

"Wait, that's them on the other line. I'll call you back."

I'd barely hung up the phone when it rang again.

Bbrrrrrrrriiiiiiinnnnnnng!

"They're at twenty-five million dollars now. I told them you're going to Oakland."

"What??" I said, panicked. "That was like three minutes and five million dollars! Shouldn't we take it?"

"Trust me," he said. "This is why you pay me, to do this. Wait—that's them."

Every time the phone rang it felt like another million dollars. We finally reached $30 million.

"*It's gotta be time!*" I said. "I don't want to lose it!"

"We won't!" he said. "I'll know when it's time from the tone of their voice. Hold on!"

It was San Diego. They were up to $32 million—an increase, but they were slowing down. One thing was clear though: they didn't want me on that flight to Oakland.

Bbrrrrrrriiiiiiiinnnnnnnnnnnnng!

"I just talked to Oakland," my agent said. "They know you're at thirty-two million, but they still want you to fly up."

"What? At thirty-two?" I said. "That's real leverage. What about Pittsburgh?"

"I'll call you back," he said.

Click!

The next time he called back, San Diego was at $40 million.

"Forty million dollars?" I said.

"Forty million dollars," he said.

"Is this it?"

"This is it."

I was quiet for a second.

"How you know it can't get up to forty-one?" I asked.

After all that, suddenly I wasn't satisfied with forty million—*double* their initial offer.

"Trust me," he said. "You pay me for this moment. This is the moment."

He was right. It was.

I never left for Oakland. I got back in the exact same car that had brought me to the airport and went back to the Chargers' facility to sign my new contract—$40 million over six years. The biggest contract in Chargers *history*.

But I'll be honest with you. After all that suspense, all that buildup and anticipation, signing the contract itself felt like a letdown. Of course I was thrilled to sign—I had been waiting for this moment forever, it felt like. My entire life, really. Forty million dollars wouldn't just mean that I was set. It wouldn't just mean that my mama, my dad, my sister, and my daughter would be taken care of. This was *generational* wealth. It meant that even my *kids'* kids would begin their lives in a better place than I had. I had just moved the starting line for generations of my family to come.

But my fantasy of what it would feel like had been so big, so spectacular, there was no way the reality could live up to it.

I got to the San Diego office, and it looked like a pretty normal office. They gave me a pen, and it was a pretty normal pen. They showed me the contract, and except for a couple extra commas and zeroes, it was a pretty normal pile of papers.

The oxygen I was breathing was the same oxygen I had been breathing a few hours ago. The sunlight was the same sunlight that had been shining on me earlier that morning.

The people with me when I signed, even a lot of them were the same. My same old GM from Buffalo, who was now GM at San Diego, had brought a lot of guys with him, coaches, scouts, assistants. All guys I knew, all the same.

There was no bolt of lightning from the sky. No earthquake or thunder or grand revelation.

It just was.

Then I called my parents and my sister. I told them the news in detail. And I thought back to everything we had shared together as I grew up. My mama letting me snuggle up next to her in bed on week-end mornings. My dad coming and taping all my games. My sister always standing up for me on the playground every day after school.

They'd always been there for me. And when I talked to them that day, not *one* of them asked me how much I signed for. They didn't ask how many years it was for, what my signing bonus would be—nothing.

All they cared about was me, what my experience had been—and the fact that now they could come to every single one of my home games.

It brought tears to my eyes.

I looked up at the blue California sky and realized it was brighter than I had ever seen it before.

CHAPTER SEVEN

DAT DUDE GOES TO SAN DIEGO

IT WAS **9:30** a.m. on game day in San Diego—*any* home game— which meant the Dat Dude Circus had officially arrived at my house.

Cars and trucks parked three or four deep in my driveway and lining my street. Parents, sister, uncles, cousins, second cousins, long-lost friends, and future ex-girlfriends, at least twenty people, usually more, most of them driving in from LA for the day. Maybe some cats I played high school ball with, maybe a few of my daddy's old work buddies from the Post Office, maybe a few random strangers they picked up along the freeway, slowing down their rides, rolling down their windows, shouting at the top of their lungs.

"Anyone wanna come to a football game!? Qualcomm Stadium! My son's playing! Number 75! Free tickets!"

(Of course they weren't close to free, but no one paid any attention to silly details like that at the Dat Dude Circus.)

My mama, Tiki, and my niece, Charne, all in their custom blue, yellow, and white bedazzled Chargers jerseys with my number on them. My mama's jersey had "Dat Mama" emblazoned on the back; she'd already become a celebrity in her own right at the games, leading cheers and raising a ruckus from my own personal seats in row 17 on the 50-yard line, right behind our bench. My daddy was just as proud in his own quiet way, still that same guy who'd showed up at all my peewee games with his camcorder.

It was early but the liquor was flowing, people offering me sips of orange juice with who knows *what* in it—all of which I politely declined. Master P blasting on the sound system.

People hanging in the kitchen having breakfast or watching the pregame show in the living room with my dad. People out back, grilling, playing by the pool, or shooting hoops on my full-size court. People talking shit about how great I was gonna be later that day, self-promoting their family like a bunch of early LaVar Balls.

"You gonna get two sacks today, man! I know it!"

"Kansas City think they can stop you? Ain't *no one* can stop you!"

I was crying laughing because it was good to feel the love. Suddenly my life had become a grown-up, big-time NFL version of my childhood. Surrounded by family and friends, eating breakfast before my peewee games, everyone getting hyped—except now there was a guest house, a swimming pool with palm trees coming out of it, and a court (with bleachers!) that could convert from basketball to tennis to volleyball, and let me tell you, Doug Flutie would come over and *destroy* people in basketball, the first dude who really earned the nickname "Dougie McBuckets."

But I also had a job to do—a job that supported all this. And my job was playing football.

My first year in San Diego, my teammates had given me a new nickname, "Dat Dude." It was a name that put me at the center of our world. A name that could mean anything to anybody. Having a lot going on in my life—from DJ'ing parties to supporting charities— had always fueled my fire. I was a guy who *thrived* on more activity, who worked even harder the more I took on. That's what "Dat Dude" was all about—on an even bigger level.

"Who's that guy in the game getting all those sacks, then dancing like crazy on the sidelines?"

"Oh, that's dat dude."

"Who's the guy who started that foundation to help underprivileged kids?"

"Yep, that's dat dude."

"Who's the guy who showed up at the event in his Ferrari, ordered three pomegranate margaritas, spun a few records, and now he's making the keynote speech?"

"Dat dude yet again."

I had become the consummate franchise player, doing everything, being everywhere. Fully immersed in San Diego Chargers' life, working my ass off on the field, connecting with all the fans at events, using my brand-new foundation to support education in my community, and having a whole lot of fun doing it. The team even named me Man of the Year for how active I was in the city.

We literally turned it into a business, with Tiki taking point on the merch and two of our teenage cousins acting as all-purpose utility men—the Nizzles, we called them, in honor of Snoop Dogg. She'd send the Nizzles out to the parking lot after games to sell official Wild Style T-shirts at twenty dollars a pop to help support my foundation.

With me taking photos and signing autographs nearby, we couldn't crack the boxes open fast enough. Anytime I made an appearance at an event, Tiki would send out word.

"Activate the Nizzles!"

I loved everything I did. It made me a better person *and* player, but football was always my top priority. Not everyone around me understood that.

As much as I loved entertaining people at my house, I made damn sure I didn't buy no huge mansion. Sure, I had a gigantic back-yard where everyone could chill, but the house itself? That was a nice little two-bedroom ranch, one room for me and another one for Morocca when she visited, because as much as I loved my extended, *extended* LA family, I knew that if I had a big-ass house, none of those dudes would ever leave. They'd set up camp, invite a few friends, and live off the fat of the land for weeks.

Shit, when I first went house hunting in San Diego, the girl I brought along for the ride asked the real estate agent when *we* could sign the sales contract. We. This is someone I had been with for a month! She wasn't some kind of shark—just a normal, grounded person. But get people close enough to smell that NFL jackpot, and they can change quick.

On those San Diego game days, I wanted to be Dat Dude for everyone who came over. Dat Dude who bought everyone tickets, who covered all the food and drinks, who kept the music blasting and the pool heated to just the right temp. Dat Dude who slapped all the backs and never seemed to have a care in the world. Who just kept the circus going on and on forever.

But I also had to be Dat Dude who got ready to put his body on the line a few hours later. Who had to focus and prepare. Who had to go out and earn all the money everyone spent.

On those Sunday mornings, sometimes I felt like my guests—the family members I'd barely even met before, the friends of the friends of the friends—didn't really care about that part of me. The part that had a job to do. They just wanted to use me. They just wanted the scene. Hell, sometimes they just wanted to borrow money we both knew they'd never pay back. But I knew what was up, and I never, ever let my guard down.

A couple hours before the game, I'd get ready to head out to the stadium. People would pour out my front door as I got into my car. My sister blowing her air horn, streamers popping off everywhere, folks waving and laughing and wishing me luck.

I'd hit the highway traffic and blend in immediately, just one car in a thousand. Just another dude going to work on a Sunday afternoon.

MY WHOLE FIRST season in San Diego I played with fire in my foot.

It happened in the last week of training camp, days before our first game against Washington. A normal play in practice, getting double-teamed the same way I had a hundred times before, using the same twisting technique I had used a hundred times before.

Except this time, my foot made a sound.

POP!

And just like that, it was broken. A fracture in my fifth metatarsal, something they call a Jones fracture. I had to have surgery in week one of the season, and doctors put a metal screw in my bone that I have to this day.

The team? They were panicking. They had just made me the highest-paid player in Chargers *history*, and now their multimillion-dollar investment was out for at least half the season with a hunk of metal in his foot? San Diego had drafted well that off-season, picking up Drew Brees and LaDainian Tomlinson, plus a few other studs in free agency, and the pressure was on, especially with an all-new front office almost entirely imported from Buffalo. They needed to show results. This was supposed to be a big year. And then just like that . . .

POP!

But me, I was still wearing that same cape I had put on to get over my back injury the year before. They weren't the only ones who had something to prove. I knew they bet the house on me, and I wanted that bet to pay off. If I was getting paid, I wanted to play.

Fuck being out for eight weeks, I told the trainers. I'll be back in two.

Say what?

Two weeks, I said. I only need one little thing—help me put out this fire in my foot.

Don't get me wrong—there was no way I had finished healing. But as far as I could tell that pin was holding everything in place structurally. I just had to get through the pain. Every second of every day, it was like there were actual flames eating away at the flesh inside my foot. I could visualize them charring my bones and joints.

My trainers were the ones with the bucket of water—literally and figuratively.

With a week to go before our third game, I spent every practice sitting on the sideline, watching, visualizing myself getting reps as I iced my foot in a bucket of ice water.

Then, only two weeks after my surgery, exactly like I promised, I suited up for our home game against Cincinnati. An hour before kickoff, they gave me a different kind of "ice bucket" for my fire foot. This one came at the tip of a needle, along with a healthy dose of shit they told me would make it feel better—without ever telling me what it was, which was standard practice back then.

I sat down on the trainer's table, and they took out the needle—or at least what they called a needle. This thing looked more like a baby's arm, it was so damn big.

Oh fuck! I thought.

Teammates walked by, smacking me on the back, trying to be positive.

"You got this, dog! You got this!"

Except I knew they were really thinking "*Shit*, I'm happy that ain't me."

I watched as the doc shoved it deep, deep into my inflamed joint. Past muscle, past cartilage, almost to the bone. It was like your first bite of ribs, and you're gnawing with your teeth, trying to get that meat—except it wasn't a damn rib, it was me!

He wiggled it around slowly, telling me to let him know when he reached the epicenter of pain. Meanwhile I was biting down on a towel, doing my best not to shriek like a little baby. Because this was the NFL, and we did *not* shriek in the NFL.

Finally, after an eternity, he found the center of the pain.

It improved, the pain went down. Except something still wasn't quite right. I could still feel it. They taped me up, I jogged out of the tunnel like everyone else, but it still felt off.

Game time. I ran out on the field for my first series—*okay*, I'm thinking, *I can definitely run, that seems fine, right?* I was picking up my assignments, but still something felt off.

Whistle blows for another play. An offensive lineman, big 340-pound dude named Willie Anderson, comes in high to block me. I see it, feel it, sense it—*he's coming in high, he's coming in high!*—so I duck low. Willie goes right by me. Nothing between me and their QB and I drive him into the ground.

Sack!

The adrenaline hits my foot like a crack of lightning.

POW-ZOW!

The pain vanishes, my confidence goes sky-high, and I think, *I can get a sack on one foot? We gonna be alright.*

Of course, the next day that fire came right back—*oh hello, remember me?*—and the process started all over again.

And that was how it went all season long. I'd spend the week watching practice and icing my foot, on game day I'd get the baby-arm needle from hell, then I'd go to work. I finished the season with 13 sacks, 2.5 more than the year before, and was named All-Pro and started in the Pro Bowl.

I didn't practice once the entire year. Not once.

I felt invincible. I had played the entire season on a single foot, and I had turned in the best performance of my life. Hell, only a year earlier, I had recovered from major back surgery in only six weeks and still went on to get double-digit sacks! But by cutting short my rehab and living off nothing but willpower, adrenaline, and lots of shots two seasons in a row, I had made a deal with the devil.

I just didn't know it yet.

I WAS ON PINS and needles when I met Junior Seau for the very first time.

You're talking about a linebacker who had been to the Pro Bowl ten times, who had been the NFL's Defensive Player of the Year *and* Man of the Year. Who I had grown up watching dominate as a college player at USC, who played D like me, who was *from* San Diego originally, a true hometown hero. This wasn't just Junior's defense. This was his city. This was his team.

And here I was coming in after one breakout year, and all of a sudden *I* was the highest-paid player in Chargers history. Somehow *I* was the big splash.

I was searching for my locker, finally found it in the back right corner, when all of a sudden behind me I heard:

"Buddddddddy!"

I turned around and there was Junior with a huge grin on his face. I caught my breath. What was he gonna say? Were we gonna be cool?

"Junior!" I said, as cheerfully as I could.

"Buddddddddy," he said, laughing. "Don't spend it all in one place."

Whew. I exhaled immediately. He could've just done the typical athlete thing, just a quick "What's up," but he did more than that. By making a joke about the elephant in the room, by embracing the obvious awkwardness, he actually got *rid* of the awkwardness. I was incredibly grateful.

I also learned one of his favorite Junior-isms: he called everyone—*everyone*—"buddy." Part of it was because he was friendly as hell. But part of it was because I don't think he could remember anyone's name. So to him, we all became "buddddddddy."

That's how it was with the players on the San Diego team, a tone completely set by him, the Chargers' consummate veteran. Professional, driven, highly focused, but also a band of brothers. Or in this case, a band of buddies. Guys who had a lot of fun with each other—but who'd also have a lot of fun fucking with you if you weren't careful. I fit right in.

Junior would invite a bunch of us out to dinner at his own restaurant, Seau's, and his mama would bring out trays heaped with rice and teriyaki island chicken that we'd absolutely destroy. The night would end, and I'd search for the bill.

"Buddy, we got it!" Junior would say. Guy couldn't say no to anyone.

But he had his ways of getting you back, alright.

My first day at camp, one of the players asked me if I wanted to join Junior's Breakfast Club. Sure, I figured. Who doesn't like breakfast?

"Naw, man," he said. "Not *that* kind of breakfast club. This is Junior's workout before the team workout. Every day at 5:00 a.m."

Shit, that was early. But I wanted to prove I deserved my contract. I wanted to earn my respect. So I was there the next day, bright and early at five in the morning. But I found out fast that the Breakfast Club wasn't just about working out—it was about *paying* out.

It started out normal enough, about fifteen of us doing superfast super sets together. Then I finished up a set on the bench, wiped it off, and headed to do pull-ups.

"Got 'em!!" one of the Clubbers shouted. "Wiley left the bench sweaty!"

"Budddddddy, that's a hundred bucks," Junior said, that undeniable smile on his face.

One hundred dollars?! For leaving a couple drops of sweat on the bench? Can I help it if I'm one sweaty motherfucker?

They'd get you for almost anything. You can't hit your ten reps, that's a hundred dollars. Forget to stack your weights, that's another hundred dollars. I swear they made up new rules as we went along. One thing's for certain though—if you got fined, you never broke that rule again.

By the end of the year, there must've been $10,000 in the pot. It made for a nice little postseason celebratory dinner for the members of the Club—and it also kept me focused and working out all season long, even if I couldn't practice because of my fire foot.

The longer I was in San Diego, the better we all got to know each other, the crazier it got.

At the Pro Bowl, Junior would nonchalantly ask me what room I was staying in at the hotel, so he could "stop by later to say hello." Uh-huh. Right. Next thing I knew, I'd be checking out and the concierge would present me with an entire *portfolio* of charges Junior billed directly to me at the pool. Somehow I'd bought drinks for everyone at the hotel—five times over.

"Buddddddddy," he'd say, with the sweetest smile, and just like that, you'd be asking him if he didn't want to charge dinner to your room too.

We'd go out at night, all the boys from the Breakfast Club, and he'd buy everyone rounds and rounds of tequila, daring you to keep up with him—then you'd find out the next day he was paying the bartender to serve him nothing but water the whole time. Didn't matter to Junior though—he'd still make your ass work out at 5:00 a.m.

I finally wised up and started doing more eating than drinking, but that didn't stop me from having my own adventures.

My second year of training camp, we were based on a small college campus. Now, training camps are a lot of hard work, but they can also be a hell of a lot of fun. After a late dinner with some teammates, I was driving back to my room with one of my boys in my Ford Excursion. Two in the morning, *bumping* Trick Daddy's "In Da Wind," I mean the bass literally rattling the entire steel frame of that big-ass truck.

Bummmmm Bum Bum Bummmmmmmmm!

My Excursion was brand-new, and when I bought it the dealer pulled me aside and gave me some friendly advice.

"This is one of the biggest trucks on the market, okay? That's a *lot*

of vehicle. It's gonna take longer to brake than you're used to. Be
careful."

I was extra careful—careful to turn that music up as loud as possible.

We had only about two blocks to drive that night, down a long
hill to get home, but about halfway there I suddenly sensed something was very, very wrong.

"Hold up," I said, squinting. "Why are we in the air?"

BOOM.

Just like that, we were no longer in the air—we were on top of a
parked Hyundai. Let me repeat: we were *on top* of a Hyundai.

I kept my foot on the gas, and then we were no longer on top of
the Hyundai, we were in front of it. Being the responsible citizen I
am, I pulled over and left a note on the windshield—or more accu-
rately, where the windshield *should've* been. Because all that shit was
gone.

"My bad," I wrote. "Call me."

I added my number, then drove my truck back to my place and
went straight to bed.

Knock knock knock knock!

Still groggy from sleep, I answered my door sometime after 4:00
a.m. It was a police officer and the head of team security.

Behind them, strewn down the street like a bunch of automotive
bread crumbs leading to my doorstep, was a long line of mufflers,
exhaust pipes, bumpers, and spark plugs stretching all the way back
to what was left of the Hyundai.

I took a deep breath and gave them my most winning, Junior
Seau–esque smile.

"So. You all get my note?"

———

THAT DEAL I made with the devil? It finally came due.

My back surgery in Buffalo and my broken foot in San Diego had taken a massive toll on my body. And over the next two years more injuries continued to pile up. In season two with the Chargers, I suffered what the team doctors initially diagnosed as a "bilateral groin sprain," which supposedly meant I had somehow sprained both sides of my groin.

In the off-season, I learned what really happened. I had torn my abdominal wall. After surgery to attach my hip to my abdominal muscles, the doctor visited me in the recovery room and looked me in the eye.

"That's the worst tear I've ever seen. I can't believe you played with that injury."

Neither could I. I had started the season healthy and racking up sacks faster and earlier than I ever had before, with three through the first three games—on track for a sixteen-sack season. I was even named AFC Defensive Player of the Week for the very first time. But after my injury in game four, I went on to have three more sacks the rest of the year.

I, the Chargers' marquee defensive end, had only six sacks that season—my lowest total since my third year of professional football.

In season three with San Diego, I got yet another injury, this time to my shoulder. It started out small, as a strained AC joint. But because I kept playing with it, because I put my career and my team before my health, by the time the season was over I had torn both my labrum and my rotator cuff, requiring yet another surgery. Not only that, but I finished the year with only three sacks.

That was my lowest output since zero sacks my rookie year, when

I hadn't even developed my pass-rush technique and I didn't even play much behind Bruce Smith. My huge sacrifice didn't amount to shit—except for more injuries.

But what was really different wasn't the injuries—I'd had injuries before, plenty of them. What was different was my ability to heal.

After I played my first season with the Chargers on one foot, I thought I could come back from anything. If I had a bad game, I'd figure out what went wrong, and the next time I'd do it better. And if I got hurt, I'd get surgery, rehab, and I'd come back, better than ever before.

I was like the Superman of getting better. Until all of a sudden I wasn't.

I tried everything. I worked with outside physical therapists, even my original combine trainer, Mike Boyle, who'd gotten me prepared for my Pro Day seven years earlier. I worked out like crazy, rehabbed like a madman. I had the big contract, but my attitude was nothing but fifty-third man on the roster—no star mentality, no entitlement at all, just working my ass off. But it didn't matter.

That move I used to make like clockwork? It started to get a little rusty. That running back I used to chase down? He just turned the corner for a first down. The QB I used to sack? He just got off the pass right as I was reaching out to grab his arm.

I was still defending the run like a beast—that never dropped off for me. But San Diego hadn't signed me for my run-stopping abilities, they signed me because of my speed and power. And boy, was my power feeling lonely. The speed was gone, that step was gone. The sacks were gone.

Every play I wasn't at my best started to erode my confidence. No confidence was fine, I could deal with that. But actively doubting myself was a whole lot worse.

Some of it was that I was getting older. I was almost thirty, playing a game where grown men—grown *young* men, in the prime of their lives—hit each other at top speed over and over and over again, and my body couldn't recover the way it used to. Some of it was the accumulation of injuries. But a lot of it was what I had done to myself—when I forced my body to come back way too fast from my injuries. Putting your team first might sound honorable, but it ended up being stupid—for both me and the Chargers.

To meet my new team's expectations—to meet my own expectations—I had pushed myself to the limits and notched the greatest season of my career. But I never really recovered.

For the first time, the pilot light was out, and there was no turning that motherfucker back on.

After the shoulder injury, LaDainian saw me working out in the weight room. Now, this was LT's third season, and he was already a beast, running with a fire, with a purpose, with a spark. The same kind of spark I used to have.

"Ay, Wiley," he said. "Why don't you look like you have fun no more?"

And I realized he was right—I wasn't having fun anymore. Not just in football, not just in my career, but in the rest of my life too. I wasn't dating or going to parties like normal. I was sinking back into something like my depression from high school, back when I would lie on our living room floor, the TV droning on in the background as I stared into space and lost myself in thought.

One night, the Monday after a game, I woke up around three in the morning. Like thousands of men and women every single night, I had to go to the bathroom.

There was one minor problem. I couldn't move my body.

I was hitting what we players called Toradol Tuesdays—that

horrific moment when all the drugs, all the painkillers we took to keep our bodies barely functioning during games, finally started to wear off and all that pent-up pain came crashing down.

Except now I wasn't just experiencing pain, I was experiencing complete system shutdown—in all but one critical organ, my bladder, which was demanding immediate action.

I tried to start small, take things slow. Let's try to roll over here, okay? Don't have to stand, don't even need to sit up. Just a roll, that's all I ask.

Nothing.

I rocked my body back and forth. Slightly at first, didn't want to be too ambitious, then faster, faster, faster, gaining more and more momentum until finally—finally—at last—*yes! I did it!*

I rolled over.

And I knew right then and there that that was the best I was going to do. Which left me with a quandary on my hands—or at least below the belt. My bladder wasn't gonna wait for the rest of my body to recover from football.

But no matter how bad it got, I couldn't let myself pee my bed—I just couldn't.

See, when I was growing up, I peed the bed all the time. I wanted to stop, of course; I hated being the pee boy. But I couldn't control it. I was cursed with what my family called the Wiley bladder, still have it to this day. I legit have to pee every eighteen seconds. Give or take a millisecond.

Finally Tiki, who shared the room with me back then, couldn't take it anymore.

"Teddy Bear, your nasty ass still peeing in the bed and you thirteen!?! What the hell is wrong with you!"

I hadn't peed my bed since. Now I was in my twenties, the Wiley bladder was about to explode and my body unable to move, and I could still hear her voice ringing in my ears. I had to do *something*. Just not . . . that.

Then I saw it. A solution. A plastic Tropicana miracle.

A half-full container of orange juice right next to my bed. A whole gallon, and close enough that even I could muster the energy to reach out a single hand, open my fingers, and take it in my grasp.

The first thing I thought was, *I don't want to waste all this orange juice.* So I actually tried to drink it. After two gulps that barely made a dent, with my bladder screaming in agony, I thought, I am absolutely gonna waste this orange juice.

I put my man in there and let go.

It was heaven. Pure relief spread over my body. I finished up, screwed the cap back on, and slept like I was thirteen years old all over again.

The next morning, my broken body, my bladder, and I woke up and got ready to destroy ourselves for football all over again.

I'D BEEN A DJ since the moment I got a tape deck at the age of eight. It was a Toshiba, with manual buttons that I could use to mix everything I recorded off the radio. Play, rewind, play, rewind, and the next thing you know I got my own custom DJ track.

I had music in my blood. My dad and my mama had a monumental record collection—took up almost our entire living room. Only a couch, a TV, a few of my trophies, and records, everything from Hall and Oates to Tom Tom Club—that was our living room. And I was not to touch *any* of it.

"Don't you *ever* scratch my records!" Mama yelled at me when she caught me spinning one of her albums.

"I ain't scratching them, Mama!" I tried to explain. "I'm staying in the groove! You don't understand! They just *call it* scratching!"

Next thing I knew, every single one of my parents' records was marked with their initials, which might as well have spelled out a simple phrase: "Stay the hell away."

So when I first started making NFL money back in Buffalo, you *know* what I was gonna do.

I got my own records, my own turntables, my own Triton keyboard and ASR-X beat machine—I mean some Dr. Dre–level equipment. Back in California over the off-season, I'd meet up with my old high school friends from FAY—that's "Fuck All Y'all," in case you needed reminding—and we'd rap, make beats, and write lyrics. Our shit was so good that when I got back to Buffalo, my teammates started coming over to make their *own* music. Now that stuff wasn't nearly as good, to be honest, but still—it was ours.

Next thing I did was take on the Bills' pregame track. When I got there in 1997, about the only thing they played while we warmed up was Bon Jovi's greatest hits, plus maybe some Rolling Stones if they wanted to get really diverse.

Then you'd look around at all the guys stretching to "Living on a Prayer," and eight out of ten were brothers! Now how the hell were we gonna get hyped to "Beast of Burden"?

I brought Buffalo's PA a mix tape suitable for public consumption, and overnight we went from Bon Jovi to Mystikal. I even recorded a little introduction right at the top.

"This is Wild Style!"

Opponents would show up at our stadium, hear the good stuff, and tell me I had to start DJ'ing their stadiums' pregame music too. I stuck with my home turf in Buffalo, but still, before you could say

"No Limit Soldiers," hip-hop was everywhere, playing before every game at every stadium in the League.

Coincidence? I don't think so.

Over the years, I went on to DJ for everyone from Kanye to Out-kast to Run-DMC.

But here's the most important part of all: The whole time I was making music on the side, my football didn't suffer at all. In fact, it was the exact opposite. I *fed* off my music. Music fueled my fire, helped push me to get better, to go from zero sacks my rookie year in Buffalo to thirteen sacks my first year in San Diego. I climbed the mountain with turntables on my *back*.

Do some athletes thrive by devoting their entire existence to their sport? Sure. But not me. I worked hard, but I never wanted people to see me sweat.

There was a reason I was Dat Dude. I enjoyed being balanced. I embraced being different. It didn't make it harder for me to be a great player—it helped. The dating, the parties, the community engagement—and yes, the DJ'ing—all of it made me the player I was, just like it had my whole life.

And that was fine as long as I racked up double-digit sacks in a season. But once I started to struggle in my second year with the Chargers, people started asking questions.

Why does he spend so much time DJ'ing?

Why does he work so hard on his foundation?

Is he really committed to his team?

Shouldn't he be more focused on football?

Sports talk radio, writers, fans looking for easy explanations for my lack of production—they all started saying it. Saying that the big paycheck had made me soft, that living so close to my home in LA had become too much of a distraction.

Seriously?!? Look at my output, look at my numbers! I played my best year of football *after* I got paid—thirteen sacks!—and I was playing hurt on one foot!

None of them could see how hard I was working in practice. None of them knew I was training every morning at 5:00 a.m. with Junior and the Breakfast Club. None of them watched me as I rehabbed and met with every specialist I could to try to get my step back.

But that was fine, really. I had never had time for negativity in the past. What did I care if a bunch of gossips who didn't even know me gave me shit on the radio now?

Fuck 'em, right?

Then, toward the end of my third season, my agent—Brad Blank, the same guy I had been with from the very beginning, not just my agent but my friend—came and told me it wasn't only sports talk radio anymore. The San Diego front office was starting to have questions too.

Nothing too critical, Brad told me. Not yet. His contacts were telling him the Chargers wanted to restructure my contract. Keep me on the team, but lower my salary from the current $6.7 million a year to something that made more sense given my recent output.

A year or two earlier, if there had been a problem, I could've gone right to the GM, John Butler, who'd been GM of both Buffalo *and* San Diego and had signed me both places. He was not only my guy, he was also a great communicator, plain and simple.

Sure, he knew football, he knew athletes, he understood scouting and all the stats. But more important than that—more important for any great GM—he knew how to manage relationships, with both coaches and players.

If John had been around and had an issue with me, he would've come and asked me about it straight up. But cancer had taken him, tragically, not long after he brought me to the Chargers.

The current GM, A. J. Smith, was a smart guy, and I had known him as long as I had known John, but he lacked John's people skills. He wasn't a talker. I like to talk. A lot. But over the seven years I'd known A.J., I don't think we said seven words to each other. I don't even mean that in a negative way—it was simply the reality of the situation.

So I listened to what my agent told me. I listened to what Brad had to say about restructuring my contract in San Diego.

And I decided he was full of shit.

I left Brad, my agent of seven years, and signed with Leigh Steinberg. The guy who repped everyone from Troy Aikman to Warren Moon to Steve Young. The guy Jerry Maguire was modeled after. Plus, he had his hands in everything—broadcasting, branding, marketing, the whole deal. If I wanted to start branching out from football, maximize my football "brand" potential, as all the marketing gurus liked to say, Steinberg was perfectly positioned to get me any opportunity I could dream of.

Steinberg wasn't big—he was the *biggest ever*. And that, I figured, was what I deserved.

In other words, I fucked up. And I fucked up at exactly the wrong time.

The season ended. I finished with three sacks, and I had surgery on my shoulder almost immediately. Free agency started shortly after that. The day before it began, Brad called me. And kept calling me. And calling me. And calling me.

"Marcellus, you've known me since day one," he said. "Trust me, San Diego wants to restructure. If we do this, it won't even be much of a haircut. You know I wouldn't lie to you!"

I didn't care what Brad said. I was all caught up in the sauce, swirling around. The only thing he wanted was to get me back as a client, I thought. He wasn't thinking of me, just himself.

Besides, Leigh Steinberg had told me everything with San Diego was cool. I was still young, he said. Just needed to recover from this injury, and I'd be fine.

And what about my coaches? After the season I had met with the D line coach and the defensive coordinator, and they told me I was all good. They knew I needed surgery, knew their defensive scheme hadn't given me as many rushing opportunities, knew I was still great against the run, promised me it would all work out.

And my GM? I hadn't heard a thing from him.

Finally I lost my patience with my old agent.

"Damn, Brad!" I said. "I'm not signing back up with you! Just leave me alone, man!"

The other end went silent. Finally he sighed.

"Alright," he said. "I'll give you some space."

The next day I woke up in my LA condo, alone in my bed. It was 8:12 in the morning—I still remember the clock.

My phone was next to my bed, vibrating like crazy. I picked it up and started checking my voicemails as I turned on ESPN, my normal routine. But as soon as I heard the messages, I knew something was up.

"You gonna be alright, dog!"

"They trippin', don't worry about them!"

"Hit me up as soon as you get this!"

What the hell is going on? I thought.

And then I saw it. The ESPN ticker, scrolling across the bottom of the TV screen in what felt like slow motion:

"CHARGERS . . .

"RELEASE . . .

"M . . .

"A . . .

"R . . ."

But I didn't even need to see the rest of the letters of my name. I already knew I had been released.

I dropped my phone, lay back in my bed, and stared at my ceiling, just for a moment. I got up and walked into the bathroom. I put my hands on the counter and looked at myself in the mirror.

I wasn't ashamed. In a weird way, I wasn't even shocked. I understood that this was a business. I knew lots of guys who had been traded or cut. Happened all the time. Hell, I had been fighting for playing time since my very first year of peewee, when Stais Boseman had overshadowed us all. I knew that football was winner-take-all.

No, what got me wasn't the fact that I was cut—it was *how* I got cut. After everything I had been through with the Chargers, they didn't have the guts to call me to tell me it was over. Not a meeting, not a voicemail, not even an email. There was no handshake or looking me in the eye.

Hell, other than Brad—the one guy who actually had my back—no one else had even let on that anything was *wrong*. And when Brad tried to tell me, of course my ego didn't want to hear it.

Nope. After three years of my working my ass off for the Chargers—playing on one foot, tearing my abdominal wall to shreds, wrecking my shoulder—the GM, A. J. Smith, didn't tell me a damn thing.

Instead, they let me find out on ESPN.

CHAPTER EIGHT

WHAT'S YOUR WORD?

NINE OUT OF the top ten times my daddy's been most excited in his life had something to do with the Dallas Cowboys.

He'd sit down on our living room floor to watch his games. We had one of those old floor-model TVs, its giant wood frame about five times bigger than the actual screen—thing was more furniture than tube. He'd sit stretched out on his butt, every ounce of his being focused on that game, taking it in. Watching, watching, watching. Then suddenly . . .

"ALRIGHT!"

Tony Dorsett would break a run, dodge one defender, two, three, dancing along the sideline.

"ALRIGHT!"

And let me tell you, somehow, someway, this dude, who barely ever broke a sweat in his daily life he was so even-keeled, would actually start to *levitate off the ground* he got so damn excited.

Seriously! He wouldn't use his hands, wouldn't use his legs or his feet. Somehow, all at once, his body would shoot into the air and hover there, electrified, for what felt like four seconds.

"ALRIGHT!"

It was the only word he ever used, but somehow it embodied a wider, more poignant range of emotions than the finest Shakespearean sonnet or pretty much any chapter from *War and Peace*. I'd invite friends over so they could experience his near-religious fanaticism.

"Dog, you gotta come watch my daddy watch a Cowboy game. You'll never forget it."

I never really knew what it was about Dallas that brought out my dad's inner emo. He had been born in Texas—Tyler, same town as Earl Campbell—but that didn't explain the depth of the connection he felt. For him, maybe, it was his one big release. The only way he knew how to let go and express whatever emotion he had bottled up inside.

Hell, if you got him talking about Tom Landry, the Cowboys' legendary coach, you couldn't even get him to shut up. Not just about football either—he'd even get jacked about whatever Landry was wearing that day, insisting he was the best-dressed man in all of sports.

Me? My dad *maybe* got *almost* that excited for one or two of my big plays back in my peewee football days. Maybe when I got drafted. But nothing that made him levitate, that's for sure.

Then I got released from the Chargers. And all of a sudden I found myself with an opportunity that I—and definitely my dad— had only dreamed of.

My new agent, Leigh Steinberg, had received some calls from a handful of interested teams. I definitely wasn't the hot commodity I had been when I came to San Diego, no crazy bidding war for me this time. But one team was showing the most interest.

Then, only a week after I got cut, the deal was done. It was official. I was gonna play for the Dallas Cowboys.

WHERE THE HELL is Bill Parcells?

It was my first day in Dallas, and from the moment I arrived, the Cowboys definitely showed me the love. They ended up signing me to a four-year, sixteen-million-dollar contract—not on the same level as my Chargers' pay, but four million bucks a year wasn't chicken feed. Even with all the injuries, even with my body not healing as fast as it used to, I was still only twenty-nine years old, hadn't hit the dreaded thirty yet. This would be my eighth season in the League, my fifth as a starter. I wasn't some sucker coming in to compete for a spot. I was expected to be the man, in the top echelon.

They showed me all the facilities, introduced me to people, took me on a tour of their locker room, and gave me a prime corner locker before I had even taken a step on the field.

But all I could think was, *Where the hell is Bill Parcells? Why haven't I met my new coach—the dude who brought me here in the first place??*

I met with Jerry Jones himself, who was sitting behind a big wooden desk. Something about his big gleaming smile said he knew you were gonna agree with him when he was done, no matter what he said. And he was right!

He pumped my hand, told me how thrilled the Cowboys were to have me in their organization, and gave me what he called "a little welcome gift"—a small wooden box containing a single expensive-as-fuck pen (I googled it later). For all the money all the other teams had given me—and boy, I appreciated that cash—no one had ever thought to get me a gift before. As much as people liked to clown the guy, made him their punching bag, I really liked Jerry Jones.

But still no Bill Parcells.

I had an introductory press conference in a couple hours, me and Keyshawn Johnson under the media's glaring lights, and I was starting to wonder if I was going to meet the world as a Dallas Cowboy before I even had a chance to meet my coach face-to-face.

But I finally got the message. Parcells wanted me to come to his office. Immediately.

They didn't have to ask twice. Parcells obviously had a reputation in the League among players. As a bully, as a genius, as a father figure. As quite possibly one of the greatest, most quintessential football coaches of all time. I was a little nervous, but more than anything I was excited.

I was on "America's Team," the biggest franchise in the country. A hell of a landing spot for someone who'd just been cut. All I wanted was a single year without another injury. And if anyone could mentor me, help me come back bigger and better than ever, make sure I got the chance I needed, it was my new coach. I was ready for the complete Bill Parcells experience.

I took a deep breath and knocked on his office door.

"Come on" was all I heard from inside.

I opened the door, and he was there. Or at least I thought it was him, because all I could see was a big, rounded back—the back of a man busy writing on a board.

"Hey, Coach Parcells," I said.

Nothing. No response.

"Uh, nice to meet you?" I said. It came out as more of a question than a statement.

Still nothing. Until finally, after what felt like an eternity, he turned away from the board, and after all that time, all that writing, left behind a single word in big, bold letters:

DRUGS.

Alllllllllllright then.

My new coach took a seat behind his desk and motioned for me to sit. He looked me right in the eye, studying me. I shifted in my chair uncomfortably.

"Marcellus," he said, "have you ever done drugs?"

My mind raced. Was he talking petty weed in my dorm room, or crack cocaine and *Boyz n the Hood*? I'd never touched any of the hard stuff, of course, but like any red-blooded American capitalist, I'd smoked two or three times before.

So obviously I answered him as straight and clear as I possibly could.

"No. Absolutely not."

Honestly, I don't even think he heard my answer. In his own mind, he was already starting to preach.

"I had a player," he said. "A player I cared so much about, the greatest player I ever coached. The player's name was Lawrence Taylor. This player could do anything. No matter what came his way, no matter what obstacle I or anyone else put in front of him, this player could overcome it all. My God, what a player."

Player, player, player. He probably said the word "player" about twenty times.

"But what pains me to this day," he said, "is that I didn't challenge the *person* to be as great as the *player* was."

My coach pointed at the board.

"There is a word that can be written on that board that could get in the way of your greatness, Marcellus. I don't know what that word is, but I want you to work hard to make sure there's nothing on that board I can write for you. That's what you gotta figure out to be a great player and a great person. What is your word."

Now, in hindsight, I think I understand what Parcells may have been trying to get at. To Parcells, comparing me to LT, one of the greatest defenders of all time, was a compliment (and a stretch, to say the least). It was an attempt to tell me that if I tapped my potential, I could be great. But at the same time, there was a reason I was in his office instead of back in San Diego making over $6 million a year. Somewhere during my career, Parcells may have been saying, I got off track. In his own way, he may have been trying to get me back on.

But at that moment? Just hours after I had arrived at my brand-new team? There was only one word that was going through my mind after Parcells's little speech: *fuck*.

As in, what the *fuck* is this dude talking about?

TRAINING CAMP STARTED a couple months later. And miracle of miracles, the Cowboys decided to hold it off-site, in Oxnard, California—north of Los Angeles, and a short drive away from my father's home. All he had to do was throw on his brand-new Marcellus Wiley Cowboys jersey and hop in his car, and he could watch his son play for the team he loved almost every day.

It was like the greatest gift I could give him. He probably levitated all the way there.

On the first day of camp I walked out to the field with Coach Parcells. Now, training camp isn't only an opportunity for the players to get back in football shape and work the kinks out after the off-season. It's also a chance for the coaching staff to scrutinize the hell out of them. For a lot of them, it meant their very livelihoods hung in the balance.

Bill Parcells took that scrutiny to a whole new level.

He stopped at the door of the practice facility, in just the right spot to be able to see the entire field. He scanned it twice. Right to left. Then left to right. And proceeded to break down every single detail of every single person there.

See how wide his stance is? He'll be lucky if he makes the practice squad.

See where his hands are on his block? I don't even know why we invited him.

See how heavy he runs? He's done. He doesn't know he's done, but he's done.

He was like Sherlock Holmes meets *Good Will Hunting*. This was some serious seeing-the-matrix shit.

There was a time when I would've joined him in tearing people apart, and enjoyed myself too. A time not too long ago, in fact, back when my position at San Diego had been all but guaranteed, and it was only *other guys* who had to worry about being on the chopping block—aging, declining vets and undrafted rookies hanging on by the skin of their teeth.

But now? Months after getting unceremoniously dumped by the Chargers, a team I had called home for three years?

Now, for the very first time in my career, *I* was the one who felt vulnerable. Now *I* was the one worried about being judged.

Best of all (that's sarcasm right there, in case you missed it), I was about to do pass-rush drills. The same test that always made me a little self-conscious. The same test that got me stuck to the fence—literally—my first year in Buffalo. The same test that put me on a virtual island, man against man, all eyes on me.

Not only that, but I was going up against Flozell Adams, six foot seven, 340 pounds, five-time Pro Bowl offensive tackle. For a first test, this was like getting integral calculus.

I got in my stance, waited for that whistle, all my nerve endings waiting to fire . . .

And I did alright, I guess.

I mean, the whistle blew, and I hit the guy, but I didn't get much push, it wasn't my best move. Dallas wasn't paying me millions of dollars for "not my best move."

A few people on the sidelines clapped for me. One of those polite golf tournament claps. No real meaning to it, just perfunctory.

I looked over at my dad, standing there in his number 75 Wiley jersey, watching. Silent but proud.

I gritted my teeth, got ready to go again. I was gonna be facing Flozell in practice for the rest of the season, potentially for the next four years of my contract. I knew I needed to make a statement, not just to him, not just to everyone watching, but to myself. I fucked up the first time; now I was gonna be better.

Except I wasn't.

Flozell stopped me. Again. No shame in that necessarily—this guy was their star offensive lineman, after all. But I was supposed to be a star too. I had been a star once.

The polite applause came again. Even less convincing than it was the first time, or at least that's how it sounded to me. But that was nothing compared with what I was about to hear.

"Wiley, is that all you got?"

I couldn't believe it. Parcells—my *coach*—had walked to the middle of the field and was chewing me out in front of everyone. Everyone including my dad.

In an instant, I flashed back to his office, the board, the single word "DRUGS" scrawled in giant letters at the top.

Was this it? Was this my word? Not "drugs," but just plain "done"?

Parcells stared at me. I could feel him picking me apart, like all those other players. I could feel him drilling into me with those sharp blue eyes. I didn't know what to say.

He shook his head in disgust, turned around, and walked away.

AFTER ALL THAT, deep down I still believed. I knew that only one in a million athletes ever even made it to the League in the first place. Now I was gonna be that one in another million who pushed past multiple injuries, who was reborn to success one more time.

Plus, I had a secret weapon. My mama.

My mama may not have been a Cowboys fanatic like my dad, but she was a *force.* And I don't mean that in an abstract way. I mean she was so big and so strong she could literally move you out of the way if she chose to do so. She was six foot one, 250 pounds, every inch of her absolutely gorgeous, with hands as big and strong as my own.

Whenever I had been injured before, whenever I'd had a bad game, she was the one who had picked me up. She was the one who had turned me around.

Whenever she would take my hands, I would feel the little dent she had in her left palm, that old scar she had from when she was a girl, and it was like all her energy was transferred to me. Somehow everything was okay.

So when she flew to Dallas before our first game, I figured that was why she was there. After all, I was already dealing with yet another injury, a hip pointer—a big, knotlike bruise I got on the point of my hip when I hit the ground hard in practice. Why else would she be visiting?

She sat down with me in my new house. Now I'm not embarrassed to admit that this house was exactly the kind of place you'd expect out of a dude making millions from the NFL. We're talking marble everywhere, fake Greek statues indoors that were bigger than me, a gigantic palace. The designers who'd lived there before had it designed symmetrically, with two almost identical wings, so I could split it exactly in half—the right side strictly for having a ball with my friends, the left side strictly for personal time, chillin' and resting.

A visit from Mama was entirely a left-side affair.

She sat me down on the couch and took my hands in hers. I felt that dent, and already I started to feel a little better, a little stronger.

"Teddy Bear, you gotta be strong," she said. "I love you no matter what. You know that, right?"

Here it comes, I thought. *Her "you gotta go hard this year" speech, how I gotta play through that doubt.*

"I know, Mama. I love you too," I said. "Everything's gonna be good. I'm gonna get right and play better, I promise."

She opened her eyes, a little surprised, and she laughed.

"Boy, I don't care about that!" she said. "You know how happy you've made me? Look at you and what you've accomplished! What more could I want?"

I frowned, confused.

"Then what . . . ?"

She sighed.

"I'm not feeling well," she said.

"What do you mean?"

"Well, I went to the doctor, and they found a lump. I got breast cancer."

She said it like she might as well have been announcing that she needed to go to the store for some bread. My mom was beyond casual when it came to her own trials, like they were meaningless. I, on the other hand, was not so laid-back.

"What are you saying?" I said. "Breast cancer!?"

"They found it early," she said. "Everything is gonna be good."

I stood up.

"I'm not playing this year, Mama. I'm going home with you. I'm gonna be there for you."

"No, you finish what you started," she said. "If you could do something for me, I'd tell you to come, but you can't. You gotta stay here and play."

"I don't want to play!"

"I want you to play."

So I played. Because she wanted me to, I played.

And on the field, I sucked.

Once I knew my mama was sick, I didn't care about anything else. I had always loved playing football, sure, but that was never what *drove* me. What pushed me to succeed was my family, fighting for them, struggling to get us all out of the hood. Sure, the other stuff was fun too—the money, the girls, the fame—but that's not why I did it. Mama was. And now, she was fighting for her life. Nothing else mattered.

You want me to stop a running back? My mom has *cancer.*

You want me to sack a quarterback? My mom has *cancer.*

You want me to worry about what Bill Parcells thinks? My mom has *cancer.*

I ended the season with three sacks. The flame of my passion was blown out.

IT WAS MOMENTS after the Cowboys' last game of the season, against the New York Giants. We had lost the game 28–24, and we finished the year 6-10. Nothing short of a disaster. I had sacked Eli Manning minutes earlier, I was on my way to the press conference, and I was ready to explode.

I was bubbling over with frustration. About my mama, about how I had played that season, about what I figured Dallas had planned for me.

Football was a business: San Diego had taught me that the hard way. And no business would want to keep paying $4 million a year for a guy who totaled three sacks in a season. I figured Dallas would cut me loose. It was common sense.

Plus, I had seen how Parcells managed his players, and he was not the kind of coach who put up with any shit. At the beginning of the season, I had seen Parcells almost come to blows with one of our wide receivers, Antonio Bryant, after Antonio got fed up in practice and threw his jersey in Coach's face—and Coach threw that shit right back at him.

The whole thing got broken up in a flash. Six weeks later, Antonio got cut.

A teammate of mine I knew from San Diego, Leo Carson, was close to Parcells. Leo tried to convince me that my spot on the team was safe, no matter what I thought. He tried to get me to cool off, told me everything was gonna be fine. Dallas was gonna switch schemes to highlight my run-stopping ability, and Parcells was gonna give me another year. There was just one thing I had to do.

"Just shut the fuck up," Leo told me. "Don't say a *word* to anyone, and we alright."

Me? Shut up? Yeah, right.

I got to that press conference, and I couldn't wait to talk. I didn't want Dallas's empty promises. I didn't want Jerry Jones's fancy pens. The fans had been saying all year long that they thought I'd be better, that I wasn't worth the money. Fuck it, I didn't want that either.

I was tired of the noise. I wanted to set the record straight before anyone else could do it for me. I had sacked Eli Manning, for fuck's sake! I couldn't wait for the first reporter to ask me something—anything. They were gonna taste napalm.

Then no one asked me anything.

Shit, I thought, *what if I don't even get my chance?*

Thank goodness I got that sack on Eli—the press had no choice, they had to talk to me sooner or later. And when they did . . .

Boom.

I owned up to my poor performance that year—then I went off on Jerry, I went off on Bill, I went off on the entire organization, saying that they had used me wrong all season, that they had no one to blame but themselves for how I had played. That wasn't true, of course, but I didn't give a damn. I wanted to do damage.

"You stupid! You so stupid!" Leo told me on the flight home. "All you had to do was shut up, that's all! Man, you fucked up!"

He was right. A month later they cut me. News delivered courtesy of ESPN, just like before.

THE MOMENT THE season was over in January, I got rid of the house in Dallas and moved back to Los Angeles so I could be close to Mama during chemo.

She was a strong person. She'd had surgery shortly after they discovered the cancer in the fall. It was supposed to be three hours, but instead it lasted eight. When I asked her why, all she would tell me was, "Oh, they just wanted to make sure they got everything."

But I could sense it was more than that. I could sense that she was holding back, just for us.

On March 2, it was another sunny day in California, like all the rest. I got up in the morning, drove to an appointment with my chiropractor, Doc Murray, a close family friend. I was waiting in the lobby when my sister called.

And just like that, she told me Mama was gone.

Doc Murray had tears in his eyes.

"I'm so sorry," he said. "I'm so . . ."

He couldn't finish his sentence.

I rushed out of the office and jumped in my car. It was my powder-blue Ferrari. I bought it for the flash, but for once I was going to use it for the speed. I hit the highway, raced down the shoulder, flying over debris, passing people like it was nothing.

I kept thinking, *If you get there fast enough, you can save her. Gotta go faster, faster.*

But deep down another voice kept telling me it was too late, she had passed away.

I arrived at the hospital and ran in. I had to see her. I didn't care if it was too late. I had to.

They took me to her. She was lying a few feet away from me. I kept daring myself to touch her. *Do it,* I thought. *You have to touch her. You can't let yourself get distant. That's* your mama *lying there.*

I took her hand in mine, just as she had done so often to me. I felt that little dent, that source of so much love, so much energy, that mark that was uniquely her. It was already cold.

I knew she was gone.

I knew something else too. After all that time, I finally knew what my word was. It wasn't "drugs" or "done." It was "family."

My word wasn't my weakness. It didn't stand in the way of my greatness as a player *or* as a person. It was my greatest strength. What motivated me, what kept me grounded and bound me to this world.

After my mama passed on, my family continued to be my support and my life. The universe shifted for my grandma. She had lost three sons before, each to violence, but my mama had always been her favorite, and she had done nothing to earn her death sentence. Mama hadn't gotten into a fight or joined a gang. She had gotten sick.

Tiki, my sister, it took a chunk of flesh out of her. She's still affected to this day. Goes to my mama's gravesite every couple weeks, on every holiday, every birthday. Always making sure the grave is tended, always keeping the flowers fresh.

And my daddy? The guy who almost never showed any emotion for any reason?

I saw him cry for the very first time.

CHAPTER NINE

THE REVEREND OF JACKSONVILLE

DAYS BEFORE DALLAS cut me, I saw an old friend.

It was the weekend of February 5, 2005, and Jacksonville was hosting Super Bowl XXXIX, the Eagles versus the Patriots. I was in town for the game, and so was my former agent, Brad Blank.

It didn't matter that I wasn't playing. See, the Super Bowl is more than just a game for the players, agents, and execs who are connected to pro football. It's almost like our annual professional convention. During the day, a guy like me could get paid to appear at different events, a luncheon for *Sports Illustrated* or a panel for Toyota. And at night? That's when all the best parties were. Dudes would chill, forget about all the rivalries of the season, and give each other love. Maybe clown you a little if you had an off year, but all in good fun.

The two of us went out to dinner at a Ruth's Chris Steak House—an NFL staple—and then went for a walk along the harbor. Jacksonville is a massive city, but kind of sleepy, and everything there feels like it's right on the water.

I had learned a lot since I had let Brad go in San Diego—about the game, about myself, about life. My mama was battling cancer, and I was coming to terms with the fact that I wasn't the same unstoppable player I had been four years ago when the Chargers made me the highest-paid player in franchise history. Hell, the way things looked, I might never be that guy again.

Dallas hadn't cut me yet, but the writing was on the wall—and Brad knew it.

"You've been through a lot, man," he said. "You need to come home, go back to an agent who'll take care of you—the person *and* the player."

He was right. I was dealing with enough uncertainty in my life. I needed a guy I could trust, someone who'd known me back when I was just coming up. I had fucked up when I fired Brad over a year ago, but now that my career was about to take yet *another* turn, I wasn't going to make the same mistake again.

Brad came back onboard, and the season after the Cowboys cut me, he brokered one of my best deals yet, right there in Jacksonville with the Jaguars.

Now, when I say "one of my best deals," I'm not talking about the money. At two years and $1.8 million, that wasn't even close to what I made in Dallas.

But the arrangement? That was ideal for where I was at in my career. I was still making good money, and unlike San Diego and Dallas, Jacksonville didn't expect me to be *the man* as soon as I stepped off the plane. They didn't assume I would start. They didn't give me the best locker on the team. And they damn well didn't give me any speeches about Lawrence Taylor and drugs.

They'd give me a shot at starting, but I was gonna have to *earn* it, like everyone else. That's all I wanted—a shot.

And if I didn't start? Alright, I get it. I'd still be great at stopping the run, and Jack Del Rio, Jacksonville's coach, knew how crucial it was to have a strong veteran presence in the locker room. He was a former player, a linebacker for five different NFL teams. Jack understood that character in football was important, not just youth and athleticism.

The Jaguars had a bunch of young studs who needed to be exposed to a guy like me, a guy who'd been through it all. I wouldn't be overbearing, I wouldn't be preachy, but in a way I'd act as their reverend. And that's what a bunch of them ended up calling me—Reverend. That and "Old Man."

Who knows? Maybe—just maybe—I could draw on all their energy to give myself one last burst at the end of my career.

If not? Well, lots of people came to Florida to retire. Maybe I would too.

I LIKED FLORIDA.

Sure, Jacksonville wasn't the most thrilling city, but I had lived in Buffalo for four years, and that did me fine. Besides, Jacksonville was a quick jump to Miami.

And Miami? That was *exactly* what I needed.

A few months before I started with Jacksonville, I sat down with a few of my boys at our usual spot on the boardwalk, the old Cardozo Hotel. It was a perfect Friday afternoon, sunny and warm, not even 1:00 p.m., and we were already having ourselves a little hydration situation.

A lot of guys like to change things up when they go out, run around trying to find the newest hot spot. Not me. The last thing I wanted was one of the big, crowded places on Sixth Street and Ocean flooded with guys—half of them in the League—shouting "Hey, baby!" at every lady in a five-foot radius.

The Cardozo was perfect, almost quaint. On Thirteenth Street, a block before shit got crazy. We could see the ladies walking by right before they hit that war zone, right before everything went full metal jacket.

There were four of us in our crew. We'd known each other for years, and we all knew our roles.

Jabari you already know from back in my grade school days when we'd go on walks to Yee's. He was the angel. Straight-A student at Cornell University, the kind of guy a girl wants to take home to Mom and Dad. If a woman was sitting with us and we started getting loud, she'd look at Jabari the Angel and think, it's cool, everything will be alright.

If I had a wingman, Rory was it. You might remember him from back when I was at Columbia. He was on the team with me, then made it to the Cardinals' practice squad, but now he was a Wall Street guy, polished, married, and pretty as hell. If a girl saw me, she might be a little put off at first—I'm loud, I got the jewelry and the tattoos, I'm the NFL player acting like he's somebody—so Rory was the guy who'd run interference. As the married dude, he was just playing along, completely nonthreatening, like "Don't worry, ladies, this soldier don't have no gun."

Then you had Cheema. He was the guy who didn't give a damn. We could've seen Beyoncé strutting by—hell, we could've seen five Beyoncés—and he'd go in without fear, consequences be damned. He was like our long-range missile—90 percent of the time he'd explode harmlessly in the ocean (*Eeeeeeeeew!*), but when he connected with his target, there'd be major pyrotechnics.

Finally there was me, Dat Dude. Nothing less than pure class, of course, having fun with a new, remixed version of cakin'.

Sitting there sipping our beverages, we saw four women walking down the street, heading toward the chaos that was Sixth Street. One Cuban, one black, and the other two checked too many boxes in the ethnicity column to name. All dressed up because their day probably wouldn't end till tomorrow.

But nothing disrespectful from us. Naw, we came up with a game that let us go at *each other*, that made *us* take the criticism. And rightfully so! They were all in six-inch heels and we were in flip-flops—and *we* were supposed to be the cool ones?

We called our game "Rank Us."

"Ladies, excuse us!" called out Cheema, the man without fear. "Can we buy you some lunch?"

Note that he asked them if they wanted lunch—not drinks—to put them more at ease. Then before they had a chance to say yes or no, before they could even start to consider how to answer, I chimed in.

"There's one thing," I said. "Before you sit down, there's one condition. You gotta be brutally honest when you're hanging with us. No half-truths, no being polite or diplomatic. You can't hold *anything* back."

That got them past the entire quandary of accepting lunch from four perfect strangers and onto honesty—which, as you know, is my favorite subject. Not only because I love to speak my mind, but because I want the people around me to speak their minds as well. "Never shut up" is always a two-way street.

"Girl, I can't be completely open with these guys!" said the Cubana. "I don't know them!"

"Tell the truth," said Rory the Wingman. "You ain't even honest with your girls and they're your best friends!"

That got a laugh, broke the tension.

"I don't know," one of them said.

Jabari the Angel came in to save the day.

"Come on! What do you got to hide?"

Curiosity got the best of them. They were apprehensive, but they wanted to know what kind of game we were playing. I filled them in as soon as they sat down.

"Rank us," I said.

They looked at us with blank faces. My boys were grinning, following my lead.

"Say what?" said the Cubana.

"I want you to rank us," I said. "If you see us out on the street or at the club, which one of us you gonna talk to first, and why? And remember, you gotta be brutally honest."

"And forget about the fact that he's NFL," Cheema said. "That can't mean *anything* here."

After a lot of hemming and hawing, the African American woman finally confessed:

"Fine. Jabari."

We exploded, acted like this was the most controversial decision anyone could possibly make.

"Jabari!" I said. "That guy? What you see in him?"

"I don't know," she said, giggling. "I just said his name, there's no reason!"

"What do you mean you don't know?" Jabari said, mock offended.

"Like, you don't even know what you like in a man?" Rory said. "Like you don't even know what you're attracted to?"

Now everyone was laughing, loose, and having fun as the ladies got used to wielding their new weapon. (Alright, it probably didn't hurt that we were paying for all the food and drinks.) In fact, they were having so much fun that a few minutes later they helped us meet even more new friends. They did everything, from asking the new girls to join us to telling them they'd have to be brutally honest.

"Naw, girl!" the Cubana said to one of our new friends. "Which one of them would you talk to first? You gotta answer!"

Four hours later, it was the four of us guys sitting at our original table—now four tables—with twenty-six women. There was no need to run around trying to find a party, because we had all created the party together.

My favorite part? I got to enjoy the sociology of it all—observing a bunch of ladies who barely even knew each other as they interacted, navigated the situation, and claimed their territory. It just happened that that "territory" was me and my single friends. Some of the women would stick around for a few hours, some of them would make it all the way to the next morning. But the ones who had the most fun weren't only there for us guys—they were laughing, talking, and kicking it with each other too.

Yeah, I thought. I think I can get used to this whole Florida thing.

MY FIRST FALL in Jacksonville, the Jaguars gave me the chance to compete for a starting spot, just like they promised. And I worked my ass off, just like I always do. But as hard as I tried, my former capacity for excellence was gone.

I was a shell of what I had been. Had no resemblance to the athlete I once was. The years of injuries and rehab had finally caught up to me. Like I'd been driving a car around with the "check engine" light on for eight years, and by the time I finally made it in to the mechanic, the engine was destroyed. All those off-seasons I had spent rehabbing instead of improving my overall skill had set me back. I had spent all that time trying to get back to the old me, instead of trying to build an even better new me. And remember—pro football is a game of inches, of tenths of seconds. The difference between running a 4.6- and a 4.8-second 40 is the difference between a star and just another guy. And I *definitely* wasn't running no 4.6.

But in the locker room? That's where I knew I could still shine. That's where I could make my mark.

It's crazy to think of me as a wise old veteran, I know. Shit, I was only thirty years old when I started in Jacksonville. Thirty years old, and those dudes were calling me "Old Man"! But in a game where the average career is just over three years long, I was practically a senior citizen.

These guys were barely older than twenty. The same way I had grown up watching Bruce Smith and Junior Seau destroying quarterbacks every autumn Sunday on TV, they had followed me and my career.

"Oh man, when I was in high school you were killing it!"

"Fuck, dog, I remember seeing you and your pad in San Diego on *MTV Cribs*! That Hummer you drove was dope!"

And I used that cred to talk to them, to make a difference. I had grown up always thinking about not just my next step, but the next step after *that*. Planning, strategizing, working to get to the NFL, yes, but also preparing for life after my football career. That's what took me to Columbia University in the first place. I *knew* football wouldn't last forever. I wanted to master the game *within* the game.

But the young studs on the Jaguars? For them there had only ever been one game in town—and that was the game they played on the field.

"You went to school for academics?" they'd say, shaking their heads in wonder. "That shit is crazy."

"I ain't even preaching right now," I'd say—even though I totally was. "Don't you think I wanted to go to a big school and have fun like y'all? Of course I did. But you gotta start thinking about what you want to do next *now*, before football is over with."

I tried to help them the best I could. I tried to relate. But honestly, most of the time I felt like the old-timer in the office who's spent his entire life working with paper, pencils, and filing cabinets, then suddenly gets a computer and says, "What the hell are all these buttons for?"

One day I was in the training room, my home away from home, dealing with a smaller injury, chilling—literally—in the cold tub. A rookie walked in and joined me. He'd just signed for a lot of money, or at least a lot of money for him, and he started telling me his life story.

This dude was from almost the exact opposite background as me. White, rural, grew up in a town so small he didn't even talk about the town, he referred to his county.

"I didn't grow up in the county," I told him. "But I did grow up *on* the county—like county welfare checks."

County Dude laughed.

"Man, I still can't believe how much money I'm getting paid right now," he said. "It's like I'm set for life. How the hell am I supposed to think about the future?"

Now to you that might sound stupid, maybe even spoiled. *Typical pro athletes being lazy and not working hard.* But think about it: What would you do if you won the lottery when you were twenty-two? Would you keep working as hard as you did before? Would you stay focused?

"Yeah, I get it," I told him, trying to play my role as reverend. "But is money really your only motivation? If you really feel like you're set in life, you're gonna be set with your accomplishments too. You're never gonna achieve anything great for you and your family."

He nodded slowly.

"I hear ya, man. I hear ya."

The next day, County Dude and I were walking to practice. We couldn't actually practice, we were still dealing with our injuries, but still—we had to go.

"Come on, Wiley," County Dude said to me, breaking off to the parking lot.

"Where you going?" I said.

"Going to my car to blow some," he said. "Come on!"

"Hhhhhell naw!" I said, drawing out that first "H" for emphasis.

One, I don't blow. And that refers to weed, for all you straight-and-narrow people out there. I'm strictly a hydration guy.

Two, for me, attending practice was an almost sacred responsibility. Both because of the contract I had signed with the team *and* the expectations I had for myself. It had taken me every ounce of my being to climb this mountain, and I wasn't about to loosen my grip—injury or no.

"You go on without me, dog," I said. "Catch you later."

Should I have tried harder to get him to do the right thing? Part of me thought so. That was my role on the team, after all, to serve as a positive example. But at the same time, there was only so much I could say and do. Ultimately, these young cats had to make their own decisions.

Needless to say, County Dude didn't last long on the team—or in the League.

Fast-forward a few weeks. I'm hanging at another teammate's house with some of the younger dudes, watching *Monday Night Football*. At first, it feels like business as usual. Conversation goes from video games to girls to the game we were watching. Same old shit I've been a part of since I first joined the League, no big deal.

Then all of a sudden it got to the advanced topic of who's the toughest guy in the room.

Next thing I knew, this dude went to one of his bedrooms and came back with a gun longer than a crutch.

"Ain't *nobody* fucking with me!" he shouted. "I got something for 'em!"

I mean, shit. I freaked myself out when I was holding on to a gun that was smaller than a water pistol eight years earlier. Now these cats were playing around with assault rifles like they were toys? All it took was one guy drinking too much and getting caught up in the moment, next thing you know we'd end up as one of those fucked-up stories you read about in the news. No way to leave either—that would just trigger the dude. All I could do was sit there and try to de-escalate the situation.

"Alright," I told him, using a little humor. "No one's fucking with you, Ram-bro. All good."

The gun made its way back into storage, and the night continued.

Things didn't get much better at the Christmas party. One of Jacksonville's lower-level backups—we're talking a dude who was one transaction away from getting sent home—brought a date from out of town to the party. Nothing weird about that—most of the guys with wives or girlfriends brought them along. The *real* problem was all the single dudes on the team.

Now, Backup Guy thought he had to spend the night working the room, talking up all the coaches, the assistants, the interns—basically, whoever had an official role on the team, he had to kiss their ass, because that's how he was gonna keep his job. Meanwhile, his girl was spending *her* time with some young millionaires at the bar.

Or at least she started with them at the bar. One minute she was there, next minute she was outside with one of them in his car. They finished their business, came back in like nothing happened. Backup Guy still working the coaches. He went home that night thinking he networked well, and she went home thinking *she* networked well.

All I could think was, *I know I used to be y'all. But please tell me I didn't used to be y'all.*

Now, as crazy as Jacksonville might sound, it wasn't *that* different from the other teams I had been on. Sure, Buffalo was a pretty chill scene, but that was a veteran group of players. But take your typical NFL team with a bunch of young guys who suddenly find themselves with more money than they ever dreamed of, and you're gonna find some pretty wild shit. Back in my day, I was not immune. They didn't call me Wild Style for nothing.

But I was starting to realize that my partying prime had passed. I hung out with the young guys on the team, but I didn't feel the same joy I had once felt, didn't feel present, didn't feel connected. I wasn't into guns and crazy Christmas parties anymore. (*What happened to me??*) I had more fun relaxing and having a nice time with my boys at the Cardozo. I enjoyed chilling more than chasing. I wasn't Wild Style anymore—I was Old-Ass Man, all at the age of thirty.

These kids I was preaching to lived their lives as close to the line as they could get. More and more, I was asking myself why I was on that line with them.

I WAS BACK ON my old field in San Diego at the center of the action. My heart was pounding, my palms were sweaty. I had *never* been this nervous after a game.

But here's the thing. I wasn't even there to play football. I was there as a broadcaster. A broadcaster who desperately needed to land the biggest interview of my young career—with LaDainian Tomlinson.

LT was one of the biggest stars in all of football, he was my former teammate, and he had just lost in the playoffs to New England in the last seconds of the game. The Chargers had been heavily favored, they had been almost unstoppable during the regular season, and now, when the stakes couldn't have been higher, they had choked. And I had to ask my old friend *all about it.*

Can you say "awkward"?

Honestly, when it came to broadcasting I barely had any idea what I was doing. I was still on Jacksonville's roster—we hadn't made the playoffs, so I had some time on my hands. I'd done some spots with a few different programs, guest hosted some radio shows, made a bunch of appearances on the *Best Damn Sports Show Period.* And I kept getting invited back, so I figured I was doing something right.

But I hadn't done *anything* like this before—being an on-field correspondent, not at some meaningless preseason game on some local radio station, but at a big-time playoff game for the NFL Network itself.

The San Diego factor didn't help. Being on my old stomping ground made me feel more self-conscious. I even saw a few of my old jerseys sprinkled in the crowd. I had returned—not because I was dominating the game, which would've felt triumphant, but because I was a broadcaster, a step removed from the game. This place had been the source of some of my best memories *and* some of my worst. It was like I was caught in an emotional tug-of-war between the good and the bad.

Not only that, but even though the NFL Network had the power and prestige of the NFL name behind it, it had only launched in 2003 and was still a new outfit. So it had nowhere near the power of the old guard: ESPN, NBC, CBS, FOX.

They called me up, asked me if I'd be their on-field correspondent, and I said sure, why not? I gotta get a postgame interview with LT? What, so I just talk to the guy? How hard could it be?

Yeah, right.

When the game ended, there wasn't some neat, orderly Q&A session out there on the field. Nope, they released us reporters like a pack of wild dogs onto that turf, and LaDainian was our single prey. He was the Chargers' star, which meant it was his team, which meant it was his loss. And the media wanted at him.

We engulfed him in a massive scrum, elbows flying, people beefin' and buckin'.

Vvvvrommmmmm! Pow-pow!

I may have had years of swim moves and beating double teams on my side, but this journalism shit was gangster. In a weird way, it was even harder than being on the line, because in football there was no pretense—if you wanted to move someone out of the way, you shoved them the fuck out of the way, drove them into the dirt.

But in the reporters' scrum you had to be more subtle. No one could *see you* knocking fuckers down, that wasn't allowed. You just had to do it, somehow, with body blocks and expert mic positioning, because you *had to get* that interview.

"LT, over here!" one reporter shouted.

"A word about the loss, LaDainian!"

"LT, over here! LT! LT!"

He wouldn't give those dudes more than a single stone-faced word, the usual cliché of "disappointing," as he kept making his way steadily toward the locker room. And honestly, who could blame him? The dude had just suffered one of the most devastating losses of his career, and now we wanted him to *talk about it*?

But I had a job to do, so I did it. I finally managed to slide through the scrum, get face-to-face with the man himself, and use the one weapon I truly possessed—the same cred that made me feel awkward in the first place.

"Hey, LT!" I said. "I'm doing a little correspondent work for the NFL. You mind talking to me for a minute?"

He looked at me for no more than a second—then smiled and took his helmet off.

"Marcellus!?" he said, giggling good-naturedly when he realized it was me. "Yeah, man!"

Now LT may have seen a lot of those reporters around over the years, probably been interviewed by them each a dozen times or more. But he hadn't only seen me around—we had actually *played* with each other, worked out with each other, chilled in the locker room with each other.

Was it weird interviewing a guy I was friends with? Who was still killing it in a game I was thinking of leaving behind? Yeah, I won't lie. But playing with each other for as long as we had, we had developed a mutual respect. That was a good thing, a powerful thing. And now it was paying off.

LT did a real, full-on interview with me, right there on the field. Giving me the purest, most dope-ass answers I could've hoped for. He came alive, talked like one guy talking to another, like a real human being, not just a football player. As all the other reporters tried to jam their mics and tape recorders in my way so they could steal the answers he gave me.

We finished the interview, and LT walked away, the scrum moving after him, still jostling, pushing, and shoving.

"LT! LT! LT!"

He sighed, shook his head, and went back to his one-word answers.

I laughed. Maybe being on the other side of the camera wasn't so bad.

ANOTHER DAY IN the Jacksonville locker room, another debate.

"But what the fuck you gonna do *after* football, Wiley?" one of the D linemen said. "How you gonna make more money than you making now?"

"Look, dog, I admit it," I said, "I don't know yet. But I'm gonna find it."

"Man," someone else said, "if you haven't even found it, why the fuck you gonna leave?"

As usual, it was ten on one. A bunch of D linemen, a few other dudes—and me. Jawing, sniping, philosophizing, having fun. Big as shit, loud as shit, interrupting, talking over each other. Like at a barbershop, except instead of talking about Joe Louis and Cassius Clay, we were talking about our lives.

It was my second season with the Jaguars, and a couple weeks earlier I'd had an epiphany. I'd been playing in a home game, and I'd gotten a stinger. Not super uncommon—somehow you'd get smacked in the head, and a wave of paralysis would suddenly extend from your earlobes to your fingertips on one side of your body. Shake it off and move on, no big deal.

Except I'd been getting at least one a game, which was a lot. And this time the other team was playing a hurry-up offense, so I hadn't even had a chance to shake it off. Finally my coaches called a timeout—not for my one-armed ass, but to talk things over.

I'd peeled myself off the turf and looked up at the owner's suite. I could see the Jaguars' owner, Wayne Weaver, behind the glass. He was leaning down, playing with his grandkids, not even paying attention to the game. He finally straightened up—just long enough so he could grab a hot dog and take a big, fat bite.

Ain't that a bitch, I had thought. I can't even feel my arm, and this dude is up there playing with his grandkids and eating a hot dog.

I hadn't felt any anger. All I knew was this: I needed to get from down *here* to up *there*. I needed to make money without all the broken bones and torn ligaments. More mind, less muscle. All gain and no pain.

I needed to get me one of those million-dollar hot dogs.

"Look," I told the guys in the locker room. "You know how many injuries I've had? I'm trying to play with my kids when I get older!"

I saw a couple dudes nod at that. We'd *all* had those concerns.

"Besides," I said. "I already accomplished what I set out to accomplish! What else I got to prove?"

"Fuck 'proving,'" one of the wide receivers said. "A game check is your fucking proof, man! That money!"

He waved some cash in my face as everyone busted out laughing.

"But Wiley already got that long money," a linebacker said, finally taking my side. "That's why he don't need to care! And he got that nerdy-ass degree!"

"Fuck that," someone said. "Reverend gonna try to use that fancy degree of his, but he gonna find out that shit ain't nothing!"

"Y'all can talk about whatever y'all want," I told them. "I'm just trying to get that hot dog."

More hooting and hollering. I'd told them my hot dog story right after it happened.

"A fucking hot dog versus a game check!" the wide receiver

shouted, holding his dollar bills up in the air. "I'm gonna take *game check* every single time!"

Everyone just crying laughing, we moved from debating to our other two favorite pastimes. Slap boxing, this playful fake fighting where we'd take turns just *barely* smacking each other in the chins. All at top speed, our hands whipping through the air.

Zzzziiiipp! Zzzzzzzziiiiiiipppppp!

Or, if not that, then the next most-obvious activity: playing table tennis. And hoping that Coach Del Rio didn't show up, because that motherfucker was like a serious Olympic-level Ping Pong player, slamming and spinning that ball all over the damn place.

In a sense, the other guys on the team were right. I really *didn't* know what I wanted to do after football. I'd done those media spots, of course, but still—I had no concrete plans. No passion, no goal beyond getting that hot dog for myself. My best playing years were clearly behind me—even though I was still good at stopping the run, I didn't get a single sack over my two years with the Jaguars. But no matter what I decided to do, odds are it wouldn't pay nearly what I could make playing in the NFL, at least not initially.

But when it was all said and done, I didn't care what anyone said, didn't care how many games of table tennis I lost. I'd heard shit like this my whole life, since back in high school when cats were trying to convince me to leave St. Monica's, to put off working out till later, to commit to a big-time college program instead of Columbia.

People had been trying to get me to shut up and go along with the herd for years. And the only thing it did was make me more determined to speak my own mind. To trust my instincts. And my instincts told me it was time to move on to something bigger than playing ball.

When my second season with Jacksonville finally ended, I told my agent, Brad, that I was done for good. My old friend refused to believe me.

"Are you shitting me?" he said. "I'm getting all these calls from the Giants! Why turn down all that money? They *want* you!"

Brad was right, the Giants did want me. They were saying all the right things too. That I'd be coming back to New York City, practically my second home. That I'd get "vet rules" in practice, which meant I'd only have to practice when I felt like it. That I'd be focusing on the run and would get a financial bonus for every sack I still managed to rack up.

It was tempting, I'll admit it. So tempting that I wouldn't go as far as to file my retirement papers with the League so I could start collecting my pension. But I still wouldn't commit to playing another year.

"I don't get it," Brad said. "You're not up to it? Why?"

My financial adviser didn't even want to ask me why. His job was money, plain and simple, and he thought I was crazy for not saying yes, probably would've ordered me back if he could.

And then Michael Strahan, the Giants' star D-end, decided to hold out for more money. So the Giants really poured that syrup on thick.

Come on, just come and play. Who knows? Maybe you can have a chance to be the star one more year. Just one more year. Just do it.

All the usual voices, all the usual whispers, goading me, trying to convince me, like Al Pacino in *The Devil's Advocate* or some shit. The devil doesn't wear red and carry a pitchfork—he dresses up, puts on that makeup, and makes himself look *good* to get you down that path.

Then, finally, right as I was thinking about maybe—maybe— giving the NFL one final shot, all of a sudden my knee started hurting.

Nothing big, nothing major, just sore. Sore in a way it hadn't been since one of the last times I had a monumental decision to make, back when I was starting high school and my growing body was struggling to keep up with my ambitions.

I hadn't realized it at the time, but facing the challenge of my painful joints back then had matured me in a way I never would've experienced if everything had come easy. I understood what it meant to face adversity. To feel betrayed by your own legs. To have incredible success and then have it snatched away from you. But I had also learned what it meant to persevere. To confront the possibility of failure—and rise above it. I could've kept sitting in our living room, watching TV, staring at the wall, thinking about how unfair life was. I could've given up football altogether. But instead Jabari and I had started training, lifting, running. I worked twice as hard as I ever had before, and it had paid off—both physically and personally. Back in high school, those aching joints had made me tough, turned me into a more thoughtful, layered, introspective individual.

And now, right on the cusp of having to make another gigantic choice—between one more year of football with the Giants and finally putting the game aside to go after that magical hot dog—my painful body came back to rescue me once again. Force me to make the hard decision.

I told Brad I was out. My knee was too sore, and my decision was final. I filed my retirement papers. Shortly after I did, my knee started feeling fine again.

After almost an entire lifetime devoting myself to football, the universe was telling me I was making the smart choice.*

---

*Then again, that ended up being the season the Giants won the Super Bowl—without me. I guess even the universe ain't right about everything.

CHAPTER TEN

EXACTLY ME

ONLY A FEW months into my retirement, and all I could think was, *Man, those motherfuckers in the Jacksonville locker room might've been right about staying in the League!*

Don't get me wrong. I loved all my freedom at first.

Wake up every day in my house in Beverly Hills at whatever time I wanted. Yawn. Walk to the kitchen, pour myself a bowl of cereal, watch some TV. Next thing you know, it's almost 11:45 in the morning.

Shit! What am I gonna do for the rest of the day?

Go to your closet, stare at all your clothes, trying to pick out something to wear like it's actually an accomplishment or something.

Man, I chose a pair a pants! That feels good! I wonder who can hang out?

Spend the afternoon driving around in your Rolls, going shopping, laughing at all those civilians locked up in their offices working 9-to-5s.

Look at that, it's already 7:30! What club or house party can I go to?

Next thing you know, you're waking up, who knows who's lying next to you, and you go through the exact same routine all over again.

And again. And again.

And again.

Suddenly I realized why people always warned you not to stay on vacation for too long. My friends would always tell me the third night in Vegas was the worst. Well, how about the thirtieth?

There actually was such a thing as *too much* chilling. Especially at the age of thirty-two. You know how many people my age were retired? No one! How much shopping can one man do? How many accessories can one man purchase? How many fake errands can one man run in a day? It was flat-out boring.

Sure, there were investments to manage, events to speak at, that kind of thing. But nothing in a boardroom can match eighty thousand people cheering your name at a game. Nothing.

I started putting on weight, started getting bigger—but not the good kind of big. Even though I was working out every day, it was nothing like working out to get ready for a game. Even exercising ended up being chill. I lost my drive, lost my passion, lost my focus.

At least during the off-season I had other athletes to hang with. Then the 2007 season began—and all the texts from my former teammates started rolling in.

How that next career looking, Wiley?

You just waking up? We got practice!

You getting fat, dog! You ain't nothing!

I'd hit 'em back after they had a bad game:

No sacks and all your fingers broken—how's that treating you?

They'd text me a photo of a stack of cash.

This treating me just fine, thank you.

I'd shake my head and laugh. What could I say? For all my locker-room talk about the importance of thinking ahead, I still needed to find a new passion to replace football. If I wanted that million-dollar hot dog, all gain and no pain, I needed to figure out how to get there. I needed to find a new purpose.

It ended up coming from the last place I expected it. On Halloween Day.

JUST BEFORE OCTOBER 31, 2007, I got a call from ESPN asking me to come to their studio in West LA to do a quick appearance on one of their shows for Halloween. I checked my incredibly busy schedule and told them that somehow I'd find a way to make the time.

The bit the producers had in mind was silly. I was supposed to get on camera and compare football players to characters from everyone's favorite scary movies. But I had fun with it.

In my imagination, the Patriots' super-intense safety, my friend and former teammate Rodney Harrison, morphed into Chucky from *Child's Play*. The Seahawks' offensive tackle Walter Jones, a quiet dude who would just stalk cats on the football field, turned into Jason from *Friday the 13th*. I sold that shit, poured all my excess creative energy into my performance.

When I was done, it was time to return to my meaningless life.

Then I got a call.

"Marcellus, that was amazing! Can you do another one next week?"

Hell yeah, I could!

This time they flew me out to Bristol, Connecticut, their world headquarters. A lot of people think of Bristol as boring and sleepy, but I had lived in Buffalo and Jacksonville, so that didn't scare me. I'd done bits in Bristol before too, so it didn't seem too out of the ordinary until I got off the plane and was greeted by two very official-looking executives.

"Marcellus," one of them told me at dinner. "Let me share this with you so we're all on the same page. If things go well tomorrow, they may offer you a bigger opportunity here."

"Oh," I said.

Honestly? The bigness of the moment didn't even register for me. After all, ESPN had access to tons of former pro-athletes, dudes with much bigger names than me, people like Emmitt Smith and Jerry Rice. We're talking former superstars and Hall of Famers.

Why the hell would the world's premier sports network want to take a chance on me?

Turned out that my past, my experience, wasn't a *disadvantage*— it was the exact opposite.

See, every NFL locker room has four levels, what I like to call the "Four Corners." Corner One is your lowest level, the guys who are always worried they're gonna get cut. The bubble players who might not make the team or make it in the League.

Corner Two is the guys who got the job security, they got a place on the roster, but no one's counting on them to make plays like the stars. They're solid but not special.

Then you got Corner Three. *Now* you're a star, you're that dude. You're balling out. You know it, and they know it. Not only do you have security, but you can push the boundaries and get away with it. Sleeping in meetings, showing up late, changing the play call when you're on the field. You want it, it's yours.

Finally there's Corner Four. You reach Corner Four as a player and you're on your way down. You're still on the team, but everyone knows you ain't what you used to be—and no one expects you to ever get there again. If you're lucky, you end up like me in Jacksonville—a reverend, someone respected. If you're not lucky, you end up a ghost of your former self.

Now think about your NFL franchise player, your superstar. How many of those corners have they experienced? Most of them know just one—Corner Three.

In fact, they get so used to it, they become institutionalized. They don't even understand how to live in a world that doesn't hang on their every word or laugh at their every joke no matter how bad it is. All they know is everyone around them constantly adjusting to them.

Suddenly they get out in the real world, and life isn't so simple. Now they have to adjust to everyone else. Now if they want someone to laugh at their joke, they actually have to be funny. It might sound stupid to you, I know—but that shit ain't easy. It's hard to adapt to a new reality.

Then you got me.

How many of those corners had I experienced? At one time or another, I had occupied them all. (And not all of them by choice, mind you.)

Corner Two my first couple years in Buffalo, Corner Three my first couple years in San Diego, and Corner Four in Jacksonville. True, I was never entirely a Corner One guy, but because I got drafted out of Columbia there were a lot of question marks when I joined the League. A lot of people wondering if I could cut it at the highest level. So I knew what it felt like to be doubted, to have to prove myself and overcome the odds.

I already knew how to adjust to everyone else. I could read a room. I knew if I didn't say something legitimately funny, all I'd get was silence.

But best of all, I had another corner that other players didn't even *know* about. A fifth corner that existed outside the locker room altogether.

I went to Columbia. And Columbia didn't just give me a great book-smart education—it taught me about bagels and donuts. It helped me understand the world *outside* of sports. The people who never stepped foot onto a field. The people who didn't know how to tackle and could barely even throw a ball. Real people. Normal people.

In other words, the people who actually watched—and worked at—ESPN.

I understood *their* perspective, not just the athlete's perspective. I knew how to take them into the locker room, where I could show them not just Corner Three, but all four.

Not just the red carpet, but the backroom, the alleyway, and everything in between.

So when ESPN told me I had a shot that day, I stayed cool, I took nothing for granted, and I went to work. The following day, they put me on show after show. Guest appearances, cohosting, commentating—you name it, I did it. And best of all, I *enjoyed* it.

I'm not the nervous type, but there was something about those last few seconds right before we went on air. I could hear the countdown through my earpiece.

Five, four, three . . .

Then that red light on the camera would turn on.

Boop!

And I'd get that rush, I'd get *juiced*—almost as good as walking through that tunnel onto the field—and I'd realize that what I was about to say was going out to millions of people everywhere, out to the *world*. And I was hooked.

I loved to show people those four corners. Loved translating the game in ways people could understand, using stories, personality, and even my understanding of sociology to bring stats and plays to life. I was communicating, making connections—with the other hosts and with my audience.

Not only that, but I'd finally found a job where I'd never have to worry about getting injured ever again. The ruptured discs in my back, my broken foot, my torn abdominal wall—they'd all robbed me of living up to my potential as a football player. Never again.

I could feel the pilot light of passion flickering. I could feel myself heating up. And it felt a lot better than the last ten months of retirement.

Finally, I was invited up to the fourth floor. The executive offices. I went behind the frosted-glass doors and it felt like a whole different world. No one I had ever seen on air before, no one I'd ever even met, and yet these were the ones who were actually in charge of every-thing. These were ones who actually called the shots.

At the end of the meeting, John Skipper shook my hand. The president of the network. He looked me in the eye and smiled.

"You're a Lion," he said. "And I like Lions."

The Lions were Columbia's mascot. He was an alumnus, just like me.

I got the job.

For the very first time, I was in the right building, on the right floor, in the exclusive ownership suite. I was playing the game within the game, and I was winning. I was gonna get that hot dog.

IT STARTED OUT like a typical night in Los Angeles.

It was December 2011. I pulled up at the club for my boy Dennis Northcutt's birthday party. I was chauffeured there in my custom-converted stretch Excursion, two big captain chairs in the back, a few flat-screen TVs, and a license plate that read "DAT DUDE." TMZ was out front, flashbulbs going off everywhere, as me and Dennis, a wide receiver for Jacksonville, get out of my crazy-ass limo and take our time sauntering to the front of the line at the door.

Then I saw her.

She was walking toward the club with a friend of hers. She was wearing an incredible dress with a long sleeve covering one arm and the other arm sleeveless, kind of reminded me of Flo-Jo. She had muscles like Flo-Jo too, chiseled, all jacked-up, put me to shame.

"Excuse me," I said. "Where you get those muscles from? You ran track?"

Now, that might sound like a line—and a very corny one at that. But something about this woman brought out the Teddy Bear in me. I wasn't just dropping a line—I really wanted to get to know her.

Her name, it turned out, was Annemarie. Yes, she had run track. And she had a whole lot of other things going on too.

Not only was she not from LA, she wasn't even American. She was Canadian, from Vancouver originally. And everyone knows Canadians are the nicest people.

Not only was she not a model or an actress, she was a hyper-educated professional, a nurse anesthetist.

Not only did she check all the boxes on my wish list, there was something more about her, something different, something I couldn't quite put my finger on yet.

But whatever it was, I knew it was right.

I grabbed my boy Jabari, my oldest friend in the world, while he was on his way in and pulled him aside.

"Look, tonight is Deno's night, so I'm gonna party my ass off for him. But whatever happens, don't let me fuck it up with her—because I'm gonna marry this girl."

Now, you know me. I've got a history of falling in love, and falling in love hard. Hell, I got engaged for the first time before I had even finished college. But Annemarie wasn't the only one who was different in this equation. I was too.

A while back, I had played in a celebrity pool tournament in Miami. Yet another classic Dat Dude adventure. Hanging with other stars, partying till late at night, searching for my next ex-girlfriend. And of course I found one, and of course we decided to go up to my hotel room later that night.

The elevator doors were sliding shut when suddenly a big-ass paw reaches in and stops them from closing.

A big-ass paw belonging to one Michael Jordan.

"What's up, man," I said.

"What's up," he replied, the perfect gentleman.

Now MJ was in the tournament too. I usually suck at pool. But the more I drank during the tournament, the better I got. I drank enough to make it all the way to the semifinals, and my table was right next to MJ's, so we got to talk a lot of shit to each other. I would've even played him in the finals if I hadn't scratched on the damn cue (by that point I was *too* drunk). So he and I were acquaintances, very casually.

But the way my girl came onto him? There was nothing casual about it.

As soon as he stepped in that elevator, she dug right in. It went from "I really respect what you've accomplished" to "those shoes of yours are sick" to "so what floor are you staying on anyway?"

He was staying in the penthouse. I was on the seventh floor.

You can guess where she wanted to get off.

It felt like the elevator was moving in slow motion, like the technology was doing its best to torture me. When we finally got to floor seven, I stepped out into the hallway.

"Alright, I see you later, big dog," I said to MJ.

"Alright," he said.

She didn't move an inch.

MJ looked at her. I looked at her. I wanted desperately to be anywhere else on the face of the earth than in that hotel. And finally MJ put me out of my misery.

"Wiley, you got a wild friend here," he said.

The tension was broken. The elevator beeped, and my "friend" realized she had to go home with silver that night instead of gold.

But I started to realize something myself. Something a lot more important.

My boys had always tried to tell me that I should look for someone who cared about *who* I was, not *what* I was—but to me that didn't make sense. What I was *was* who I was—I was a football player! What was I supposed to do, lie to girls and tell them I worked for the telephone company?

But now I got it. Here I was in my mid-thirties, going out and drinking like I had in my twenties, meeting someone whose name I wouldn't remember in a week—and then having to worry about her trying to go home with Michael Jordan instead.

Something had to change. *I* had to change.

Flash-forward to the night I met Annemarie. It was my friend's birthday, so I made sure I gave him a good time, but every ten minutes I'd find her and check in, make sure she was okay. If she needed something, I made sure she got it.

For Annemarie's part, she got to see me not only be sweet on her, but also act the fool for my boy all night long. Dancing, clownin', wiping the sweat off my face with a towel.

And you know what? She didn't judge me for it once.

That was what made her different, *that* was that special something I couldn't quite put my finger on at first. She transcended all the usual boxes I liked to check off, because to her, boxes like that didn't mean shit. She was kind, giving, incapable of judging. She naturally thought the best of everyone from the moment she met them.

Around her, I didn't have to be a walking résumé. I didn't have to worry about being the smart guy, the successful guy, the guy putting on that cape to save his family. I could be myself, and that was all she needed.

What I told Jabari that night was prophetic. After meeting in December 2011, Annemarie and I got engaged a few months later, and this time it was meant to last. In 2014, we were married.

Two weeks after I started appearing on ESPN's *NFL Live*, my boss, Seth Markman, pulled me into his office.

"Man," he told me, "the way you approach this show, you're not long for it."

Fuck, I thought.

"And that's a *good* thing," he added.

NFL Live was exactly what you'd think it would be—a football show. I put on a suit and tie, I talked about third and goal and *x*'s and *o*'s, and I was very good at it. But I did more than that too—I told stories. I talked about characters and painted a picture of life in and out of the League. I didn't limit myself to *x*'s and *o*'s—I talked about *I*'s and *U*'s, people and their personalities. That was my special sauce.

And that's why, as well as I was doing on *NFL Live*, Seth thought I could do even more.

Back before ESPN had even hired me permanently, Mike Golic had told me the same thing when I'd guest hosted *Mike & Mike* with him for the first time. The night before the show I'd stayed up poring over the subjects we were scheduled to talk about. Memorizing stats and facts like I was back hanging with Three-Piece-Suit Guy on Columbia's campus. I wanted my first time guest hosting the show to be flawless. I wanted to get all the numbers down perfectly.

I passed that test alright. I told my stories, I went off script, *and* I peppered everything with stats and facts. Then after the show, Mike gave me a little advice—to focus on what made me unique.

"Bro, your storytelling is insane," he said. "Anyone can tell you yards per carry. But only you can tell your stories. Never abandon that. Make it your go-to move!"

After my first two weeks at *NFL Live*, I noticed the show started utilizing me more for the intros and conclusions. In other words, the parts that were more personality-focused and less about hard sports. The parts that let me take you into the world of football my own unique way.

I stayed there for three more years. A step in the right direction, but still a lot of *x*'s and *o*'s. At that point, ESPN didn't focus as much on personality-driven shows; it was much more of a hard sports network. And besides—I was a former football player. Naturally all I should do was talk about football, right?

Then I found the perfect spot. *SportsNation*, hosted by Michelle Beadle and Colin Cowherd. Sometimes I'd join the two of them as an analyst, and we all had such great chemistry that I started subbing in for Colin as co-host whenever he was out.

These guys weren't arguing over stats, they weren't taking themselves too seriously, they weren't even wearing suits and ties.

It was relaxed. A conversation. Michelle and I were eating Munchos on a couch, watching sick highlights with our guests, and saying, "Dude, did you see what he did?" It was like hanging in a living room or at the bar with your boys (or, in Michelle's case, your girl). We talked about every sport, and no sports at all.

We played beer pong with Gronk, and we had the Migos, Kendrick Lamar, Rae Sremmurd, and many others perform in studio. On another episode, we even got Drake on tape talking major shit about Kendrick during an interview. (Of course, after watching the interview Drake's publicists wouldn't let us *air* that tape, but still—we got it. Take my word for it.)

When Colin and Michelle decided to go to other programs, the powers that be wanted me to start hosting *SportsNation* full-time. Of course, I wanted to too—but not in Bristol, where it was produced, and where I'd been shooting my segments up till then. I needed to be close to my home, my family. I needed to be in LA. Guess what? They wanted me bad enough to move the show to California. I felt like I was back in my NFL free-agent days, except this time instead of going from Buffalo to San Diego I was going from Bristol to Los Angeles. I became host alongside Charissa Thompson at ESPN's new LA studio, a huge upgrade from what I was doing before. Eventually the show expanded to three full-time hosts, and I've had the chance to host with amazing talents like Max Kellerman, LZ Granderson, Cari Champion, and even Michelle again. Not only that, but the location was great for my family and my home life.

Most important, I got to be me. Simply and exactly me.

MOROCCA, MY BABY girl, had just graduated high school.

She lived in Connecticut with her mom and her stepdad, so after the graduation ceremony we all went out to celebrate at a Mexican place. In Connecticut.

Let's just say I wasn't there for the food.

My baby was all grown up. Tall, athletic, she had run track in high school, and she was about to start running on the college level, for the University of Connecticut. I was so proud.

After eating—or at least pretending to eat—we all went around the room, each of us giving a short speech to congratulate her. And for once, maybe the first time ever, we were all there, her entire family. Me and Annemarie; Tiki and my Columbia godmother, Jackie Blackett. Kim and her husband, Anthony, a great guy who did as much as anyone to raise our daughter; and Kim's parents too. Morocca's brothers and sister. Everyone.

Morocca stood up to say a few words herself. She panned the crowd, took us all in, black, white, mocha, married, divorced, remarried. A real-life modern family.

And she started crying.

It had taken a long time to get to this dinner, to get to this moment.

As she had grown up, I had done everything I could to be there for her, given that most of the time I lived thousands of miles away. She spent a lot of time during the summer with me. Whenever she could visit, I would fly out to Connecticut on the first flight that morning, pick her up from home, then fly back with her to LA that same day. The longest commute in America.

But the reality was that I simply wasn't there every single day. Her mom and Anthony were. To Morocca, they were Mom and Dad. To

Morocca's Connecticut friends, for many years, Anthony was the only dad they knew about. Not out of any sort of malice toward me, but because it was easier, more convenient, to talk about the one dad who actually lived at home. In a way, it reminded me of my own family life growing up. On the surface, a perfect Universal Studios family. But look a little closer, and you'd start seeing all that plywood. You'd realize that shit was a lot more complicated.

For a lot of her childhood, Morocca lived in that bubble. I won't lie—the situation made me angry. But I suppressed my anger, both because I wanted what was best for her and because I partly blamed myself—rightly or wrongly—for the position she was in. I never wanted her to have to deal with the dynamic of a divided family, and I wanted to do everything I could to make it easier for her. Even if that meant going with the flow when the significance of her LA family was downplayed.

As she got older, though, the bubble started to burst under its own weight.

Her friends might overhear her talking on the phone with me, doing something as simple as saying, "Bye, Dad."

Wait a second—I thought your dad was in the other room. Who were you talking to?

It got even more complicated as my profile grew on ESPN.

Wait, your dad is Marcellus Wiley? I knew your last name was Wiley, but I didn't know you were that *Wiley. Why didn't you tell me! I follow him on Twitter!*

The next thing you know, I'd be at her high school track meets and people would want pictures with the two of us. We'd always say yes, then Morocca would smile and shake her head after.

"You know they don't want a picture because of *me*, Dad."

Imagine yourself in her situation. Imagine you grew up keeping someone naturally out of the conversation, and suddenly it's thrown right in your face. That's not easy to handle.

She didn't ask to be stuck between two families, on two sides of the country. It was the reality we gave her, and she had to deal with it the best she could. Now that she was older, though, at least the two of us could talk it through. That meant the world to me—to simply be able to listen to her concerns. To hear her pain. To be there for her emotionally, even if I couldn't always be around physically.

At the restaurant after her graduation, Morocca wiped the tears from her eyes.

"My whole life, this is all I ever wanted," she said. "My family to be together and love each other."

That's right. That's my daughter.

I KEPT UP WITH Junior Seau after I left San Diego.

I'd see him around at parties, at charity functions, or maybe we'd grab lunch. I noticed his wattage was a little lower, like the glow he used to have wasn't quite as bright. Nothing I chalked up to any serious problems. He just didn't seem quite as joyous, quite as jovial, as he once had.

Maybe this was a good thing, I thought. Junior enjoying retirement, finally learning how to tell people no instead of picking up every single check at his restaurant.

It was all relative, anyway. A low-wattage Junior was still happier than 95 percent of humanity. He was one of the greatest players ever, yeah. But somehow he managed to be an *even better* person. No ego, no arrogance. I'd never met anyone like that before. Still haven't. He was an angel.

The day Junior died, I was on air when our producer said he

needed to talk to me during break. We were live on my radio show, *Max & Marcellus*, on ESPNLA with Max Kellerman, so all I could do was wait.

Shit. I hated having to wait.

"Look," he said at the break. "I don't know if this is real or not, but my friend is a fireman in San Diego, and he just told me Junior's dead."

I started googling like crazy, checking every news site I could to see if it was true, to figure out what had happened. I texted Junior himself, hoping that maybe, by messaging him, I could somehow make it not be true.

"Hey buddy," I typed, using his favorite word. "You good?"

Nothing. Not a word from anywhere or anyone other than my producer.

The show kept airing, but I wasn't paying any attention. All I could do was keep hitting refresh on my cell, hoping for some kind of news.

Suddenly my phone lit up. In my mind, it plays back to this day like it happened in slo-mo. I looked at my screen, but it wasn't him, it wasn't Junior. It was Orlando Ruff, another former Chargers teammate.

"Did you hear?" he said.

And I knew. Just like that, I knew for sure Junior was gone.

Junior, the most positive, vibrant personality I had ever known, had taken his own life. Later lab studies of his brain demonstrated that he was suffering from CTE, most likely caused by repeated impacts to his head from decades of football.

What was hardest for me wasn't learning about the CTE. I've had bouts of depression in my past, in high school and during my last season in San Diego, but I overcame them both, and they felt like natural human responses to the adversity I was facing at the time. Because CTE appears as direct damage to your brain, there's no way doctors can tell if you have it until after you die. I may have it, I may not. I have no way of knowing, but it's something I have to live with. I may feel fine now, but anyone who thinks banging your head a million times over twenty-five years of games and practice *won't* have repercussions is kidding themselves.

All of that I grimly accept, because I have no choice.

No, what was hardest for me was finding out that the Junior I loved, the Junior I believed in, the Junior I had modeled myself after, had stopped existing long before his suicide—and I hadn't even noticed. My friend was depressed, he was hurting, he was wounded inside, but I kept believing it was the same old Junior. There was a perception deception. On his part, and on our part too.

Sure, part of it was that Junior tried to hide that pain from us. He chose to suffer silently instead of sharing his burdens with all his friends, even though we would've gladly helped him. But how much of it was something I simply didn't *want* to see?

Maybe I couldn't bear the idea that this man who had inspired me for so many years was actually destructible? Maybe it was too tough for me to come to accept that someone who'd been so strong, so vital, could be brought down at such a young age? Maybe I was worried, deep down, that someday that would be me?

Whatever it was, I had missed the signals, and I hadn't been able to help.

I didn't know it then, but it wouldn't be long before I'd encounter health signals of my own. Something very different from CTE, but just as impossible for me to ignore.

CHAPTER ELEVEN

A REAL HYDRATION SITUATION

MY WORKOUT AT Freddie Roach's Wild Card Boxing Club in Hollywood went exactly like it always went—great, and without me getting hit a single time.

When I walked in, Freddie was there sitting behind the front desk like he did every day of the week. Freddie's one of the most legendary trainers of all time, coached guys like Manny Pacquiao, Miguel Cotto, and Julio César Chávez, to name a few. Freddie boxed himself for about eight years, hell of a career, but ended up getting Parkinson's disease, his soft-spoken words not always too clear. If anyone understood what it meant to sacrifice for his sport, Freddie did.

The dude was a superstar, but he still loved to work the front desk at his own gym. Mild-mannered, friendly, but with this aura that lets you know you should never test him. He's an alley-cat fighter. A guy who would go through a brick wall if he wanted to whip your ass. So you make sure he never does.

Freddie trained all the greats, so naturally he didn't train me at all. I'd go in and work with another guy, Ernie, doing drills, working the mitt and the heavy bag—and never, ever, letting anyone lay a damn hand on me.

People teased me all the time. *Why you learning to box if you never even get hit?*

Man, I was thirty-nine years old. I'd been through enough of the real thing in my life. Didn't need to *pay someone* to try to whup my ass.

Just wanted to go into the gym, get my workout in, fire up my heart rate, and hone the technique I never wanted to use. And that's exactly what happened that summer day in 2015.

Until I walked out of the gym, folded myself into my Porsche to go to work, and my hamstring locked up. Out of nowhere. Couldn't even move it.

Shit, I thought. *Here it comes.*

ANYONE WHO'S HEARD me on the radio or seen me on TV knows my *favorite* situation is a *hydration* situation. Going out, chilling with some friends, enjoying a cocktail or seven during the afternoon, the evening, and sometimes, if I'm really having fun, making it all the way to morning.

That's what I call the *perfect* hydration situation.

Then there's the other kind of hydration situation—one that doesn't involve alcohol at all. It's the kind that actually inspired the term in the first place. That one ain't so great.

It actually all started with my aunt, back when I was eight years old. She was young herself, only twenty-eight, and she died of kidney failure.

Kidney failure? You can die from something like that? It was tough for my eight-year-old brain to comprehend, but one thing stuck with me, something both my mama and my grandmamma drilled into my skull, saying it over and over and over again:

Drink water. Your aunt died because she didn't drink enough water. Drink. Water.

That was my *real* hydration situation—and according to them, it was life or death. So ever since I was a little kid, you better believe I was drinking the fuck out of water.

But sometimes I still didn't get enough. I learned that lesson the hard way when I played at Columbia.

I was in spring training for my last season when it happened the first time. I had been drinking a lot of water—but getting by on a typical shitty college diet of Pizza Hut and Taco Bell. I was on the field, working like crazy, playing both offense and defense, when suddenly I experienced my first-ever total-body cramp.

It's difficult to describe to anyone who hasn't experienced it, but imagine that each one of your body's muscles is a rope, and all of a sudden, without warning, all at the same time, they all get pulled tight, to within a centimeter of snapping. Every muscle without exception, from ear to toe, bulging out of your skin and feeling like it could pop wide open any second. When I say "ear," I mean it—I can literally remember my ear being pulled tight against my jaw, my skull.

Every part of me locked up. I was unable to move.

My teammates had no idea what to do with me. I was placed in a cold tub and given a saline solution IV to hydrate me. When I was finally loose enough to walk without support, I went home and slept. My body was young and healed quickly.

Fast-forward a few weeks to our first game of the season, against Harvard. I walked into the locker room at halftime, sat down on the bench, and couldn't stand up again. They gave me an IV. I walked out for the second half with blood still soaking through the gauze they had patched me up with. I played the second half, and we won in overtime, 20–13.

If you thought I drank a lot of water before all that happened, you should've seen me after. I had a bottle with me wherever I went, and I upgraded fluids—from water to Pedialyte, this miracle drink for kids that was just water and electrolytes, without as much sugar as sports drinks. That stuff was my elixir. I never left home without at least a gallon of it.

Then I got to the NFL.

I kept on the fluids. If it's possible, I drank even more. Pedialyte? I couldn't get enough.

But that was nothing compared with the painkillers. Take my history of injuries and add it to the normal wear and tear of playing in the League, and that's an equation for a lot of hurt. I'd go to the team docs, and they'd dish them out—painkillers and more painkillers. Pills and shots, little pricks, and giant needles right to my joints. Before games, after games, during the week.

They flooded my system for years. Saturated my body, my blood, my kidneys. Never really left my system, no matter how much I tried to wash them out with more liquids.

That day in 2015, after my morning at Freddie's gym, all those painkillers finally caught up with me—and left me moments away from being on dialysis for the rest of my life.

_____

I WAS IN MY car outside Freddie's, I could feel the rope in my leg stretching, tightening, locking up, and I tried to stay calm. I had to get to ESPN for a pre-production meeting with my *SportsNation* crew. All the way downtown, probably a thirty-minute drive. I wanted to get to work, had to get to work, never missed work, I had never even been late in eight years.

Remember your routine, I thought. *Breathe. Straighten it out. Slowly. Slowly. Slowly.*

I breathed. I slowly straightened it out. And of course, I guzzled the last few drops of my Pedialyte.

I started the car. I could feel the cramps spreading, but I tried to ignore it, pretend it wasn't happening. I was right on the edge—*right there*—and if I admitted it was happening, if I gave in to the spreading pain, I knew it'd be over. I'd fall over the edge and right into that abyss.

I hit Highland Avenue, in the heart of Hollywood, and suddenly I realized I couldn't even brake—my body was so straight and so stiff I couldn't even move my foot off the gas pedal. Just kept going, picking up speed on a street where there's tons of traffic and a light every few blocks.

Finally I managed to jerk my body over to the side, get my foot off the gas. I couldn't put it on the brake, but at least I wasn't speeding up. I started coasting, nudged the steering wheel, and slowly rolled to a stop on the side of the road.

The first thing I did?

Used every ounce of my remaining motion to cradle my cell against my head and call work.

"Hey, yeah, this is Marcellus. I'm gonna be a little late, but I'm coming. Yep, all good, just a little late, that's all. Cool, see ya."

I told you—I refused to admit that anything was wrong. Couldn't go off that edge.

I shifted my tightening body in my seat and managed to press the gas again. I have no idea how, but somehow I managed to make it, block by block, mile by mile, all the way to ESPN. Pulled into the massive underground parking garage that's right below the gigantic building.

Drove into a parking spot, came to a stop, and that was it.

That motherfucker went off the edge.

Everything locked up. Everything! I was still trying to talk myself down, tell myself that everything would be okay.

I ain't that old. I'm still the same guy who finished that game bloody from the IV. This isn't even football, this is a parking lot! Just need a few minutes and another Pedialyte! I'm fine!

I tried to open the door. I couldn't.

I wasn't fine.

I was helpless.

WHEN YOU'RE PLAYING in the NFL, you're not married—you're on a date. It might be a long date, if you're with the same team for a few years, but it's still only a date. There's no real commitment, and there definitely ain't no unconditional love. You're constantly trying to impress, constantly trying to earn that affection—that playing time, that spot on the team.

If you have a problem, you're not gonna go to your date to advertise that shit. You're gonna try to show them your best self at all times.

Now maybe if it's something small, sure. If it's something simple they can fix, like a cramp—great, here's some salt tablets, here's some pickle juice or Pedialyte. They'll fix it, and you'll stay on that date.

But if it's something big? Like a problem with your kidneys? No way. They ain't looking into that. They don't even want to know. If it's something big, you're out of here, and they're finding someone else to go to the prom.

That mentality, that complete imbalance of power, explains how a guy like me and, really, everyone else who played the game in the '00s, the '90s, and earlier ended up gorging ourselves on painkillers. In some cases, maybe many cases, to the point where we get addicted. Because we were always covering up the issue, always getting just right enough to keep on playing, but never, ever, going deep enough to really fix things.

Just keep playing. Just stay on that field. No matter what, don't let that date end.

It started in my rookie year, at Buffalo. A pretty simple injury, plantar fasciitis, which feels like a bunch of needles in the arch of your foot. That led to wearing a plastic boot while I slept overnight and had therapy during the day, along with taking a mystery painkiller that I still don't know to this day.

Just walked over to the trainer, told him I have a problem, and it was, "I got you, baby." Slipped me a little manila envelope with a little magic pill. No written instructions, no sit-down consultation, just "Take this and you'll feel better." And I did.

Then year three came around, and all of a sudden the little envelope wasn't enough. By now I was getting more reps—not only practicing, but playing for real. And when you start playing, you start feeling shit. Not even injuries, per se, just colliding with three-hundred-pound dudes at full speed over and over and over again.

What did they have for that? Toradol. A little pinprick in your butt before every game, and bam, you ain't feeling shit anymore.

Now that I've educated myself, I know you should take Toradol only in controlled situations under strict medical supervision. But back then, we didn't know a damn thing. We wanted to stay on that date, so most starters were taking it every single game.

In my fifth year I went to San Diego, and right around then I also started taking Vioxx. Don't get me wrong—I didn't stop taking the other stuff. In fact, there was a whole routine, a pill-taking balancing act we all used to make sure the painkillers maintained exactly the right kind of high.

Vioxx you took day to day, to get you through practices, off-days, and life in general. No way you stuck only with Vioxx on game days, though, because if you did that, you felt the hell you were going through. So on game days you added those Toradol butt pricks. Make sure you save those only for games, though, because you start taking those and your body will get used to it. If your body gets used to it, then what you gonna do on Sunday, bro?

It's like Pac-Man. You wanted those little Vioxx dots to get you through the maze, but you saved those big Toradol energy-dots for when you really need to go crazy and start taking out those ghosts.

Then there was the *next* next-level stuff. The needles and the Lortab.

That also started with the Chargers, my very first year, when the foot surgery I needed in week one looked like it was gonna put a quick end to what was supposed to be my biggest season.

That's when the needle came out—you remember that, right?

Long as a baby's arm, stabbed right into the middle of my joint and wiggled agonizingly until they found the epicenter of the pain, all while I was biting on a towel trying not to scream.

I did that before every game that season. And for the rest of my career, each time I had a major injury the needle came back out. Those "strained groins" in my sixth year (really a misdiagnosed tear in my abdominal wall, but who's counting), the AC joint separation that led to a torn labrum and rotator cuff in my seventh year, then in my eighth year a hip pointer. Needle, needle, needle, every single game.

No needles during the week, though, so the docs threw another pill in the mix, stronger than all the others—Lortab. Google it and you'll see "high risk for addiction" is the first thing they list.

Maybe that Vioxx wasn't quite doing you right, or maybe you needed more than a Toradol prick before a game—no problem, pop a Lortab and you got that *boom!*

I wasn't the exception—I was the rule. Players talked about the painkillers they were on like runners talk about the shoes they wear.

How you feel? You hurtin'? You just hurtin' you should try out the Vioxx. But if you hurtin'—*like* hurtin' *hurtin'—well, you gotta go get that Lortab.*

Honestly, how would we know any better? We had doctors, medical professionals, giving us this shit. We had no doubts or questions. We were hurting, we knew these guys went to school for this stuff, so we deferred. Anything to stay on that field, earn our pay, keep that date going as long as humanly possible.

By the time I left the League after ten years, my tolerance for meds and pain was crazy. I'd go to a doctor and he'd poke me with something and say, "What, you can't feel this? Really?" I couldn't even find a massage therapist because no one pressed hard enough.

The drugs had affected me in other ways too. Ways I didn't even understand yet. But I was about to learn.

MY PHONE STARTED ringing in the car. Somehow I barely moved my hand enough to answer my cell, pressed the speakerphone because I couldn't get it up to my head.

It was my coworkers at ESPN. The meeting had started, and for the first time *ever* I wasn't there on time, so they were searching for me.

I told them I was parked downstairs in my car, my body was completely locked up, I couldn't move a muscle—but not to worry because I'd be totally fine in a minute.

Yeah, right.

Thankfully for me, when my cohost on *SportsNation*, Max Kellerman, heard that, he didn't believe a word of it. He knew something wasn't right. Max was the coolest, smartest guy in the world, but he was always nervous when it came to health and safety. Total germophobe, doesn't even like shaking hands, worried he might get cooties or some shit. Usually *I'm* the dude who tells Max to chill out and relax, but for once I'm glad he freaked.

He came down and found me in my car, straight as a board and completely immobile.

"Marcellus," he said, "something wrong? What's going on?"

"Naw, naw," I said. "I'm good, dog! I'm just locking up. I just need more Pedialyte!"

That's right. My dumb-ass still wanted to make it into work.

"You're crazy," he said.

"I'm good, I swear! Just bring me a Pedialyte, man!"

"I'm calling Dr. Klapper."

That's Dr. Robert Klapper, my friend and the director of orthopedic surgery at LA's Cedars-Sinai Hospital, one of the top hospitals in the nation. He also hosts a weekend radio show for ESPN and would do guest spots on our show all the time. Max called him, told him my symptoms, and Dr. Klapper said I had to go to the hospital immediately.

"Naw, naw," I shouted. "Pedialyte!"

"You need to get to the emergency room *now*," he said.

"I can't even move!" I said. "How the hell am I gonna go?"

By now a small group had formed around the car of this massive, completely immobile former Pro Bowler. It was officially a scene.

"*Shit*," Max said. "We can't even get in his car to get behind the wheel! He's too big!"

They called a big Uber SUV. Working together, a few of the guys slowly pried me out of the car, laid me in the back of the truck, and took off for Cedars-Sinai.

By this point even *I* could tell something was intensely, dramatically wrong with me. I was starting to black out. I felt like I had no more water left in me, no more blood. I was all dried out and brittle.

It hurt so bad that it didn't hurt. I felt it, and I didn't feel it. I was beyond pain.

We arrived at the hospital, and for the first time that day I felt afraid.

Hours earlier I had been going about my day, having a normal workout—not even getting hit!—on my way to work, and now here I was in the ER!

There was something about the tone of the doctors' voices, these serious people in their sterilized scrubs, examining me with creases in their foreheads and concern in their eyes, and saying, "We need to make sure you're okay." Throwing around terms like "renal failure" I had never heard applied to me before.

Something about it all told me that something was wrong, *this was not normal.*

My wife, Annemarie, arrived, thankfully, and talked to the doctors, used her training as a nurse anesthetist to decode what was really happening, and told me, for once, to shut up, listen, and do what they said.

They put me on an IV, pumping me full of substances I couldn't even pronounce, and then into an ambulance to take me to another hospital.

This wasn't football anymore. This wasn't "throw him in a cold bath and give him some Pedialyte." They were putting me into an ambulance for an extended stay at the hospital. I'd never been in an ambulance before. They couldn't even say when I'd be able to go home again.

This was real.

As the EMTs placed me into the ambulance, still barely able to move, I thought back to my childhood best friend, Corby.

When I was eleven years old, Corby got hit by a car while he was riding his bike. When I got to the hospital, they wouldn't let me see him because I was a minor and I wasn't family. He was about to be medivacked to another hospital for emergency surgery.

I begged the doctor to let me see my friend before he left. Begged him.

"Alright," he said. "Look out there—we're about to transport him."

I looked outside. I saw the blade spinning as they rolled him into the helicopter on the gurney. He was lying there. His head in a neck brace, his body wrapped up in white like a mummy.

That was the last time I ever saw Corby alive. Never even got to say goodbye. My only release was sobbing in my grandma's arms.

I thought of Corby then, and wondered how much pain he had

been in as they had taken him away. Wondered what his final thoughts had been in those last few hours before he died.

The EMTs strapped me in and closed the ambulance doors. I was still hooked up to an IV. We drove off to my second hospital that day.

BY THE TIME I retired from pro football, I was like Pablo Escobar with all the dope I had stored up—not just in my body, but in my medicine cabinet. Any pill, cream, or needle prick I hadn't used over the last ten years, I had kept and added to my arsenal.

Funny thing was, I didn't use any of it after I quit the game. I've heard of people with addictive personalities, and I guess I just don't have one. Only things I've ever been hooked on were Hawaiian Punch, tacos with ketchup, and Cheetos—love that salty crunch—but drugs? Nope.

I grew up around addiction, I had family members addicted to the worst of the worst, crack, you name it. I've heard all the reasons they got addicted, and I empathize. But it's not for me. When I was done with painkillers, when I didn't need them for my livelihood, that was it, I was done.

But I still kept every last one of them, all in my own personal safe. Didn't throw out a single pill.

There was something psychological about it, I think. Even though I never used them, it comforted me somehow *knowing* they were there. Just in case. In case of what, who knew? It could've been as dumb as falling off a skateboard. But whatever it was, I knew I wouldn't have to worry about going to some doctor who'd look at my busted leg and say, "You're fine! Have an Advil!" Advil was too weak to work on me, because I'd built up a crazy tolerance over the years. So if something bad happened to me, I always had my Pablo, my strong stuff, to fall back on. Who needed Advil if I had ten-year-old hydrocodone? That shit wasn't going anywhere.

Until one day in 2012, six years after I played my last snap, Annemarie found it all.

She wasn't my wife yet, just my girlfriend, but she was staying over a lot. Things were getting serious. Then she saw my treasure trove of painkillers, and she realized things were serious on a whole other level.

"What the hell is all this?" she said, laughing despite how completely disturbed she was. "Is all this *yours*?"

"Yeah," I said, kind of defensively. "It's from back when I played."

"You took *all* these?"

"Well, not all at once!"

"Where are the recommended doses? Or the instructions? Or even the doctor's name?"

"What?" I said, completely ignorant. "Why would I need that? They just gave us packages, worked fine!"

"Do you know how old some of this stuff is? It's from, like, the Stone Age! You can't keep pills like this around! This shit is dangerous!"

To be fair, my oldest pills were from my first season in Buffalo, about fifteen years prior, which definitely is *not* the Stone Age. Although, yeah, pretty damn old.

But Annemarie didn't want to argue semantics. She knew medicine, she studied it. If anyone knew how dangerous all this stuff was, she did.

Even though, deep down, I knew she was right, I didn't want to give my Pablo up. She had *no idea* what I went through in the NFL. Four different teams, multiple surgeries, countless collisions, and most of all that constant pressure to never show pain, to never show fear, to never even *admit* you might not be able to play. She didn't know. She *couldn't* know.

"Look," she said. "What you went through was like guerrilla warfare. I know I didn't experience that personally, I get it. But you have to let me bring you back to civilized society."

I realized that I hadn't been holding on to all those drugs just because I was worried I might fall on some skateboard—hell, I didn't even own one. I was holding on to something else too. The life I had lived, the entire culture of living fast, playing hard, having access to whatever I wanted whenever I wanted it, and always wanting more— and never giving a fuck about the consequences, even if my own health was at stake.

It's weird, but there was actually something appealing about always being on that date in the NFL, even if I was the one who could get dumped. The excitement, the risk, the uncertainty. Always having to be at my best, to push myself harder. And yeah, to take a bunch of painkillers if that's what I had to do.

Six years after retiring from football, I still hadn't let it all go. The drugs might not have been addictive, but the lifestyle—that was.

Together, she and I threw away my ten years' worth of pills and packets.

Two years later, she and I got married. The year after that, I was in the hospital.

My lifestyle wasn't ready to let go of me just yet.

AT THE SECOND hospital, they continued to pump me full of fluids, chemicals, everything they had. They ran test after test after test. Poking me, prodding me. My wings were clipped. My muscles had regained their functionality, but they were still cramped, in a deep pain. My body was so dry, so dehydrated, that even though I was hooked up to a catheter, no urine came out for a day and a half. I usually peed every twenty minutes! I wasn't going anywhere.

The doctors threw a bunch of Latin terms at me when they told me what happened, but it all came down to this: despite all the water I'd been drinking, despite all the bottles of Pedialyte, I had somehow suffered from severe dehydration to the point where I lost kidney function.

After all those years of painkillers, my kidneys had been thrown completely off balance. The filters hadn't been functioning right, and over time massive amounts of protein had built up in my bloodstream. Until finally, suddenly, the whole damn system shut down.

That's what the doctors said. But none of them could break it down like Annemarie.

She knew my spirit. Knew that if it had been up to me, I never would've even gone to the hospital in the first place. I'd still be back in the parking garage, frozen stiff, asking for another bottle of Pedialyte. Hell, even now, even after all this, deep down I still really just wanted to go home!

"Marcellus," she said, looking me in the eye, "you have to remember that you're the same person who had an entire cabinet full of capsules, needles, and anything else you can think of when we first met. Whatever you took before, whatever you've been through, is still affecting you. There's *no way* a single workout should ever do this to you."

"I know, baby" I said. "I get it."

"I don't think you do," she said. "You retired early for a reason. You want to raise a family. We both do. I don't want you to leave me early. You have to slow down and take better care of yourself. I need you."

That was all she needed to say. I flashed back to when I was seven years old and I had made the decision that I would take care of my mama, my dad, and my sister for the rest of my life. I had to put my entire family on my back and carry us all out of South Central.

That's what I had to do now. This wasn't just personal anymore, wasn't just about me. I needed to be better for her, for my family, for the children she and I wanted to have. This was business.

I stayed at the hospital for three days and two nights.

My first day, all my numbers from all the tests still looked bad—and it felt like they were running a new test every five minutes. Despite all the fluids and everything else they were throwing at my system, nothing had changed.

On day two, I stabilized. I wasn't good yet, but I was at least out of trouble.

Finally, on day three, my numbers significantly improved. I was in the clear. I packed my things and got ready to go home to be with my wife. I was going to take it slow this time. There was no big game I had to play in that afternoon. I could afford to ease myself back into the real world.

The doctors told me I was fortunate. If I had waited two hours more to get treatment, I wouldn't have needed three days in the hospital—I would've lost my kidneys forever. I would've been on dialysis for the rest of my life.

A YEAR LATER, IN 2016, I joined a players' class-action lawsuit against the NFL, charging the League with violating federal law by giving us powerful, prescription-level painkillers without the medical guidance, oversight, and caution required by the DEA.

I gave depositions and countless press interviews, joined by dozens of other former players. I felt a responsibility not only to myself, but to my brethren in the game, to my craft, so I followed through.

The NFL, big surprise, denies it all—even though multiple team doctors testified that they violated regulations. And a lot of the charges have already been dismissed by a judge, partly because of a bunch of technicalities and the usual legal nonsense that protects giant companies from admitting they screwed up. But honestly, that doesn't bother me.

What am I gonna worry about—the money? They can keep their eighty-eight dollars or whatever it would've been after the lawyers' fees.

I just wanted the world to know what we went through, and I wanted the League to be held accountable. Not even necessarily by paying out extra money to guys whose health they ruined—though they should—but at least by admitting there was a problem and allocating resources to study and improve players' health.

Stop looking at players as adversaries—or at best, as an expensive date who can be tossed out if someone better comes along. Instead, look at us as partners. Realize that investing in us as people isn't only good for us—it's good for the business too. It's good for the game.

Thanks to that lawsuit and a ton of other outside pressure, there's already been progress.

Teams can't pass out pills like they're candy anymore. Vioxx—stuff I used to take all the time—was actually withdrawn from the market by its own manufacturer after it was found to increase the risk of heart attack. Toradol is still around, but the medical supervision is more rigorous, the dosage more controlled, and most of the other stuff has been banned unless there's legitimate medical need, and not just to get guys back on the field.

But that's only a start. A huge problem isn't medication, or even concussions—it's the whole system of team doctors.

These are medical professionals who took an oath to put their patients' interests first. Who are their patients? The players. But who pays their checks? Who gives them sideline seats and celebrity perks? Who do they report to every single week with updates on who can play and who has to sit? The teams.

Our doctors don't report to us—they report to the coaches, the general managers, the owners. Because of that conflict of interest, it's virtually impossible for our health to come first—instead, the team's profits do.

That system isn't going to change anytime soon, so players have to act to protect themselves—by hiring their *own* doctors. Something the owners shouldn't just tolerate but encourage. The same way that almost every player puts together a business team right before he joins the League—agent, financial adviser, business manager—he should put together his own health team too. Doctor, chiropractor, movement specialist. A group of people who aren't his second opinion, they're his first. They don't even have to be full-time. Just a team of trusted specialists who know everything about you, your entire history from day one, and who are paid to be on call if and when you need them—a small price to pay compared with an NFL salary. And a football career that could be far longer and far more lucrative with honest, unbiased medical care.

At the same time, we need a change in the culture itself. A culture that currently values the short-term reward of a player getting back in the game as quickly as possible instead of the long-term benefits that come from a longer, more stable recovery. A culture that's willing to sacrifice someone's knee or ankle or back as long as it means the team wins *this* game, or makes the playoffs *this* season.

Well, what about the next game? What about the next season, or the next five seasons after that? What about the entire life a player has to look forward to after retirement? Getting a player's health right, making sure that a joint, muscle, or bone is fully healed before they see the field again—that's not only good ethics, it's good business, and good sports. Over time, it means more wins for everyone.

A cultural shift that profound won't be easy. It won't be fast. But it can be done, and it needs to begin with all of us. Owners, general managers, coaches, players—and fans.

SINCE I CAME within hours of losing my kidneys forever, I've become incredibly careful. I take it slow, like Annemarie said. I do it for her. I do it for my family.

Of course I still drink my fluids, and Pedialyte will always be my best friend. But now I watch my sweat levels when I work out, and I flush out my system with CKLS (Colon, Kidney, Liver, Spleen) herbals.

Most of all, I'm trying to be less stubborn, trying to listen to friends like Max and my wife and trust that they have my best interest at heart—even if deep down I'd rather hold on to those pills, that Pedialyte, that NFL lifestyle I enjoyed for so long.

Now, anytime I'm talking to Max and I get him on a point, he stops me.

"Hold up, Marcellus. Don't forget I saved your life."

He's right.

And I never will.

CHAPTER TWELVE

BIGGER THAN ME

WHEN MY SECOND child was born two years ago, I had no idea what was coming out.

These days almost everyone finds out whether they're having a boy or a girl a long time in advance. They want to be able to plan better, pick out colors for the nursery, pick out exactly the right things for their registry, whatever.

Not me. I wanted to be surprised, even managed to convince Annemarie to go along with me, as much as she was dying to know. I wanted a blank canvas.

Embrace the unknown, savor the uncertainty, never run away from it, like I had in life.

Then in the hospital, I saw that second "umbilical cord" come out, and I knew I had a son. He had some of the longest fingers I'd

NEVER SHUT UP   257

ever seen on a baby, gigantic mitts like his mama's. I held him in my arms and I was in an emotional free fall. No anxiety, no external pressures, nothing but loving this kid that Annemarie and I had made together.

I will forever deal with the guilt I feel over my experience with Morocca. People would call me a parent, and I'd feel like a fraud. No matter how much I loved her, I wasn't there for her as much as I wanted to be. I wasn't involved in her life the way my parents had been involved in mine. I wasn't a full parent—I was a parent lite.

Now, with the birth of my son, here was my shot at vindication. I would give him everything I'd wanted to give Morocca—and more. I had been hoping for this opportunity, the chance to be a full-time parent, for years. Now it was finally game time, and I realized there was nothing I could've done to fully prepare for this experience.

You can't understand what it all means until you finally get in that game.

Physically taking care of him consumed every second of every day. Can't stop, won't stop, so many details to constantly manage. He messes up his diaper, so then you put new clothes on, but now he wants to eat, so he gets food all over his clothes, so you put new clothes on, except now he messes up his diaper all over again, so it's time for another set of clothes!

As a football player, I was used to having those details handled for me. I was the performer in the equation—I showed up at my locker and there was my fresh, clean uniform all laid out for me and ready to go.

Not anymore. I became like a parental MacGyver, making shit up as I went along.

But more important than all that—and twenty times more challenging—was the process of raising him, nurturing him emotionally, psychologically, spiritually. How would I support him while giving him enough space to be himself? How would I inspire him to greatness while giving him enough room to fail? How could he stay "hungry"— motivated—even though I'd make sure he'd never want for anything? What was the right balance?

We named him after me, Marcellus Junior. I was named after the greatest boxer of all time, Cassius Marcellus Clay, and I always felt like it gave me power. With a name that fresh, you gotta do something in this world, you gotta amount to something. I wanted my son to be blessed with that mark of greatness the same way I was.

But as he grew, I never actually called him Marcellus. Wouldn't even use his initials, MJ, like almost everyone else did. The only thing I called him directly was "Big Man"—or, when I talk about him to other people, "Lil' Man." No proper name at all.

As much as I liked "Marcellus," I realized he had to create his *own* name for himself. To turn into the man *he* wanted to be. To embrace the unknown, savor the uncertainty, the same way I had before he was born.

Is giving him that freedom always gonna be easy for me to respect? Hell no.

Our future is wide open, but life isn't as simple as it was when I was growing up. He and I will have to make choices about our lives, hard choices. Including about football, the sport that got us here in the first place.

I GREW UP JUST twenty miles from where I'm raising my son. It's just a thirty-minute drive from the Valley to the hood. But it's a whole other world.

Where I grew up, if you were walking down the street or going to the store, you didn't say nothing to nobody. Look straight ahead, don't wear the wrong colors in the wrong places, and always watch what those fingers were doing—you couldn't even make the peace sign, because it was one bent knuckle away from a gang sign. The first concussion I ever got wasn't from playing football, it was from playing on the swings, when a couple dudes from the VNG Bloods decided to throw me off for fun, leaving a hole in my head and—nine stitches later—a scar I had for life.

In the Valley, there isn't just a street and a sidewalk; there's a bike lane and a stroller lane. The park doesn't have gangs, because it's too full of parents and kids having playdates and planning meetups, because *everyone* has kids. And there definitely ain't no Yee's restaurant, but there are eight—eight!—different yoga places within a mile if you want to get your stretch on.

Where I grew up, I didn't have options. I'm not just talking about yoga—I'm talking about life. Sure, I was able to choose not to fight, because my sister fought for me. And yeah, I was able to pick Columbia instead of a big football program because my parents sacrificed for my education and I got good grades. But past that?

I *had* to carry us on my shoulders. I *had* to get us out of the hood. I *had* to put on that cape when I was seven years old, because no one else would. There was no choice, no decision to make—it was succeed or die trying.

And if I wanted to fly? *Football* was my fastest way to the clouds.

My son? He doesn't have to think about saving his family. The only thing he has is options. He won't just go to the best schools, he'll go to the best *pre*school. He can be anything he wants to be, no matter what.

That's not all positive either.

It's something I talk about with my former teammates all the time, other guys who started from nothing like I did. We got where we are today in part because of all that adversity. It was like pressure grinding away at a lump of coal, making us hard as a diamond. We got that dog in us because we were hungry.

How do we put that dog in our kids if they always got a full belly? How do we make sure they sparkle like diamonds if there's no natural pressure shaping them?

For kids like ours, that need has to be internal. It has to come from within, springing from a place of pure passion for whatever it is they do. Sure, I know successful people—including athletes—who grew up not wanting for anything and naturally had that desire. But possessing it isn't a given.

The fact is, having so many choices in life isn't easy. It can be paralyzing; it comes with its own kind of pressure. For me, a lack of options was actually freeing. Liberating. I had no choice but to drive forward. If I hit a wall, I just found a way around it—or through it. Stopping wasn't even in my vocabulary. But my son, he'll constantly wonder if he's going in the right direction or the wrong direction. When he faces adversity, he'll hear a voice whisper, "Go ahead and give up, you've already got everything you need anyway." The world will expect entirely different things from him than it did from me. It'll judge him on an even higher level.

Now *that's* pressure. And that's why my support will be so important.

Right now, Lil' Man's favorite thing in the world is going to the zoo. And I don't mean in some casual "let's go laugh at the monkeys" kind of way. I mean this kid wants to go to the zoo *every single day*. He's fascinated by animals, watching them, studying them, identifying them.

Museums too. He's obsessed with dinosaurs. I might look at a dinosaur and say, "Yeah, that's a dinosaur." But he'll say "triceratops" or "brontosaurus" or "stegosaurus." The boy ain't even three, and he knows more about this shit than I do!

So what happens if he comes home one day and says, "Dad, guess what? I wanna be a zoologist."

Alright then. Back when I was playing at San Diego, I always knew that every home game I could look in the stands and find my mama there, cheering like crazy and wearing her bedazzled "Dat Mama" jersey for all the world to see.

If my boy wants to be a zoologist? Find me a lab coat, because I got my BeDazzler and rhinestones ready to go, and he's gonna have "Dat Dad" cheering him on every single day.

But there's one decision Lil' Man could make that wouldn't be so simple for me to accept.

Playing football.

It's the *only thing* he could choose at a young age that I would not allow.

Don't get me wrong. He could be great a football player. There's no way to know for sure, but I look at him and can't help thinking, "Shit, this kid is built to dominate on the field." He's already huge for his age, those big mitts keep getting bigger, and with parents like his—his mama ran track and played college basketball—he's bound to be athletically gifted. And I'd love it if he plays sports. Basketball, track, swimming, whatever.

But that's not the problem.

The problem is that I know better than almost anyone what a lifetime of football does to your body—no matter how big, strong, and fast you might be.

Forget about all the injuries I dealt with in the past. Forget about almost ending up on dialysis for the rest of my life. I'm talking about the physical strain I deal with *now*, in the present, twelve years after I played my last down.

Remember how I needed to use a juice bottle to pee in the middle of the night when I couldn't get out of my bed back in San Diego? I *still* keep an empty orange juice bottle next to my bed to this day. And one in my car. And one in my office. (I make damn sure I keep them separated from the real OJ jugs. Twice I've taken a shot right to the head by accident, and trust me—pee is a lot better going out than it is coming in.)

Now, part of that is my Wiley bladder. Sometimes it sneaks up on me, and better to be prepared than to dribble all the way to the bathroom.

But the other part—especially at night, in bed—is how hard it can be to move. Once I get up, once I get going, I'm alright. But getting that engine started, getting that pilot light lit, that's a constant struggle. I have to *will* my body to move, battle the hurt, the aches, and the inertia that come from years of slamming myself at top speed into three-hundred-pound men.

Hell, *right now*, as I'm writing this, my neck is in massive pain. Not because I slept on it funny, but because all those stingers I got playing for Jacksonville love to say, *"Remember me?"*

Then there's my future. Like I said, there's no way for me to know if I could end up suffering from CTE. There's simply no test doctors can do while I'm still alive. My mind is clear now, thankfully. But I'm only forty-three years old. Who knows how I'll feel ten, twenty years from now. It's a possibility I have to accept.

But I don't have to accept it for my son.

In grade school and junior high, the most I'll let him do is play flag football. No tackle. That's a big decision for me—after all, full-contact peewee football was a huge, formative part of my childhood.

But like I said, I never really had a choice. I always knew I had to develop my mind, of course, but football was our number-one path out, and I knew it.

I also didn't understand the long-term damage I was doing to my health. No one around me did. But even if someone had, even if someone had taken the time to explain the science to me, I was too young to really comprehend the consequences at that age.

Before he hits his teens, Lil' Man will be too young to understand it too. Which is why I'll make that decision for him and keep him out of full-contact ball, whether he likes it or not.

That'll change once he gets to high school.

I'm not stupid. If I try to forbid him to do something he truly wants to do when he's a teenager, it'll only make him want it even more. Besides, I want him to take responsibility for his decisions.

But just because I won't forbid him doesn't mean I won't advise him. Very, very firmly.

You see all your friends playing video games? You sure you want to be out there dislocating all your fingers instead?

You hear that sound it makes when two helmets collide? That rrrahhhh!? Think about your head in that, your developing brain. That what you really want?

You sure you don't want to play a sport where if you get hit they give you free throws instead of NoDoz?

I'll advise him for his sake *and* mine. Because honestly, all it takes is for Lil' Man to trip on our stairs, and I feel his pain all the way down to the roots of my hair. If I have to watch him on the football field when he's older, I have no idea how I'll get through it.

But if he wants to play, if he truly has a passion for football, if he's willing to sacrifice his body the same way his daddy did—I will get through it. For him.

I will support it. For him.

And I'll hope and pray that he chooses zoology instead.

I'M NOT THE only person who's reconsidering his attitude toward football.

The fact is, by the time Lil' Man is old enough to play, football could be a very different sport.

People talk a lot about the TV ratings decline for NFL games, which I think is actually exaggerated. TV ratings are dropping not so much because people are watching *less* football—they're watching it in completely *different ways.* Live streaming, social media, the internet, that's how tons of fans consume sports now, none of which is measured by traditional ratings systems. Five years from now those ratings systems will be caught up, and my guess is we'll realize the overall numbers are about as high as they ever were.

If anything, live sports—especially football—is one of the few things that's keeping people watching old-fashioned cable and network TV, because people want to watch it as it's happening. No one is going on Netflix and Hulu to binge-watch recorded games from five years ago. Yet, anyway.

But let's be real. Football's reputation has taken a hit.

When I was growing up, my father wasn't saying what I'm saying about football now. He never would've kept me away from peewee football. More and more parents are, at the very least, doing what I'm doing, and keeping their sons out of full-contact football until they reach at least high school. Peewee football has already seen big declines in its enrollment rates.

Hell, my former teammate Drew Brees only played flag football in grade school and junior high, and that dude's a future Hall of Fame quarterback! If it worked for him, why not everyone else? The guy even went on to found his very own flag football league so his own little kids wouldn't have to play tackle themselves.

The facts about football and health are impossible to ignore. From movies like *Concussion* to high-profile stories about former players like my friend Junior Seau. People love the game, but we also love our kids. We want to protect them—no matter what their age.

Unfortunately, the NFL is struggling to adapt. The world is changing by the day, and the League is changing by the decade. The people who run it are smart, extremely capable individuals. But something happens when you get to be as big as the League is—you become risk averse. You don't think about what *will* work, you focus on *what if it doesn't* work, because you're afraid you'll ruin the gravy train.

As far as health and safety goes, the NFL has finally started making *some* progress. The League already limited contact in practices and the Pro Bowl. They even implemented a new rule for the 2018 season penalizing players if they lower their heads to initiate contact with their helmets. Now I have no idea how they'll actually call and enforce that penalty—incidental helmet contact is hard to avoid—but clearly the NFL recognizes there's an issue.

The question is, how far will they go to correct it?

As my grandma used to say, one option could be to *just cut the shit*. Get rid of the battles in the trenches, make the game less focused on defense and big hits, and highlight the offensive players, the quarterbacks and the receivers, instead. Fans don't want to watch "defensive battles" that end with a score of 3–0 anyways. They like big scores, like 41–33, the final of the last Super Bowl. A game that was thrilling to watch not just because the Eagles beat the Patriots for their first title ever, but because of the fast-paced offenses moving down the field almost at will.

The way it stands now, football is less sport than entertainment anyway. The League may keep moving in that direction. That doesn't mean I'll personally like watching it—at a certain point, football just isn't football anymore. But the NFL may not have a choice.

Look at the "taking a knee" controversy sparked by Colin Kaepernick—which the League struggled like crazy to address, and which was arguably the most divisive story in pro football in 2017.

To me, the cause rings true. Not only because of all the stats and stories about police violence against minorities, but because of personal experience. My dad was generally a man of few words, but when I was nine years old he made it abundantly clear exactly what I had to do if I ever got stopped by the cops:

Don't you ever fight back, don't you ever resist, don't you ever even argue or tell them you're innocent. Getting pulled over ain't time for trial. All you say is "Yes, sir" and "No, sir" and survive. Period.

At first I felt like he was being a punk, telling me to lay down and take whatever they gave me, but I learned just how right he was—the hard way. Fourteen years old, I was waiting at the bus stop by myself, daydreaming, watching traffic roll by, when suddenly I noticed a different kind of traffic.

Out of nowhere I was surrounded by three police cars. No warning, no nothing. Just cops jumping out, aiming shotguns right at me, and shouting thirteen different commands that all boiled down to *"Get the fuck on the ground!"*

Did I talk back? Hell no!

I hit that pavement fast and hard, spread my body out in a big X. One of the officers put the end of his gun right up against the back of my head. I could feel the steel against my skin. All I could think was if I twitched a finger, if I even sneezed, I'd be dead. Just like that.

Seconds later, I could actually see one of the cops on his walkie talkie—a man simply working his job who happened to have my life in his hands—and hear him get a call that they found the *actual suspect* somewhere a few miles away.

And just like that it was over. The cops said they were sorry and went on their way, like nothing even happened. Even though I knew I was one itchy trigger finger away from getting my brains blown out all over that bus stop.

Now, almost thirty years later, I'm left wondering when I'll have *my talk* with my own son about how to handle the police as a black man.

So I *feel* this issue. But what's happened in the NFL wasn't really about the issue, it was about the owners.

If the players wanted to protest something like veterans rights, you think the owners would care? Of course not. They'd fully support a movement like that, and by forming a united front with the players they could actually influence public opinion and get something done.

But the ownership hasn't fully understood the players' concerns about police violence against minorities, for two reasons:

One, the ownership itself isn't diverse enough. Frankly, it's hard for white people to really get how bad police stereotyping of black people is because they've never experienced it. I've had conversations with lots of well-meaning people that start with questions like "They pulled you over for *that*?" Until the NFL gets more minority owners, more owners who come from a similar place and perspective to the players, they won't really get the players' concerns. Or broader society's.

Two, the NFL ownership doesn't think of the players as partners; it thinks of them as disposable employees, nothing more than servants. Some of that attitude is built right into the contracts themselves, which aren't guaranteed—meaning players can be fired at will without the owners having to pay up all the money. But some of that is just the culture of the League, ingrained behaviors that are hard to stomp out.

It doesn't have to be that way. The NBA, for example, has guaranteed contracts for its players. So owners take very special care to treat that walking, breathing $20 million with special care. Pro basketball has a more diverse ownership than pro football, and the sense of partnership to match. Until NFL owners achieve something similar, the trust deficit with players will continue, and so will the controversies. Potentially turning off both fans and advertisers—and at exactly the worst time.

The competition for viewers has heated up more than ever. The NBA is winning the conversation as the more enlightened league, and social media and all the other new entertainment platforms have splintered everyone's attention spans. People simply have more options, the same way my son does in his life compared with when I was a kid, and the NFL can't take their interest for granted.

Think about what happened to boxing.

Boxing used to be the sport of choice for kids trying to get out of the hood. Not only that, but it had broad appeal to all Americans. Everyone watched it, and young people trained for it, dreaming of being the next Muhammad Ali (or Cassius Marcellus Clay, if we want to honor my namesake).

Now? Boxing is limited to a solid core of intensely devoted fans, except maybe for a couple major events once a year. Kids have options. They want to play video games. They want to play AAU basketball. They don't want to go to the gym to get the shit beat out of them.

If the NFL isn't careful, football could wind up the same way.

Twelve years from now, when Lil' Man isn't so little, when he's about to start high school, I might not even have to have the conversation about football I'm dreading right now. He might not even care.

EVERY FEW MONTHS when I was a kid, my dad would measure how tall I'd grown. I'd stand up against a wall in our apartment, and he would mark my height with a pen. We could see my progress, week after week, month after month, year after year, against that old plaster with its peeling paint.

Now I measure Lil' Man's height. Except we don't use an old wall and a pen—we use this thing we bought off Amazon, all shiny, bright colors and pictures of footballs and basketballs. Every inch pre-marked for us, ready-made. But still keeping track of his progress, week after week, month after month, year after year.

That contrast says a lot to me about how far I've come, how far my family's come, and what the future holds for us.

When you don't have money, you think money is everything, that it's the key to all life's problems. But once you get it, you realize the important things, the meaningful things, stay the same. What makes you sad keeps making you sad. What brings you joy keeps bringing you joy. What's real is real.

A lot of people like to say they don't have any regrets, but I'm not too proud to admit I do. I regret that right when I was on the brink of reaching my full physical, athletic potential, my injuries kept holding me back. I regret that I wasn't more of a presence in my daughter's life as she grew up. I regret that I wasn't holding my mama's hand when she passed from this earth.

I'm also not too proud to admit that I have fears, especially when it comes to my health. Since I was seven years old, I've based my entire existence, my whole identity, on taking care of my family. But what happens if my old injuries break me down? What happens if I do have CTE? The idea that I couldn't take care of my family anymore, that I'd lose my reason for living, and that they, my wife, my sister, my children, would have to physically take care of me—that's my greatest fear.

But honestly? I'm an overwhelmingly positive guy. I never hold a grudge. I almost never get angry—about anything. And I'm full of hope for my future. I trust, deep down—I just *know*, I feel it—that somehow everything will all work out.

It's the same attitude that got me out of the hood, that got me into Columbia, that got me a ten-year career in the NFL, and more. I believe that all my positivity, all my optimism, acts as a deposit in the Bank in the Sky. Whenever I'm struggling, I make a withdrawal. In other words, I trust the universe, and the universe says, *I got you.*

I've got a job I love in broadcasting, where I couldn't even get injured if I wanted to. (Then again, check that—I had to have surgery to remove a node on my vocal cord a couple years ago, so I guess a guy like me can't escape the injury bug no matter where I go!) At this point, I've been commentating on football longer than I played it professionally.

I've got a house in a neighborhood where you don't have to worry about gang members throwing kids off swings at the local park. I've got a perfect wife, a daughter, a sister, and now my very own son. And all I want is for them to enjoy their journey as much as I did. Celebrating the good things and even the bad.

Celebrating life.

Eventually, when I was young, my dad stopped measuring me against that wall as I grew taller. Instead he measured me against himself, a man who was six foot three. We'd stand shoulder to shoulder, back to back, and I'd check my progress.

Now I'm up to his chin.

Now I'm up to his ear.

Now I'm even taller than he is.

That's all I want for my son in his future. Years from now, to stand up next to me and realize he's bigger in every single way. To look me in the eye and realize he has to look down. To smile his very own way and just say, "What, Daddy?"

And hope he doesn't notice the tears in my eyes.

ACKNOWLEDGMENTS

This book represents my life and my legacy, the lessons I've learned, the struggles I've overcome, and the amazing adventure I've had along the way. That's why I'd like to start by thanking my family, because they're my cornerstone. My reason to be.

No one is closer to me than my mama, even now that she's up with the angels. She taught me balance in life, how to value not just my work but my family and friends. She sacrificed and prioritized my life over hers, and I'm forever indebted to her. Mama, I'll always strive to make your pain worth it.

After all these years, my dad is still a man of principle, silent strength, and responsibility. Dad, thank you for teaching me by example that actions speak louder than words.

My sister, Tiki, fought growing up so I didn't have to. She gave me her strength and her confidence, and I'll always be grateful. She's also my memory. This book is the one time I've told my story without her helping me out—so, Tiki, forgive me if I fucked a lot of stuff up.

I want to thank both of my grandmas, Grandma Blackie (yeah, that's what I called her—deal with it) and Grandma Madear. Grandma B, thank you for being brutally honest in a world filled with deception. I hated how honest you were when I was a little kid, but now it's what I love most. And, Grandma M, thank you for introducing me to my faith, to my religion, to my spirituality. Without you I wouldn't have known it existed.

Shout-out to Grandpa Howard, who gave me my first Major League baseball, and making the world of pro sports feel real. I still have the ball too.

My aunts and uncles each taught me something special. Uncle Tyrone taught me what fresh really is, showed me that the wrapping paper can be just as important as the gift. Uncle James taught me just a little of his charm—and that went a long way. Uncle Donnie taught me that everything doesn't always work out in life, but heart is what really matters. Uncle Benefield taught me to always stand my ground and never waver in my convictions. Auntie Cynthia taught me to never stop loving what I really love. And Auntie Toska taught me how important it is to wear your emotions out in the open.

My niece, Charne, added another chamber to my heart. Lafayette, thank you for defusing the Tiki firecracker every day. And thanks to Tyran, who always looked out for me even though I didn't see him. He was my force field for the bullshit.

Deborah, thank you so much for everything you do for my dad. It makes me happy knowing you're there to watch him levitate during Cowboy games.

Kim, thank you for accepting our modern family. And, Anthony, I'll always appreciate how you made the difficult look easy.

Then there's Jabari. He might not technically be family, not biologically, but he's the closest thing to it. I've been blessed to serve as the role model for many young people in my life, but Jabari—he's my role model. Thank you, man, for being the only person I can travel outside this world with.

Jackie Blackett, there's a reason I call her my godmother. Thank you, Jackie, for loving me like your son and translating life for me—both back at Columbia and to this day.

If my family gave my life purpose, my friends gave it flavor. To all my friends now and from back in the day, thank you to the ones who've been real. Who supported me before I made it to the NFL, and after I left.

Thanks to the Goss family. Stan and Keith weren't just my muscle in the streets, they also showed me my presence has power. And thank you to the Spanos family for the respect they've given me, which was even bigger than the check.

Doc Murray, you provided more than physical therapy—you were therapy for my heart. Thank you for stepping out of your office and into our home.

Shout-out to Rancho Golf Course for being my dad's sanctuary and our playground for bonding. And to Crazy Keith and the Strange Lady, for showing me you don't have to be normal to be cool. Then there's Mr. Kinney, and his insane Bose stereo system that he always let me play around with. Thank you for introducing me to my first love—music.

Thanks to Davida Adams for liking me then for what I am now. Tiffani Greene taught me that family doesn't have to be blood. Auntie Brenda helped show me the world outside the neighborhood. And her daughter Jamie, she was my first crush.

Charice, I appreciate you for letting me tag along with the cool kid sometimes (and for being my second crush). Tiffney Cambridge showed me that age doesn't define a woman. Ms. Woods reminded me that "student athlete" started with student. Michelle Klapman and Mikel Jollett taught me that being smart was cool. Keisha, Myra, Camille were my first glimpse of beauty and brains. And thank you to

Sister Cheryl for vouching for my character, and helping me redeem my reputation.

Thanks to Na'il Benjamin—our friendship inspired me to catch up to you. And to the boys of FAY—Diarro, Ratanzi, and Marvin. I'm glad we knew who we were *not*.

Props to Yee's Chinese Food for always being the place that lets me know who's real. And to Slauson Swap Meet for having the mixtapes that set me apart from the rest of the neighborhood. And to Janet Jackson, my forever Charlene. Thanks for the extra rep.

Fatback, Cheema, and Dennis Northcutt, y'all are my sparkplugs. Never change. Tarima Levine, thank you for free-falling with me and helping me understand my self-worth. Ciroc Boyz—Omar, Terry, Eddie, Louis—I love being big kids with you dudes.

Then there's the guys I've played with over the years. You weren't just friends—a lot of you were like brothers out there on the field. We went through it all together, and I appreciate the hell out of you.

Dominique Walker, I owe you millions—figuratively!—for introducing me to football. Stais Boseman, thank you for showing me stars aren't just on TV. James "Gumby" Gray, I appreciate you for showing me success requires more than just talent—and for never telling the school district you used my address.

Matty L, you taught me that nice guys actually can finish first. You, Momma, Poppa, Cool Breeze, Jenn, and the Lenzonie crew showed me the meaning of extended family. And, Rory, thank you for being my balance on the other side of the seesaw.

Jeff "Butter" Byrd—dog, without you I'd just be a big-ass former running back teaching high school right now. Thank you for that. Brian Larson, thanks for taking it easy on me in the scrimmage. But I'm still mad you guys beat us 40–0 during the regular season. And to my Bulgarian Brotherhood—bwa!

Bruce Smith, you went from being my hero to my friend. Like a childhood dream come true. Thank you so much for letting me into your world.

Gabe Northern, thanks for teaching me to embrace my Wild Style. Ted "Mount" Washington, you showed me that a man can be a gentle giant off the field and a beast on it. Phil Hansen, I appreciate you for never looking down on me when Bruce left—and for picking me up too.

To my first football idols growing up, Eric Dickerson and John Elway. Thanks for being main characters in my dream.

Junior Seau, thank you for being an even better person than you were a player.

Curtis Conway, you were my teammate, and now you're like my family. Thank you for being the example I try to follow. Jim Trotter, thanks for being an ear for me to talk to, and for never burning me. And, Leo Carson, I get it, and I still love you.

To my boys in Jacksonville—Stroud, Hayday, DG, Tangy (Fred T. and B-Mac), and all my Duval teammates—y'all reminded me why I got into this, and why I needed to get the fuck out.

And to all my teammates from Buffalo, San Diego, Dallas, and Jacksonville—I know y'all were sweatin' that I would go there, and you some lucky motherfuckers I didn't tell everything I know.

Next, to my coaches at the different stages of my career, I appreciate everything you taught me about the game and so much more.

Coach Melvin Smith, Sr., thank you for showing me that I could be the man even as a young boy. Coach James, thanks for teaching me that hard work is hard but still worth it. Coach Moore, you taught me that your heart is the biggest muscle in your body, and that you gotta use it to keep it strong.

Coach Angelo Jackson, I appreciate how you showed me that football could take me to the next level in my life. Coach Ray Tellier, thank you for blessing my ears with the quote that didn't just convince me to come to Columbia, it became my mantra. Coach Joe White, you stayed in the stadium for me when everyone else left.

Coach John Levra, thank you for showing me the sweet science of pass rushing. Coach Jack del Rio, thank you for just plain getting it.

My strength coach, Mark McAllister, bless you for helping me make those scouts' mouths drop. James Collins, thank you for healing my pain that wasn't only physical. Mike Boyle, you convinced me I was only scratching the surface with my athleticism, and pushed me to go deeper. Lil' Man is next—and that shit is over.

John Butler was my general manager at two separate teams. He breathed life into my dreams and made them a reality. I miss you, Big Bear.

And, Bird, I know you're out there somewhere. Thanks for flying to every NFL headquarters and chirping loud. Find Number 27, and both y'all Tweet at me.

Thank you as well to everyone who's been such a valuable part of my success and happiness—in football and beyond.

Brad Blank, I appreciate how you put me before the dollar. Nick "Cobra" Khan, you're all love. In this fake world, you're the real. Amir Malek helped me put this puzzle back together, and boy is it pretty. And, Brandon, you're more than a manager—you're my Voltron. Thanks for being the bad cop to my good cop. My partner in grind.

Thank you to Jamie Horowitz, for introducing me to the big stage in media. Charlie Dixon, you never stopped believing in me from afar. Trey Wingo, thanks for covering for my early mistakes and teaching me that not being perfect was its own kind of perfection. Max Kellerman, you're my brother from another. And, Michelle Beadle, how many times can you leave me? I guess someone that talented just can't help themselves.

To everyone who had to listen to me philosophize on a daily basis—Charissa, Cari, LZ, Travis, Kelvin, and Sean, who was lucky to get out quick—thank you for putting up with me.

Garry and the whole G Train family, thank you for giving me NFL-level training—outside the NFL.

Marquel, I've really enjoyed being a part of your learning and growing. Young lion, let's roar! And, Shayna, thanks for the third hand. Keep on excelling!

A huge heartfelt thanks to my amazing editor at Dutton, Jill Schwartzman. Jill, your energy and enthusiasm gave me the confidence to share my story with the world. A big thanks to my agent at CAA, Dave Larabell, who didn't just help me find a platform for my story—he gave me the shove I needed to get it done. And, Christopher Farah, thank you for bringing my life to the page. You know more about me than my wife does, so careful what you tell people.

Massive shout-out to Columbia University, for having a reputation that affords me privileges and respect every day.

To ESPN, thank you for an amazing eleven years. You were more than just a place to work—you were my family away from home. Fox Sports, thank you for keeping my big mouth on TV. I hope you're ready, because I really don't ever shut up. Let's do this!

And I can't forget Moo-Moo and Quincy. Moo-Moo, thanks for being a traitor and making Mama happy. And, Quincy, I miss cuddling with you—and being scratched by you.

Last of all, I'd like to thank my wife, Annemarie, and my kids, Morocca, Lil' Man, and Lil' Mama, who's on the way.

Annemarie, you're the one person I can be entirely myself around, on all levels. You love me for who I am, without the degree, without the money, without the suit. Thank you for always thinking the best of me—even when I'm at my worst.

Morocca, I love you, and thank you for never letting distance get in the way of our love. Lil' Man, you're my man, and you reignited my love for life. And, Lil' Mama—girl, what can I say? You're about to be born into an amazing family, but sorry I can't protect you from your older brother.